Adventure Without

RESERVATIONS

Begins at 50

FRANK KING

i

Frank King

Published by:
BOND-KING PUBLISHING CO.
3912 206TH AV. NE
SAMMAMISH, WA. 98074

If you like this book, try these other fine books by Frank King

Travels with Doris

The Ice Lady

ISBN-978-0-578-10499-7

Cover design and maps by Sam Mills

Contents

Contents

List of Pictures

List of Picttures

List of Maps

Fellow Travel Adventurers

Author, Frank King

Chapter 2-5
Debbie Anderson

Chapters 20-22
Susan Crawford
Kathleen Crawford

Chapter 23
Norm Winn
Rick Munsen

Chapter 24
Josh Logan

Chapter 25-27
Bruce & Nadine Byers
Stan & Marilyn Jensen
Harry Morgan
Janet Wall

Chapters 15-18
Kecia Harris, Leader
Jenny Turner, Driver
Catherine Robinson
Ian and Donna Lauder
Stuart Robertson
Mannon Gosselin
Mignon Manyel

Dave Palmer
Tim Meikle
Sally Glan
Jack Ferrell

Steve Jewell
Carol Egan
Sharon Lake
Peter Pyke

Frank King

Yvonne Burnett   Jane Wells   Mark _____

Adventure Without

RESERVATIONS

Begins at 50

FRANK KING

Chapter 1
Prologue

When I was a younger man looking for fun and adventure, my elders kept telling me to be patient. "Wait your turn, life begins at forty." What a piece of nonsense! As far as I could tell, a person at forty looked pretty old and used up. And in those days someone over fifty was middle-aged and on his way out. Impatient to do and see everything, I watched my forties rapidly slip away.

In those days, before Rick Steves started his lectures on low budget travel adventures, it slowly dawned on me that I would have to initiate my own adventures since no one else seemed to care, or know how to go about it. Everyone, that is, except those young people in their twenties trooping off to far lands with their giant packs and having a wonderful time.

A few months before my fiftieth birthday, I applied for and received my first passport. I had already chosen South America for my first out-of-country destination, and was busy reading a guidebook on South America to gain as much knowledge as I could about each country I planned to visit. I planned to go to seven countries and that would take about three months. It didn't take me long to find out that travel could be very expensive and use up a lot of time if I wasn't careful. Fortunately, about that time, guidebooks came out with the words "budget," "cheap," or "traveling on a shoestring" in their titles, and they showed me ways to mitigate travel costs. Over the years, I learned to call such travel "frugal," and I have become very good at frugal travel, not to be confused with cheap travel.

For my first excursion outside the USA, I persuaded Debbie, a climber friend, that this would be a nifty trip, so with some minor arm twisting she agreed to meet me in Santiago, Chile. On that trip, I spent a little over a month in Columbia, Ecuador, Peru, and Bolivia, and the second month and a half was in Chile and Argentina with Debbie.

Since that first trip in 1979, I have traveled to seventy countries throughout the world. It was a lot more fun traveling with someone than when alone. But if no one would go, I went anyway--alone. Everyone's memories of places are different, and big changes can and do occur over a thirty-year period. So each person's adventures are different. The only things that don't seem to change are the universal kindness of people the world over, and the need for any traveler to have a good, commonsense attitude, and a little sense of humor.

2) Frugal Travel?

Frank King

Southern South America

Chapter 2
Across the Andes by Boat, Chile-Argentina

When I met Debbie in Santiago, South America, the first thing we did was get out of that big, noisy city, away from traffic, subways, and its crowds of people, over fifteen million of them. We figured there was nothing much of interest for us there, especially carrying around climbing and camping gear, boots, hardhats, and ice axes. People looked in wonder at our mountain of gear and murmured "alpinists," as if we were aliens from a different world.

We took the first bus out, and headed for Puerto Montt, population one hundred thousand, which was the farthest south we could get in that part of Chile. We were still over a thousand miles, as the crow flies, or about fifteen hundred miles via boat from Chile's southern major port, Punta Arenas, where cruise ships embarked to Antarctica. A bewildering conglomeration of islands, hundreds of them, with lakes, mountains, glaciers, and a few fishing villages filled that vast area of the country to the south without a practical way through the mess unless you owned a boat. We stayed a few days exploring the town of Puerto Montt, hiking the pebbly beaches, camping out, and enjoying seafood from the town's extensive fish market occupying a large pier.

On the first night out, we discovered what we had forgotten.

"You didn't bring a tent?" I asked Debbie in amazement.

"No. I thought you had one. You were already down here."

"I haven't needed a tent until now, because I never camped out. I stayed in hotels in towns along the way."

"Well," said Debbie, "we sure need something now,"

The next day we walked uptown and solved that minor problem. We bought two blue plastic tarps large enough to provide us with ground cover to sleep on and a roof to keep us dry in the rain. And that's what we used throughout the rest of the month whenever we thought it necessary to set up camp. Most of the time we simply spread out the ground covers wherever we were and went to bed.

Our next destination was Bariloche, Argentina, and I suggested to Debbie that we travel there through the Andes via the lakes route. It was touted in the guide books as one of the most beautiful trips in all of South America. The route involved crossing three lakes by small passenger ferries and by buses over the land masses between them. No outside roads serviced the area, and I wondered how they got buses and ferries into that wild remote area.

After a short bus ride to Puerto Varas, the gateway to the area, we hitched rides to Ensenada, a lonely spot on a lonely dirt and gravel back road. From that point the road carried no traffic at all, and it took us all afternoon to walk the last ten miles to Lago Todos, the first of the three lakes we had to cross by ferry. It was a long slog carrying our big backpacks and Debbie's duffle bag. This was a consequence of not paying a lot of money for a tour, but doing the trip on our own, hopefully for less money.

I don't know what she carried around in that big bag, and I didn't ask, but it was the millstone around both our necks. The only practical way we managed to drag that bag along was for each of us to grab a handle on each side of the bag and trade sides when our arms became too tired. I like to think that there was a lot of neat, beneficial stuff in that bag, but thirty years later, I'm not so sure that most of it could have been left behind.

At the end of the road, a small unpretentious hotel offered rooms for rent taken mostly by local trout fishermen. And I was relieved to see a small dock that proclaimed some sort of boat service beyond.

We walked down the pristine beach a short distance and made our camp for the night. The lake was one of the most beautiful I've ever seen, a stunning emerald green color surrounded by thick forest with no roads or signs of civilization to mar that pristine shoreline. Nearby, the perfectly shaped volcanic cone of Mount Osorno poked its summit into the blue sky. Its top was flat where the volcanic cauldron lay open and a bright white snow band covered the mountain from the top down, about one-third of its height.

We were up early enough the next day to see the people on tour arrive by bus and troop aboard a passenger ferry which had magically appeared that morning. Debbie and I negotiated a price to go with them to Bariloche. I think we saved some money, but I'm not sure. Ten years later, I did the same trip, and simply paid the asking price from Puerto Montt all the way to Bariloche and saved myself a lot of hassle.

The lake was incredibly beautiful, and for a while, we had views of Mount Osorno reflected in the still waters of the lake. Like the other tourists, we craned our necks and took picture after picture of stunning mountain views surrounding the lake. Eventually we came into sight of Mount Tronador to the south, a mighty massif covered to the top with brilliant white snow. It was easily the highest peak we had seen so far.

"Let's go there and climb that big mountain," said Debbie.

"Sure, why not? We'll be in the neighborhood anyway," I said.

We crossed into Argentina just before boarding the second ferry on Lago Frias, a small mountain lake. Then it was a short bus ride to the third lake and our third ferry ride. A bus met us on the other side and drove us to Bariloche, stopping to drop people off at their hotels along the way. We went all the way to Bariloche since we hadn't booked a hotel, yet.

That afternoon, we made contact with Raphael, a local man who advertised himself as a consultant for foreign climbers, passing through Bariloche. He owned a hardware store and was very welcoming and friendly. He stopped what he was doing, insisted that we store our packs in an extra storage room, and then took us to a café for some of Bariloche's famous chocolate drink. I didn't know that Bariloche was famous for chocolate. It wasn't on my favorite drink list, but I had some anyway. We pored over topographic maps of the area and slurped chocolate. Very pleasant. With Raphael's help, we chose to go to the mountain hut, Refugio Cerro Lopez, and climb some peaks from there.

The next morning we repacked our packs and left our extra gear in Raphael's storeroom to be picked up when we got back. We took a bus to the trailhead that led to the *refugio*, and as we climbed, we saw dazzling views of the lakes area that we had traveled through from Chile. Every detail appeared to be flat on the valley floor like a postcard. I could almost see written on the front of that giant card, "wish you were here."

Most of the guests staying at the *refugio* were young climbers, and they enjoyed their bottles of wine after supper. I'm not sure how it started, but I was soon leading a sing-along of American songs, and others led songs in languages completely unknown to me. But it didn't matter, everyone sang along as best they could no matter what language was used.

During our stay there, Debbie and I climbed two rocky peaks, one of them was class three/four named Cerro Lopez, and the other just a pimple on the ridge. We also did a long snow climb. Nothing was too technical and we had a good time while there. We finally got tired of the wining, dining, singing, and lounging about, and left the *refugio* in midmorning of a lazy day.

Our plan was to hitch a ride back to Bariloche and travel south to climb Tronador, but we couldn't get a ride. Finally, in late afternoon, a beat up old pickup truck stopped and we hopped in back with their four kids. The family was going camping at one of the beautiful lakes along the way to Bariloche. They didn't go very far before stopping for the night, and Debbie and I were stuck.

We found a secluded spot near the lake to stay the night. Luckily, we had a little food with us, but best of all, a bottle of wine from the *refugio*. The next morning I was ravenous, and we were out on the road early, hoping to get to Bariloche in time for breakfast. But we walked on an empty road for quite awhile before arriving at a bed-and-breakfast. Its most memorable attribute was the daisies that grew waist-high in lush profusion everywhere.

Debbie was curious to inspect an Argentine B&B and, in the process, we negotiated a breakfast of tea, toast, butter, and jam with the balance of our meager funds now running low until we could get to a bank in Bariloche. The tea was bottomless, and the toast came out in endless stacks, along with ample jam and butter. We went away full and happy. Arriving in Bariloche, we repacked our stuff stored with Raphael into two backpacks and two over-stuffed daypacks, thereby eliminating the pesky duffle bag. Then we took a city bus to the southwest edge of town to hitch a ride to the Mount Tronador trailhead in Parque Nacional Nahuel Huapi.

3) Mount Osorno, gateway to the lakes route

4) Stall on fish market pier, Puerto Montt

5) Refugio Cerro Lopez

Chapter 3
A Day at Tronador, Argentina

"There it is," I shouted to my partner, Debbie, trooping along behind me. "There's the hut."

Overheated by the afternoon sun, with numerous horse flies buzzing around our heads, occasionally biting out hunks of our flesh for sheer pleasure, we paused to look over at this goal for the day. There it was, an ugly building covered with tarpaper and sheet metal set amidst boulders and debris, and held in place by a network of cables. I figured the wind at times must rage through the area. It was sited near the edge of a huge glacier that extended to Mount Tronador itself.

"Darn," said Debbie, "I'll miss these big old horse flies."

Tronador rose up behind the hut like a huge white curtain. At eleven thousand-five hundred feet, it was the highest mountain in the area. The ridge we had been hiking fell away on two sides down to snowfields below leaving the hut sitting on the only bare spot left on the ridge. Despite its depressing appearance, we were glad to be there and were hopeful to get some respite from the heat and biting flies inside the *refugio's* ugly walls.

Looking down at one of the snowfields to the left, I saw that the bulk of the snow and ice formed a huge triangular fan. It rose five hundred feet from its base to meet the lip of a cliff where ice from the upper glacier continually fell over the cliff, making the fan of snow and ice ever larger.

We had started from Bariloche in early morning to hitch a ride to the trailhead at Tronador, but hitching a ride was slow and sporadic, and we didn't arrive at the access road into the park until after lunch. The park rangers had decreed that the road be reserved in the morning for traffic going one-way into the park and after four o'clock in the afternoon be reserved for traffic going out of the park. Essentially, the road was one way into Tronador until noon and then one way out from four o'clock on.

We found that hitching rides was hard in this part of the world, but the cost of tour buses, taxis, or other private vehicles was astronomical and disastrous for our budget, so we walked a lot. Now we trudged up the access road a couple of miles to a pretty meadow lying below the road off to our right. It surrounded a small lake and was partially secluded by trees and brush, and that's where we made camp for the night. Ahead of us was the top of Tronador still gleaming white in the afternoon sunlight.

The next morning we were up on the road early and easily got a ride into the Tronador trailhead. There we met Stan and Cricket from Alaska who, like us, were traveling around to see South America. They had been on the slopes of Tronador the day before, and were traveling back to Bariloche and on south in Argentina. They gave us information of what we might face doing the climb.

"We didn't try to make the summit," said Stan. "We just weren't prepared to do it, without the right equipment."

"It was awfully steep at the top," chimed in Cricket, probably giving us the real reason they made no summit attempt.

The day was already hot when Debbie and I started up the trail. I began the process of sweating out the sins of previous days and trying to dodge horse flies. Debbie didn't appear to be quite as sinful as I, but she was coping with her share of the horse flies too. After a mile or two, we entered a shady forest of Lenga Beech trees, which provided protection from the hot sun. They were huge old trees that in the South American autumn-- around April and May--the leaves turned to an orange-red color. I tried to imagine the surrounding hills at that time covered with great swaths of such flaming bright colors.

Reaching the top of a ridge we left the beech trees behind, and entered an alpine area. Now as an added incentive to make our goal, we saw occasional glimpses of Tronador to keep us going. The trail became nonexistent, lost in the cinders and rock typical of volcanoes, and we followed little rock cairns built to mark the way.

Although the valley resounded with sounds of cascading water and the occasional rumble of an icefall, there wasn't a drop to be had along the way. Everywhere, we saw rushing water, but all of it was out of our reach. Then unexpectedly we came upon a stream right in the middle of the path between two cairns. It flowed out of the cinders a few feet and disappeared back into the cinders. We loaded up on cold fresh water only to find that the climbing hut with lots of water was just over the next rise.

It was cool and dark inside the hut, and I got the impression more dirt lay inside the hut than outside. Although the door remained open, the horse flies didn't come inside and that was a great relief. We shucked our packs and met the hut master. His appearance was similar to how I thought Friar Tuck would appear right out of the tales of Robin Hood, accentuated by climbing knickers and a shirt one size too small. To keep his ample belly covered put a terrible strain on his buttons, and I kept waiting for them to pop off and go whirling through the air.

He was jovial, but spoke very little English Even so, we managed to understand that we were welcome, the only guests, and that he served tea, coffee, soup, and sandwiches. We drank some tea in front of the only window, which faced the mountain, of course. Our seats were benches on each side of a long table in the center of the room. The hut had low ceilings and the lower parts of the walls were concrete, which gave me the impression of a cave. Piped water ran continuously, night and day, into a sink, making loud, disgusting sucking and gurgling noises on its way out the drain. It never stopped flowing.

I found out that the hut master had wine, and he and I sat sipping wine while Debbie went off to wash up. I learned from the hut master that Tronador had three peaks making up its summit; Argentina Peak, straightforward and not difficult, Chilean Peak, moderately difficult, and International Peak, very difficult. I unilaterally chose to try climbing the least difficult,

Argentina Peak. The hut master described the route up including its pitfalls and the places we needed to find to make our way up and back.

From what I could understand between my poor Spanish and his poor English, the route sounded straightforward and simple. Go up from the hut toward a secondary satellite peak on the ridge running north from Tronador, and turn left above a field of crevasses. Pass the crevasses and continue up to a prominent snow ridge, then slide off left of the ridge and down a short drop into a basin. Follow the basin up to the col, the low point between Argentina Peak and International Peak, and then turn right to the summit of Argentina Peak. He said we needed to leave the hut at about three o'clock in the morning, because the snow became very soft in the afternoon. Then, he added, we should make the round trip in about eight hours.

About the time we felt comfortable being the only guests for the night, a group of four young men arrived to settle in. None of them spoke English. Good grief! When I left home, friends assured me that I didn't need to learn Spanish since English was well known. Fortunately, I had taken a crash course in Spanish, so I knew at least some words, which came in very handy. Sometimes I knew what was going on, but I had to guess at many other things. Now I guessed that two of the newcomers would climb in the morning, and two would stay behind in the hut.

We spent time in the late afternoon packing for the climb, and shared mutual interest in the gear we were taking with us. They carried two Perlon ropes, sixty-five feet long while ours was a one hundred twenty foot Gold Line. Their crampons were heavier and not adjustable. We carried all-metal ice axes, while theirs were wood-shafted. We also carried nylon webbing, carabiners, and rescue pulleys. I packed a light sleeping bag in case we needed a bivouac, and Debbie and I carried all the extra cold weather clothes we had with us. I suggested that we all go together as one party for mutual safety and support, and I thought this was agreeable to all.

I made one more trip to the *baño*, bathroom, before going to bed. This was a death-defying trip even in daylight, but by flashlight it was just plain horrendous. In a fit of bad humor, the hut master had rigged up an open platform over a twenty-foot cliff for a bathroom. The main supports were two beams that spanned the chasm, and over these he had nailed a few cross boards. Two of the boards had the outline of feet painted on them to guide the user to the proper position to use the facilities. When our feet were properly aligned with the painted ones, the bathroom was ready for use. The whole contraption had no rails and was completely open to the elements. As an added feature, the hut master had rigged up running water under the planks that merrily splashed and flushed its way down the cliff. All very sanitary.

The Argentinean contingent was already asleep when Debbie and I made our way upstairs into the dark dungeon of a dormitory. The beds were on a raised wood platform extending continuously along two outside walls separated by a half partition running down the center of the room. Two-foot wide mattress pads delineated the extent of each person's bed. It was a hard place to relax and sleep, very black and "heavy" in a room with no windows. I tossed and turned with thoughts and tensions of the climb ahead. Then entered the hut master, bringing with him the loudest foghorn of a snore I have ever heard. It was obscene.

We retreated to the farthest corner of the dormitory where we got some relief by distance and the half partition. But now what's that other disgusting noise? Directly below us in the kitchen, the drain from the sink made its terrible sucking and gargling noises as it ran out the drain. Will this night ever end?

We got up at three-thirty the next morning and went downstairs to find the Argentinean climbers busy finishing breakfast. Debbie and I got some stuff together to eat, but it was hard to get excited about eating at this time of day. The Argentinean pair seemed to be in a hurry and ready to go and, in fact, soon left the hut with only a short farewell to us. So much for my understanding of a four-person climbing party. We fumbled around for a while and headed out into the pitch black morning at five o'clock.

We quickly reached the edge of the glacier, put on crampons, and roped-up for glacier travel. I had a headlamp powered by a long life lithium battery, and Debbie had a handheld flashlight. I took the lead and Debbie switched her light off. We started up the glacier guided by the prominent satellite peak on the ridge. We saw it easily by starlight when we switched off all our lights. It was cold and our crampons bit into the hard snow with a satisfying crunch. We talked very little, lost in our own thoughts, and restricted by the little world we could see. The rope, umbilical-like, bound us together in the darkness about fifty feet apart.

I constantly swept the slope ahead with my light, but so far there had been no crevasses. The slope just kept going up out of sight. At about that time, the wind started to blow, forcing us to stop and put on our last layers of clothes--windbreakers. When we moved on, the wind picked up and blew even harder, making it difficult to exchange conversation. Although it blew from the rear, the wind was a concern; for if it was bad here, it might be far worse higher up the mountain. But then again, I have seen hard winds dissipate at dawn.

Ahead, I saw the bulk of the satellite peak where it blotted out the stars. It appeared very close, so I made a tentative swing to the left and, almost immediately, my light picked up a large crevasse ahead, so we turned and continued going up. I didn't want to play around in a field of crevasses in the dark. A little later, I tried bearing to the left again. This time we were able to keep going without running into crevasses. An hour passed and the wind shifted to blow from the front. Not pleasant, but bearable. We encountered some crevasses. Some we jumped, and others were too big, so we detoured around them.

I grew weary of darkness and kept looking east, but there was no hint of dawn yet. We carried on because there was nothing else we could do. The wind and cold kept us from loitering. Then suddenly my eyes saw a little farther and, in a short time, I didn't need my headlamp to see in the predawn light. The early light of dawn lit up the peaks of Tronador and, in a few minutes, my view of the glacier and my depth perception greatly improved. The winds moderated and by sunrise quit altogether.

Suddenly Debbie and I became very cheerful and talkative, and I felt like I'd awakened from a somber dream to a colorful world of beauty and light. By now, we were high on the mountain and could look down at the horizon where the sun was beginning to peep over the edge of the world. I didn't know of anything else that compared to watching the sun's first rays light up the high peaks in a shimmering gold sheath. The show was over much too fast, but the reddish gold color on the peaks lingered a little longer. The sun's appearance seemed foreign when the rest of the world below was so black. Debbie took pictures of the peaks bathed with tints of red and gold. Tronador dominated the landscape, and in that light was superbly beautiful. Just being there knowing that we were a part of that scene was a thrilling experience, and all thoughts of the hard work during the dark hours were forgotten.

We nibbled on some snacks and speculated on where the two Argentinean climbers could be. Then we turned uphill and the slope we were on became a prominent ridge. We should have passed this ridge to the left. Sure enough, the ridge "cliffed" out, and we had to backtrack, losing about five hundred feet and dropping into the basin that led past the ridge. For any climber, losing altitude is always demoralizing. I don't think that it's the five hundred feet climbed and lost that's so bad. It's the additional five hundred feet of elevation re-climbed just to get back even to the height reached before turning back.

Reaching the basin, we saw two tiny figures--the Argentinean climbers--way down on the lower slopes. We speculated on why they were so far behind, or how we had gotten so far ahead. We never did find out. Tact and my poor Spanish made it a difficult subject to discuss. I figured they must have gotten tangled up in a crevassed area. We felt no compunction to wait for them and Debbie, who was leading, set a wicked pace straight up the basin toward the ridge. I estimated our speed at about fifteen hundred feet elevation gain per hour. Not bad! The pace was exhilarating and we rapidly closed in on the col, the low point on the ridge. Coming to the top of a prominent ridge was always fun, because it opened up views on the other side which had not yet been seen.

This ridge was no exception, and the views from there were breathtaking of a jumbled mix of ridges and peaks mantled in brilliant white snow that lay ahead and to the south, as far as I could see. The perfect cone of Mount Osorno to the north was close by.

Close, just ahead, we finally saw the third peak of Tronador. It was surmounted by a steep snow pack that covered the entire summit. From the ridge, it was easy to determine the easiest peak of Tronador to climb, and that was Argentina Peak to the right of the col. The other peaks looked frighteningly difficult, and it didn't take much discussion to try for a route up Argentina Peak.

Debbie led off again on slopes that were much steeper now, and we ran into crevasses that required us to maneuver back and forth and across snow bridges. We ascended much slower than on the open slopes below the col. At this elevation, the snow had refrozen and formed a thin ice crust, which clinked and rattled when it broke up under our crampons. The upper edges of the crevasses were badly eroded and rotten which indicated to me that this slope became mushy once the full sun hit it. For now, the slope was still frozen and stable.

We reached the base of a steep snow and ice cliff and followed its base on a narrow lip of a crevasse, which in many places had eroded away leaving nothing. We crabbed our way across these places, but the ice cliff beside us kept encroaching on the little space we had for maneuvering. It bulged out farther into our way, so that soon our faces were next to the snow with ice axes embedded at chest height, and we felt as if the cliff was pushing us off the mountain.

Finally, the snow bank and the crevasse ended, and we faced a steep unbroken slope, which led to the summit ridge about one hundred feet above. Below us, the slope ended abruptly at the top of rock cliffs. It was such an unpleasant place I almost called it quits right there, but I judged it too far from the summit to count it as a successful climb. I offered to lead the pitch, and Debbie promised me a "bomb proof" boot axe belay.

While Debbie set up her belay, I chopped a nice platform on the slope for my first step up onto the steep slope. When I looked at Debbie's belay, she could embed only three-fourths of an inch of the point of the axe into the hard snow. Most of the axe was unsupported. Her belay was dubious at best and "bomb proof" only to the extent that no one fell. Stooped over with her arresting hand on the rope and balanced precariously on the edge of the crevasse, she was not a very convincing figure of a solid belay. But no matter, we were committed.

35

When standing on my little platform chopped into the steep slope, my chest was about three feet away from the snow, so I leaned into the slope a little and jammed the ice axe in at chest height in an arrest position. A little fear seeped into my mind. The slope felt a lot steeper on it than when looking at it. I couldn't help thinking that slipping on this slope might be fatal, especially with those cliffs below. Fear went with me each step of the way up, and I thrust my ice axe into the hard snow at every step, hanging onto it like the rungs of a ladder while I kicked-in steps with my boots.

Debbie kept advising me on the amount of rope I had left for climbing, but I ran out a couple of feet from the safety of the rocks that made up the ridge at the top. She had to come out of her belay and step up on the flat step I had made on the steep slope. When she did that, I had just enough rope to reach the safety of a moat, a depression melted out at the top of the snow slope by the heat of the sun on the adjacent rocks on the ridge. Now I had a truly secure place to belay, sitting in the depression between the snow slope and the rocks. Debbie quickly climbed to my position and arrived feeling perfectly happy and safe. I thought, *how are we going to get back down that mean slope?*

From there, it was a simple saunter to the summit where we took some pictures, before heading back. Debbie offered to belay me down the steep snow slope, and I agreed without discussion. We used slings for anchors and saved every bit of rope we could for the climb down. Even so, I was afraid it wouldn't be long enough to reach the little step I had made earlier. The snow slope kept getting steeper the further down I went, and I was unable to see where to get off. Feeling the panic and dread that I wouldn't find the right place to get off the slope, I searched franticly where I thought the way out should be.

I finally saw the platform we had started from, a little farther down the slope and to the left. Debbie had to come out of her belay spot and downclimb the slope a little to give me some extra rope. It was precarious for both of us until I put in a good boot axe belay on the platform. Debbie soon joined me, and without stopping, went on past me, past the bulging ice cliff at the edge of the crevasse to a safe place beyond, where she set up a belay for me. When I joined Debbie at her belay spot, relief washed over me and I was euphoric, for the hard part of the climb was over.

The snow had already gotten soft and would turn even mushier very soon. We met the Argentinean climbers at the col and exchanged a few words, but all of us were in a hurry to get back to the hut before the snow became impassable to walk through. They still had to climb the summit, but we moved along toward the hut as quickly as possible. Eventually we came to places on the slope so soft that we plunged knee-deep into the stuff, so it was with relief that, at about two o'clock, we reached the hut surrounded by its bare solid ground.

I sat at the table and ordered a bottle of wine while Debbie went somewhere to wash up. About five o'clock the two Argentinean climbers came in exhausted. My wine was gone and Debbie had finished washing. There really was nothing left to do here, and I refused to consider another night listening to the hut master's snoring and water sucking its way out of a pipe. So we packed up and left. We headed down the long ridge to the river far below, and made camp along its banks just before dark.

6) Debbie on lead to col at dawn

7) Tronador peaks, International and Argentina

8) Debbie hitching a ride to Tronador trailhead

Chapter 4
Town at Bottom of the World, Argentina

When Debbie and I got back to Bariloche from Tronador, we discussed what to do next. We were tired of climbing and decided to cross Argentina to the Atlantic Ocean to see the sea wildlife there and then perhaps head south to see the sights of southern Argentina. The Patagonia and Tierra del Fuego sounded mysterious and might be exciting places to visit. We took an extremely slow train across the country that in fairness had its tracks washed out in several places somewhere in the middle of the country.

Late in the day, we arrived at the small town of San Antonio Oeste and made camp in a little park overlooking the Atlantic Ocean. We were about to crawl into our sleeping bags when two well dressed young men showed up at our campsite and began talking. They were Mormon missionaries, Americans, sent to Argentina on a two-year mission for their church. I think they enjoyed hearing and speaking American English for a little while after working all day with the Argentines and listening to Spanish. Finally, after dark, they left to go home, wherever that was.

We were up and out on the road by early morning trying to hitch a ride south to Puerto Madryn. It lay close to Peninsula Valdez where sea life congregated by the thousands in colonies all around the coast of the peninsula. We finally got a ride in two dump trucks, one for me, and the other for Debbie. Both of us could have fit into one truck easily, but the drivers insisted on that arrangement.

Along with many other travelers we camped out on the city's public beach, a postage stamp-sized piece of sandy beach on the waterfront. There were way too many people trying to camp out there, and without proper sanitation, I'm sure garbage and worse was buried throughout the sand. At no charge, the price was right, but it was a terrible place to camp.

We easily got two seats on a tour bus that circumnavigated the Valdez Peninsula, which was almost an island, stopping off to see some of the seal, sea lion, and elephant seal colonies. The animals were gathered together very closely and made a racket that I could hear a half mile away and, when close to them, their smell was dreadful. We also saw several small penguin colonies, but the really big penguin colonies were a little farther south.

The next day we hitched a ride in the back of a pickup with a couple and their two teenagers who rode in the cab. They were on vacation and stopped at every point of interest along the way. We saw a lot of things, some not too interesting. But they did stop at a huge penguin colony, and we got out and walked among a multitude of penguins, waves of them. We were the only people among all those penguins. Wherever we went, they parted to open a way for us to walk through their vast numbers, and I think I knew how Moses felt when parting the Red Sea.

In midafternoon, we stopped on a pristine, lonely pebble beach, with nothing in sight for miles, except for the beached carcass of a whale. When up close, the whale became a large elephant seal, and we thought it might be dead. One of the teens patted it on the back and that mountain of blob suddenly became very alive and moved away down the beach.

Then out came the *matte de tea* paraphernalia and we were introduced to a national ritual practiced by many Argentines. They heated water on a burner attached to a five-gallon liquid gas container. While waiting for the water to boil, the host making the tea coarsely chopped up tea leaves in a mug. After pouring the mug full of hot water, the host stirred the mixture a bit, took a sip of the

43

tea, and then passed it onto the next person, who took a sip and passed it onto the next person. This went on until the mug was empty from all those little sips of tea.

Sometimes the mug was filled again with hot water and passed around again, but I've never seen a third mug of tea made. It seemed that a twisted metal straw was prescribed for use in the theory that the twists of the straw would cool the liquid a little before it burned lips and mouth. The tea was always too hot for me, and a little sip of the stuff was all I could handle anyway. The timing of this ritual seemed to be almost any day in midmorning or midafternoon, or both.

Debbie and I got tired of riding in the back of the pickup and, by the end of the second day, were heartily sick of it. We never could get comfortable because the ride was so bumpy on the gravel roads of the back country, and coping with the wind when traveling at high speeds was difficult. Our clothes, our bodies, everything we touched was coated in dust, which seemed to cling to everything. So it was easy to convince ourselves we would be better off with another ride. Anything but the back of a pickup.

That night we stayed in a cabin in a campground near the water while our hosts with their pickup went uptown to stay at a hotel. The next morning, we didn't wait for the pickup to come get us. We were out on the road early trying to hitch another ride. There was nothing. We couldn't get anyone to pick us up, and as the morning passed away, the pickup ride we had before looked better and better. We had walked to the southern edge of Comodoro Rivadavia from our camping spot where we thought the best chance of a catching a long ride south would be best.

Next to us was a ubiquitous guard station checking all vehicles and people coming in and out of Comodoro Rivadavia. The military *junta* of Argentina who ran the country had checkpoints everywhere, especially at edges of towns or states. And at each one, we had to stop for a pack inspection, show our passports, and file our names, destination, and where we had just come from in Argentina. I don't know how many ledgers were filled or who, in their right mind, would read them. The process was a pain for all travelers.

I thought we might gain a little advantage by staying close to the guard station, because everyone that came through had to slow down and stop. One of those people would surely pick us up, I thought, but nobody did. When it started getting dark, we made camp in a room of an abandoned house near the road. It had no roof and half the walls were gone, but we made a good supper and had a restful night.

Up early the next morning, we did our best to hitch a ride, but no one would consider us for passengers in their vehicles. Maybe it was because of all the climbing gear we dragged around with us. Debbie and I began discussions about the feasibility of traveling to southern Argentina and where we might go instead.

On the second day just before twilight, the guards either took pity on us, or they were just tired of us hanging around their guard shack, so they twisted a lone driver's arm to give us a ride on down the road. He went a short distance to a turn-off on a side road that led down to Puerto Deseado where he planned to visit his girlfriend. The pavement ended at that point and the main north-south route in Argentina appeared to be just another gravel and dirt back road. Just before dark, we made camp in the brush a little way from the dusty road.

On our third morning, the hitchhiking seemed just as dismal as the previous days, only now the vehicles had no reason to stop or even slow down. We despaired of ever getting a ride, and resorted to trading off hitching duties. I would try while Debbie read her book, *One Hundred Years of Solitude* by Gabriel Garcia Marquez, an author from Columbia. Then she would try hitching while I read her book. Thus, we passed the time and both of us read the same book. Then in the late morning, a miracle occurred.

A big truck stopped to pick us up. The drivers were Carlos and Victor, and I don't know why they stopped and didn't ask. We hopped aboard the big cab with all of our gear and still had plenty of room to rattle round. The cab had a built-in bed in back of the front seats and this was a comfortable place which got used a lot.

"How far are you going?" asked Debbie.

"Ushuaia," was their response, as if it was just down the road a short distance.

"That's the farthest south you can drive to in the whole world," I said, stunned by that possibility

We never dreamed of getting that far, but plans are made to be changed, and it didn't take us long to decide to go all the way with this truck if the drivers allowed us. We had originally made our objective Rio Gallegos, but now it was Ushuaia, deep in Tierra Del Fuego.

After settling in a little, I noticed that the truck was tearing along at twenty-five miles per hour. That was it; the speed never varied. At first, I thought our speed was about forty-miles per hour, but finally realized their gauges were in kilometers, not miles. I figured, at that rate, we would get to Rio Gallegos in about twenty hours.

And then to get to Ushuaia would be about another fifteen to twenty hours, which included a crossing of the Straits of Magellan and two border crossings in and out of Chile. It was a long way, and we would be a long time riding in this truck going twenty-five miles per hour.

We soon found out that our truck didn't stop for mundane reasons like lunches and coffee breaks, and rarely for a toilet. Late in the afternoon, we stopped at a gas station for some fast food and a toilet break, and that was it for the night. I asked the driver about the slow speed and got a response of *"mucho kilos."* They were heavily loaded with slabs of beef for the southern towns and would return north heavily loaded with sheep meat for the northern towns.

In midafternoon, the off-duty driver hauled out a five-gallon gas tank with burner and put some water on to boil. We were going to have *mate de tea* in the cab of the truck lumbering down the highway. How novel! Sure enough, Debbie and I got a few sips of tea through the inevitable twisted metal straw. Apparently, Victor who made the tea was a purist and provided no second mug of tea to make the rounds. One mug was sufficient.

Just before dark, we experienced the first tire blowout. I counted nine of them before we reached Rio Gallegos. The drivers didn't have that many spares, and we passed no garages, so they laboriously broke the tire out of its rim, fixed the inner tube or put in a new one, and pried the tire back onto its rim. Fortunately, they had a small air pump that worked off the truck's engine to pressurize the tire before putting it back on the axle. I figured that saved a lot of hard work pumping the tire. By hand At first, we all jumped out of the truck to try to help, but as the night passed, only the driver got out and fixed the tire. The rest of us slept through it all, although I felt a little guilty not getting up for the driver's moral support.

Morning arrived and still the truck lumbered along at twenty-five miles per hour. We passed no settlements, nothing of interest man-made, just the small gravel road that led on and on in front of us. About noon, the drivers stopped to let us out before we reached the police checkpoint at Rio Gallegos. I guessed they didn't want us in the cab when they went through, and promised to pick us up at the west end of town when their work was done.

After getting our passports properly stamped, we walked through town to its western edge. There we joined about a dozen people, all trying to get rides. It was no different than elsewhere, and only a few rides were available. As late afternoon passed, I figured Carlos and Victor had already gotten their work done and were long gone toward Ushuaia. That meant we needed a place to stay for the night, and then try again the next day. Both of us were discouraged.

But suddenly, our big truck came down the street with Carlos and Victor waving at us. They stopped and we piled into the now-familiar cab, much to the chagrin of the others waiting for rides. We crossed the Straits of Magellan, and in the gathering gloom, it was just another body of water. It was pitch black when we crossed the Argentine and Chilean border, and there we were subjected to the most intense scrutiny of our packs in all the time we spent in Argentina. They went through everything we had with a fine-toothed comb. They were particularly interested in the few drugs we had with us, and poor Debbie had to explain the peculiar items she carried for feminine hygiene. By the time they let us go, I was worried that our ride would be gone too, but Carlos and Victor were still waiting for us a little way down the road from the checkpoint.

From that point, I don't remember stopping again until we reached Ushuaia, except for more flat tires. There were so many of them I lost track, and I didn't bother stirring from my comfortable seat in the big cab, trying to sleep through it all. Early in the morning after driving all night, Victor dropped us off in town, there was no police checkpoint to pass through. I guessed the town was too small and remote for the *junta* to worry about. As a result we didn't have far to walk to a hotel.

Exhausted, we got rooms and slept until noon. Hitchhiking had turned out to be hard work. We soon found that Ushuaia was a boomtown. Huge apartment houses were going up at the edge of town, and construction workers were everywhere. We hiked beyond the town, and made camp in a meadow in a small depression that hid us from anyone beyond ten feet.

I don't ever remember staying in a place where I could walk to the airport, walk to the shipping piers, and walk straight uphill into a jumble of unclimbed mountains. We climbed one of the taller peaks, route finding our way through a jumble of ridges and lesser peaks to the top. But Debbie and I made a big mistake that day. We stopped in a store on the way, bought some food to take along, and gave the clerk an empty wine bottle to fill. She decanted it from a big vat of wine at the back of her store, popped a cork in it, and handed it over. It was so fast and simple, and cost us seventy-five cents. "That's cheaper than a Coke," I told Debbie.

When we got to the top of our peak, we ate a leisurely lunch and drank the bottle of wine. That was the big mistake. At that elevation, the wine hit us hard, and we had a devil of a time finding our way out. From

51

that day on, I never drank alcohol on a climb, never. Even if it was cheaper than a Coke.

We met a doctor one morning who was born and raised in Ushuaia. I was sure not many people living here could not make that claim. She offered to drive us to a little park where the road ended, marking the southern-most place in the world that could be reached by road. The tiny park on the shore of the Beagle Channel was nondescript, but wherever we chose to go from there had to be north.

One day, we ran into Stan and Cricket, the couple we first met at Tronador, and had a fun talk about our experiences getting to Ushuaia. In an incredible coincidence, they had stayed at the same campground in Comodoro Rivadavia where the couple in the pickup promised to meet us the next day to travel on south with them in the back of their truck. We didn't go with them, and the result was that Stan and Cricket took our place in the pickup, and they rode all over Argentina, seeing every sight available to see. They didn't mention the bumpy roads, the dust and dirt, or the raging wind tearing at their clothes. They were going to El Calafate which everyone shortened to just Calafate to see the Moreno Glacier, which was where we wanted to go too.

"How are you getting there?" I asked. "We tried getting plane tickets, but no airlines flew there from here."

"We're taking a military flight," Stan answered. "When they have extra seating available, they sell those seats to the public."

Debbie and I went back to the airline ticket office and, sure enough, got two tickets to Calafate that afternoon in a DC3 operated by the Argentinean air force.

9) The truck and drivers

10) Typical camp in southern Argentina

11) Buying bulk wine at convenience store, Chile

Chapter 5
A Mighty Glacier and Mountain, Argentina

Riding in a military plane turned out to be far more exciting than a regular commercial jet. Maybe the pilot was practicing to fly a fighter plane. He made gut-wrenching turns, ascents and descents, and soon had all of us passengers praying for a safe return to earth.

Coming into the airport at Calafate, the pilot slid the plane in sideways at full throttle, straightening out at the last minute to land amidst a cloud of gravel and dust, finally stopping thirty feet from a cliff at the end of the runway. When the passengers finally realized that the flight was over and we were safely on the ground, they broke into spontaneous applause, and I joined them.

We did a little partying that night with Stan and Cricket, and the next morning bid them farewell. They were going to hitchhike north to see Fitz Roy, a mountain known by climbers the world over, and we were going to hitchhike west to see the Moreno Glacier. The glacier was about fifty miles away, and we got a ride out there in a short time. I hadn't read much about the glacier, but I knew it was a major place of interest.

When I finally saw it, I couldn't believe my eyes. First of all, it was immense, far larger than anything I had imagined. It wound its way through the mountains for fifteen miles from its source, a huge ice cap that spawned twelve other large glaciers. The front edge of this glacier ended in the waters of Lago Argentino.

I had seen many glaciers in Alaska that ended in water, but the size of their icy snouts were puny in comparison to this monstrous wall of vertical ice, three miles long and two hundred feet high above the surface of the lake.

The front edge of the glacier was deeply fissured, and undercut by the waters of the lake as they melted out the ice below the surface. When the weight of the ice became too heavy, great chunks of it broke off the front of that huge ice cliff and slid into the lake waters.

The truly large pieces of ice, the size of a twenty-story building, broke away from the ice cliff in a series of rifle-like reports. Then sounding like jet engines at full throttle, the ice chunks went thundering down hurling a spray of snow and ice high into the air like a white cloud. The ice hit the water with a mighty splash, disappeared under the surface a few seconds, and then reappeared rolling over and moving sluggishly about in the water until the new ice berg reached its equilibrium.

With about ninety percent of the berg under water, it floated out into the lake where it eventually melted into its waters and disappeared. Sometimes the bergs hit the water to form a large tsunami-like wave that washed up on the shore from where we watched the glacial show. The authorities placed warning signs not to walk along the beach, but Debbie and I walked there anyway keeping a sharp lookout for incoming big waves.

Stranded on the shore were huge pieces of ice the size of houses. At first, I thought these were remnants of icebergs that had somehow come ashore rather than floating away into the lake, but then I realized these ice chunks were left by the glacier when it retreated.

At the time of our visit, Moreno Glacier was one of very few glaciers in the world that grew at a rapid pace. Every two to three years, part of the glacier formed a dam that cut the lake into two parts. It covered the beach and jammed our hillside view points with ice. The water behind the dam rose ninety to one hundred feet above the surface of the rest of the lake. We saw the evidence of that damming where the forest didn't start growing until ninety to one hundred feet above the surface of the lake.

Then came what the local people called the "rupture." The dammed up water finally cut a channel through the glacier, and all that water began pouring through the breach in the ice. I visualized that scene of pent-up energy as the dammed water rapidly widened and deepened the channel causing a maelstrom of roaring, rushing water that carried away with it huge chunks of ice, allowing even more water to flow into the lower lake. I would have loved to see that. However, in recent years, the glacier no longer dammed the lake into two parts. Some say it's because of global warming.

Finally rousing ourselves from the mesmerizing action of the glacier, we decided to go back to Calafate rather than camp out at this wild and lonely place. We managed to wrangle two seats from a sympathetic driver on the last tour bus left in the little parking area overlooking the glacier.

Debbie and I got back to Calafate in late afternoon and dropped into a store to buy some food and the inevitable bottle of wine. While there, we met two Frenchmen who were in a little trouble. Debbie spoke French and found that they were low on cash, but were traveling about in a rental car. They wondered if we would buy some food for them in exchange for a round trip ride to Fitz Roy. We readily agreed because Fitz Roy was at the end of a long dead end road, and we thought hitching there would be very difficult, especially after our experiences in hitching rides so far. After buying their food, we agreed to meet the next morning.

Debbie and I set up camp a short distance from the edge of town among some large bushes that screened us from anyone walking about. That night we had a supper over a real wood fire, roasting pieces of meat on a stick between swigs of wine. Just before complete darkness, a big fat moon rose over the flat desert of the Patagonia in a wonderful display of beauty in such a wild place.

We met the two Frenchmen at the gas station where they were topping off their gas tanks. The last thing they purchased before leaving town was a six-foot length of half-inch plastic tube. When I asked about that, they said it was for siphoning gas into their tanks when they ran out of gas. Fitz Roy was too far to drive there and back on a tank of gas. They expected to run out of gas somewhere on the way back. Someone would have to come along in the middle of nowhere and give us some gas. With that cavalier attitude, we jumped into the car and sped off in a cloud of dust toward Fitz Roy.

In early afternoon in the middle of nowhere, we stopped behind a line of traffic. By now, that seemed impossible because we rarely saw that many cars in one place. Up ahead a small ferry had stopped running across a large lake that cut the road and we, along with the others, were forced to wait until the ferry was repaired. No one left their place in line and hours passed. Finally we did as others were doing, made supper, and camped for the night near the car. Some actually slept in their cars.

No one complained much; it was just part of traveling in that section of the country. During the night, we heard the occasional shouting and clank of machinery as someone worked on the ferry ahead of us. Then early the next morning the ferry blasted its whistle, waking us up, and began operating again. The line of cars moved, and we moved with it.

Suddenly two people ran out of the nearby trees down the line of waiting cars. It was Stan and Cricket desperately looking for a ride. Apparently, this was as far as they had gotten in almost two day's worth of hitchhiking. They greeted us like long lost friends and the Frenchmen agreed to take them with us to Fitz Roy. I'm not sure if any money changed hands.

We lost all traffic after turning off on the dead end road into Fitz Roy. It was a long way in, but finally the road came to an abrupt end on the banks of a small river. Ours was the only car in a tiny parking area. Across the river was an uninhabited field of brush and grass gently sloping from the foothills that led into the mountains to our left down to a larger river on our right. Nearby, almost lost in the trees, was a national park guardhouse, but the guard stationed there was of little help, except to recommend that we wade the river in the morning before the snowmelt made the waters too high later in the day to get across.

For me, wading anything was disagreeable, but that little river was a raging torrent, and we all got wet to the waist. The current in some places was almost enough to pull me off my feet, and I was carrying a full pack of at least sixty-pounds. I'm always amused by the psychology of wading through a rushing stream. Not one of us used the same spot to cross, each person figuring his choice of route was a better place to use. Sometimes it took a lot of walking up and down the bank of the river to find that best place. After wading the river, I took off my boots and wrung out my socks, which was the extent of drying out my clothes. The outer clothes dried rapidly in the sun and air, but my underwear remained wet for a long time.

Before we found the trail to the base camp at Fitz Roy, we saw a little house almost lost in the trees and brush. I thought it might be a sheepherder's camp. It looked abandoned, and even though the others remained unenthusiastic, I knocked on the door anyway.

It opened immediately and a jolly bearded man invited us in to his one room that was a kitchen, living area, and bedroom combined. He talked constantly, but I didn't understand much of what he said. He told us where to pick up the trail into Fitz Roy and described other spots in the area worth hiking to.

Just for fun, I asked about buying some sheep meat, but he vigorously shook his head, "I no can sell you meat."

Then he ushered us into a second room where haunches of sheep meat hung, covering every square foot of ceiling. He looked over a few and yanked one of them off the ceiling.

"Here," he said as he pushed it into my hands, "I no can sell you meat, but I can give you meat."

I took a little ribbing from the others as I struggled to tie the unwieldy haunch to my pack so that it wouldn't hang down too far, swing from side to side, or bounce around on my back when I walked. That night we had a feast of roasted meat on a stick done on an open wood fire along with the ubiquitous wine.

The trail into Fitz Roy was about five miles long, and ended in a wooded area below the peak. We had beautiful views of the mountain, and its satellite peaks almost all the way in. It was a monolithic fat finger of seemingly unclimbable steep rock sticking up much higher than the surrounding peaks. Perversely, the base camp lay among trees tucked in too close to Fitz Roy for us to see the mountain from there. However, we climbed a couple peaks nearby and got an eye full of Fitz Roy from the top of these. It looked terribly impossible to climb, and I found out later that most climbers started at a base camp on the other side, the Chilean side, with more success than from where we camped.

When it was time to head back, we broke into three pairs, each pair to explore a different route and area on the way back to the car. Debbie and I cut across country over some high hills toward the river we had waded at the start of our trip in. The area was pristine and beautiful, and I easily imagined that Debbie and I were the first to walk through that paradise. But I knew that sheep had been here years before with herders following in their steps.

We came to a large lake and I swam briefly in its frigid waters. Debbie lasted in the water a lot longer, and I chalked it up to her being very dirty or maybe having a greater tolerance for swimming in freezing waters. The rest of that afternoon we read and lolled about in the warm sun, watching the fluffy white clouds and their shadows play across the glaciated peaks to our right and on the lower forested foothills to our left.

The next day we arrived at the banks of that little raging river and waded it, relieved when that ordeal was over, knowing we didn't have to do it again. When all six of us got back to the car, we jumped in and started the long trip back to Calafate. I was dozing in the back seat when suddenly the engine stopped running, and we coasted to a stop at the edge of the road. Out of gas. We waited the rest of the afternoon, but no traffic came by. We made supper and camped right there close to the loneliest section of dirt and gravel road in the middle of nowhere that I had ever traveled. At least we were stuck on the main road and not on the dead end road into Fitz Roy.

When I awoke in the morning, a pickup had stopped on the road beside our car. By the time I was out of the sack and dressed, the two men from that pickup had pumped some gas into our car and were ready to go on again. Apparently, seeing our stopped car, they knew immediately what our problem was, so I guessed this procedure happened often. We barely had time to thank them before they were on their way again, but I did get a glimpse of the huge gas tanks they had in the bed of their pickup.

That night we partied a little in Calafate, and in the morning went in three separate directions. Debbie and I headed for the road out of town to Rio Gallegos to start hitching for a ride. Stan and Cricket started hitching for a ride out to the Moreno Glacier, and I don't know where the Frenchmen went. Late in the afternoon, we were still just outside of town. We couldn't get a ride no matter how hard we tried. Then Stan and Cricket showed up walking out from town, and the four of us stood there awhile with our thumbs out, but no one stopped or even slowed down.

We gave up in disgust and set up camp near the road. Stan and Cricket set up a tent for the night and invited us to join them, but Debbie and I just spread out our plastic tarps and went to sleep. That night it rained, and we quickly picked up our bedding and ran for the tent. It was a three-man tent with a pole down the middle. Stan and Cricket made room for us although it was a tight squeeze with four people and gear. During the night I woke once to find Cricket snuggled close to me. *This is nice,* I thought, and went back to sleep. Next morning, neither of us mentioned that dream.

Early in the morning, we began hitching for a ride again, and by midmorning, I was discouraged. No one stopped and I didn't know of any buses that went between the two towns. If we couldn't snag a ride, I worried about how we would get to Rio Gallegos, the gateway back to buses, airports, and Buenos Aires, and our only way out of southern Argentina. Then along came the two Frenchmen in their precious car, and they stopped to pick us up.

Once we got to Rio Gallegos, we celebrated our arrival in an ice cream shop and then went once again in three directions. Debbie and I took a late afternoon flight to Buenos Aires, and in the next two days we crossed Argentina into Chile by bus. Then we flew up to La Paz, Bolivia where Debbie and I parted with a big hug and a couple of tears. She still had a month left to explore Bolivia, Peru, and Ecuador, and I went home.

I've been back to South America four times since that first trip thirty-years ago. Much has changed in that time. Access roads, parking areas, and people in parks are fenced in so that the penguins and other animals can roam the land unmolested with no interaction with people. A multitude of tour buses take visitors to see the Moreno Glacier and other neat places in the area.

The dead end road to Fitz Roy now crosses that miserable little river on a new concrete bridge to end at a new town, El Chalten, and at the edge of that town is a bright shiny new gas station. So there's no reason to ever run out of gas coming and going to Calafate. The biggest change is that the Moreno Glacier no longer advances fast enough to dam up part of Lago Argentino to create a high lake and the "rupture" phenomenon.

Debbie and I still live in the Seattle area, and we've remained good friends even though our paths rarely cross. But that month's adventure with her remained a high standard, from which I have judged many of my other trips over the years.

12) Moreno Glacier

13) Moreno Glacier

14) Moreno Glacier

15) Fitz Roy

Frank King

Fort Cochin (now Kochi) is a region in the city of Kochi in the state of Kerala, India. This is part of a handful of water-bound regions toward the south-west of the mainland Kochi, and collectively known as Old Kochi or West Kochi.

Nepal is a small landlocked country of highly diverse and rich geography, culture, and religions. The mountainous north has eight of the world's ten highest mountains, including Mount Everest. It contains over 240 peaks more than 20,000 ft (6,096 m) above sea level.

Map of the trek in Nepal

70

Chapter 6
On the Trail, Nepal

I felt like a little kid let loose in a chocolate factory. After months of planning for a long hike, I had made it to Nepal where trekking for days or weeks on trails was a way of life. I had so many choices of trails, big mountains, and strange places to see that it had been hard to pick just one area. I chose to do a trip that circled mighty Annapurna, a massive peak in the Himalayas.

According to my guidebook, the distance around the mountain was in excess of one hundred fifty miles, but in more practical terms the time required for me to walk around the peak would take about three weeks. The major obstacle was crossing the Thorung La Pass at over 17,600 feet elevation about halfway through the trek. Before this trip, the longest hikes I had ever been on were nine-day backpack trips into the North Cascades and never at such high altitudes. So along with the heady excitement and anticipation of starting this adventure was a niggling worry about whether I could do it or not.

. I traveled alone, carrying a light pack containing a few extra clothes, wool sweaters and hat, a light sleeping bag, and a foam pad. My sleeping bag was literally a bag, no zippers, and every night I scrunched into it from its open top. To save weight and space, it had down filling on top, but only nylon cloth on the bottom. I didn't plan to camp out, but expected to find places to stay overnight wherever I went. Aside from a few snacks in my pack, I planned to eat whatever I found along the way that looked edible.

I carried iodine crystals to purify the water. I only needed a few crystals, because they seemed to last forever. I carried them submerged in a two-ounce bottle of water, and the physics of iodine crystals allowed only a fixed amount of iodine to saturate the water and no more. Therefore, the two ounces of solution always had the same percentage of iodine, and adding a couple bottle capfuls of that to a liter of water was sufficient to purify even the murkiest and rattiest of water. I never got sick from drinking water, but the downside was that I never got rid of the unpleasant taste of iodine. Of course, I never had thyroid problems either.

I started out on a trail so wide it looked like a dirt road. Sure enough a short time later, a noisy tractor belching dark, obnoxious exhaust passed me hauling a wagon full of people. I watched with mixed emotions of envy and dismay as they pulled out of sight, leaving behind diesel fumes and dust hanging in the hot air. The heat made me envious of those people riding in relative comfort, but anticipation of a wilderness experience caused my dismay when I saw the trail shared by that nasty machine. Most of the people like me walked. I met them in ones and twos and in bunches. They all looked me over as they passed, obviously interested by a 'Westerner' in their midst. The women made bold eye contact, but the men glanced at me more surreptitiously.

The women wore colorful saris that made them look so graceful, and many balanced baskets, bundles, or firewood on their heads. Most men carried nothing. Among the travelers, porters plodded along at their deceptively moderate speeds carrying their great backbreaking loads. Later, I found out that most Nepalese measured distance by porter days, the time it took a porter to travel from place to place in one day. Although in good physical condition, my distance of travel in a day seldom equaled that of a porter.

Children appeared suddenly from nowhere, each greeting me with shouts of *namaste* and when I returned the greeting, they would immediately shout *miThai, miThai.* It took me awhile before I understood they wanted sweets or candy. I wouldn't give them any because I had very little and, also I didn't like to see them begging. *"It'll rot their teeth,"* I thought. I became more and more reluctant to acknowledge the frivolous use of such a beautiful greeting as *namaste,* which translated loosely as, "I greet the god within you." In today's modern world, that simple greeting meant "hello" or "goodbye." Fortunately, the frivolous greetings and requests for sweets diminished the farther I traveled from the trailhead.

Later on in the trek, I occasionally met a person who greeted me with a solemn *namaste,* accompanied with a bow of the head and hands pressed together as if in prayer. Taken by surprise whenever it happened, I would quickly return the salutation, awkwardly bowing my head with my hands held in a prayerful attitude. Whenever this happened, and it wasn't very often, a wonderful feeling engulfed me. Suddenly, I felt like a very special person. Though we might be far apart culturally and economically, the greeting made me feel close to the other person and somehow a part of his world.

In midafternoon, a pretty girl about twelve years old dressed in a sari came bouncing up the trail. She wore jewelry on her arms and around her neck, and one that pierced the side of her nose. I mentally winced. She greeted me with *namaste*, but instead of shouting *miThai,* asked me in a soft persuasive voice to visit her village and stay the night with her family.

"You are welcome there," she said. "Please come," and she pointed off to the left of my route where I saw nothing but rice paddies. I hesitated a moment thinking, *It's pretty early in the afternoon to stop for the day, but why not? This could be fun.* I followed the girl off the main trail on minor paths that wandered through the hot, open rice paddies. After some time, I began to wonder if I had made a bad decision, but the little girl beckoned me on, and I dutifully followed. I knew one of my faults was that pretty women easily persuaded me. But where was this girl taking me?

We finally reached another large trail paralleling my original route. It was definitely not a road and much more pleasant to travel with shade trees, less people, and no machines. In a short distance, we reached a small village consisting of about twelve small houses scattered on both sides of the trail. The trail widened a little to provide space for the villagers to work, play, and conduct business.

The pretty girl delivered me to her mom's doorstep and ran off on another errand. I never saw her again, and later thought maybe she was simply a young hustler bringing in paying customers to stay the night here. Yet when I saw her last, she was gaily tripping away down the trail, and before passing out of sight, turned to give me a pretty smile and a little wave of her hand. *Such a nice hustler.* The 'mom,' now more correctly, the hostess of a primitive boarding house, invited me in, and we negotiated a price for supper and breakfast the next morning, and for a place to sleep.

Looking around the bare room, I placed my head on my hands as if on a pillow and asked, "Where do I sleep?"

She pointed to a large, eighteen-inch wide bench just inside the door that I hadn't noticed before. I saw no other furnishings in the house, so I agreed and paid her some *rupees* in advance.

The villagers built their houses of rough-cut wood boards set vertically in the ground. The cracks and imperfections between them let in some ventilation and daylight, and the only other opening was a doorway so low that I had to duck my head to enter. The floors were packed dirt, and the roofs were thatch. An open fire provided some light and heat to cook meals, but with no chimney, the smoke curled about the room, slowly leaving through the open door and the cracks between the boards of the walls.

My boarding house consisted of one room where guests stayed near the door and the fire, and a piece of cloth screened off a small area beyond the fire to allow privacy for the host and hostess. A stream nearby provided water and the toilet was anywhere out of the sight of others. The village had no electricity, and during the black night, candles, lamps, and fires provided the only light, except for my flashlight.

The entire village lay in deep shade provided by just two giant trees growing within twenty feet of each other. Their branches spread out horizontally to form a protective snug canopy over the entire village. A rock wall surrounded the trees at their base, and at four feet, was too high to sit on. Later I found similar rock walls all along the route of my trek. They were called *chautaara* and were built for porters to set down their loads.

I didn't realize until later that some loads carried by a porter were so heavy, up to one hundred seventy pounds, that if dropped to the ground couldn't be picked up without help. But a porter could back up to a *chautaara*, set his load down on top and slip out of the pack harness, leaving his huge pack precariously balanced. Like truck stops back home, the porters gathered to rest in shade, eat lunch, and gossip while their rigs sat in a row on top of the *chautaara* ready to go.

A haphazard web of rope and twine held the load together, and a trump line around the forehead supported most of the weight straight down the neck rather than having the weight supported on the back. I tried using a trump line once and found it easy to use, but I almost broke my neck when I turned my head to one side. A porter didn't turn his head; he turned his whole body to one side or the other. The porters freighted every conceivable type of box, crate, sack, and basket, or cases of beer to every village and town along the trail. No matter how far the distance from Katmandu, the capital, a bottle of beer remained the same price wherever I went. I thought that was very nice, but never got an explanation of how that was possible.

Four other travelers, all Nepalese, drifted in to stay overnight. In late afternoon, a young boy about fourteen years old came by. He said he was a friend of the pretty girl. *Small world*, I thought. We got to talking because he wanted to practice speaking English. Many people in Nepal spoke some English, and young people were learning it in school. Before he left, he invited me to come to his house the next day and visit his school. I agreed to go. His home lay some distance from the village, and he promised to come for me in the morning.

'Mom' served-up supper just before dark. It was *dal bhat,* a couple spoonfuls of runny lentils over a large mound of rice. *Yuk,* I thought, *I hate rice.* She offered nothing else to eat; it was "take it or leave it," so I took it. Many of the meals I had while trekking consisted of *dal bhat,* lentils and rice. Sometimes for a change, I got runny spinach instead of runny lentils. Invariably, those vegetables were spiced hot enough to bring tears to my eyes and smoke from my ears, and I ate a lot of rice just to tame them down a little. Reluctantly, I learned to like rice, a little.

For reasons of sanitation, I brought my own plastic bowl and spoon and washed them in water treated with iodine crystals. I think I read somewhere I had to do this to stay alive or at least not get sick. When I refused to eat on the plate Mom provided, I received a contemptuous look as she dished up my bowl. Everyone else ate the meal with their right hand off plates furnished by Mom. I used a spoon and a bowl bought from home, and I felt ridiculous trying to be so sanitary.

I thought about this cultural difference in eating styles and decided that I would risk using Mom's dishes and try eating with my fingers. After supper, I got rid of my bowl and spoon. I gave them away or threw them away. I don't remember. But I still refused to use their water for washing my hands, and when no one was looking, I tossed it away and used my iodine treated water. It seemed to me to be a reasonable compromise, and for the rest of my time in Nepal, I followed that routine, using my hosts' dishes and my own treated water for washing, never getting sick, or even close to dying.

The next morning I received a smile from Mom when she dished up breakfast on her own plate, and I prepared to eat with my hand, the right one, of course. What a mess I made with food all over my hand and face! Much to the amusement of the Nepalese, I had to be taught the proper way to eat. Using the first three fingers as a scoop to pick up a mouthful of food, I transported it to my mouth, and with my elbow held high in the air, shoveled it off my fingers with my thumb. The more I did this correctly, the cleaner I kept my hand and face.

After supper, the villagers stood around in the street talking and laughing. One of them started to play a guitar, and soon a couple of men began a dance accompanied by shouts and laughter. I was embarrassed when they insisted that I do an American dance. My face reddened as I did an impromptu, awkward jig of some sort, much to the amusement and great approval of the group.

That night I shared the bench, now a hard, bare bed toe-to-toe with another man. Somehow I managed to kick him lightly when I went to lie down. I had heard that this was a terrible offense, and I apologized effusively while expecting to be beaten up and thrown out. He accepted my apology, and we lay back down. The other men lay on the bare dirt floor wherever they could find room.

Dad, in the meantime, had closed the door, the only opening in the house. It consisted of several boards laid on edge and held upright by grooves in the doorjamb. The smoke from dying embers of the fire filed the room, and I sweat in the stifling heat. I longed to be on the ground outside in the cool night, but couldn't think of a way to gracefully get away. Everyone else immediately fell asleep, but I laid there awake for a long time. Thus, I spent the first night of my long-awaited trek.

In the morning, I waited awhile for the boy I had met the day before to show up. I finally gave up and started walking out of the village, but hadn't gone far when a younger boy came running and shouting after me. My friend from the night before hadn't come because he had spent most of the night irrigating his father's fields, but I was to follow his younger brother home. The house was located past the village about a quarter mile off the trail.

The boy's family of four lived in a small, one room hut with dirt floor, adobe walls, and thatch roof. Absolutely no furniture. His mother cooked over an open fire and wore a loose-fitting dress that slipped off one shoulder or the other, exposing one or the other bare breast. The father had something wrong with his legs and couldn't stand up. He got around by swaying his body back and forth in a sort of duck walk. Surprisingly, he could get around pretty fast.

They insisted I eat breakfast even though I had already eaten. The mom served me one boiled egg and pancake-like bread with tea. At this point, thankfully, her dress covered both breasts. Everyone else had pancake-like bread and tea. To escape the smoke, we stood outside to eat, except for Mom who stayed by the fire. No one else had an egg, and it turned to ashes in my mouth when I found out they had given me their only egg. I thought of cutting it into four parts, but I had already eaten half. My God, I didn't even like boiled eggs and eating this one was simply a courtesy. The guidebooks hadn't prepared me for this.

I apologized and tried to give them money, but they said no. They didn't want my money. They tried to assure me that, as their guest, they were obligated to give me the best they had and that was an egg.

The fourteen-year-old boy took me back to the main trail after I had seen his school. The windows had no glass and the doorways no doors. A few benches sat in rows on a dirt floor. The bare, stark walls had no pictures, maps, or blackboards. He asked me to take a negative he had of himself back to the United States and make some pictures for him. He needed them to make an application to the next level of school. I readily agreed, and took down his address. When I got home, I sent him the pictures along with some money. I never heard back from him, but after all these years, I still remember that day, the day I received the best his family could offer, one egg.

Chapter 7
The Umbrella Man, Nepal

Almost everyone I met on the trail in Nepal would ask me *"kahAA jaane,"* where are you going? I answered "Manang," although it was several walking days away. Everyone knew Manang because it was a major town in that part of Nepal. They would walk along with me and converse in English for a while, and then pull away since their pace was always faster than mine. Of the various trails in Nepal, I had chosen to hike around Annapurna, the tenthhighest mountain in the world. Annapurna was a huge massif consisting of four connected peaks, and for me to get all the way around would take up to three weeks. I traveled alone on the trail carrying a small, light pack

One morning a man overtook me with a cheery, *KahAA jaane.* He told me that he was traveling to visit his girlfriend in Besisahar. He had left his home in the hills across the river the day before, swum the river that morning, and hoped she would be in Besisahar when he got there about noon. I told him she must be special for him to walk so far, but he didn't think it was too far.

He was tall for a Nepalese and carried a large black umbrella. It was very hot, and he offered me shelter from the sun in the shade of his umbrella. Back home before this trip I had planned for cold temperatures, after all this was the Himalayas, home of snow and ice, bitter cold, and the 'abominable snowman.' But no one told me that traveling through the rice fields of Nepal at five thousand feet would be hot sweaty work, so I welcomed his offer of shade that miraculously traveled with us.

He called me *baabu*, father, and was concerned about my traveling alone in the heat. I couldn't remember anyone who ever used that term, and I was flattered by his respectful use of baabu. Perhaps my graying hair and gray-streaked beard confused him. In a few places where the dirt had washed away from the trail leaving exposed rocks and roots, he solicitously took my arm to get me past those rough places. I didn't tell him about the dozen peaks I had climbed earlier that year, and simply let him 'help' me through those areas

At one point, we came to flowing water gushing from a pipe alongside the trail. He stopped to drink the water, but I held back thinking about all the germs and bugs that could be in the water. I drank water purified with iodine solution, so my water always tasted of iodine. It was horrible stuff, but safe to drink. I asked if this water was *ramro paani*, good water. He laughed and said it was pure, cold water piped directly from the ground. I threw away my iodine-tainted water and enjoyed drinking the sweet water instead.

At midmorning, we stopped at a teahouse. These places served food and beer as well as tea, and generally were places to stay overnight. The accommodations varied from just enough floor space to flake out, a bench, or a real bed. Private rooms were a rarity. Many places didn't have bedding, but no matter, I carried a light sleeping bag with me. I used my rolled-up pants and a sweater for a pillow and slept like a baby.

Several men sat at a table nearby, and the umbrella man talked to them while I had tea and *biskooTs*. These were much like Lorna Doone shortbread cookies. After awhile, the umbrella man and another older man came to my table and sat down. Umbrella man asked me if I would give some Nepalese *rupees* to the older man and his friends in exchange for a personal check. It seemed that these men had left town before the bank was open and were short of cash. They were traveling away from the bank, and I was traveling toward the bank

I thought, *Oh boy, here comes the scam.* I didn't know they had banks in Nepal, much less checks. However, they assured me that Besisahar had a bank. Umbrella man told me not to worry, that he would personally get the check cashed for me. I mentally calculated that I could afford to lose the amount of cash they required if it came to that. So I allowed myself to be persuaded, and forked over the cash in exchange for a check written in Sanskrit which I couldn't read, except for my name prominently displayed in English.

We got to Besisahar and found the bank. Outside the door, people milled about like a recently kicked anthill. That didn't faze umbrella man; he just pushed his way through the mob and disappeared into the bank with my check. I waited and sweated in the hot sun, not daring to move away from the sight of the bank's doorway. About fifteen minutes later, he reappeared with my cash. I thanked him with relief and invited him to lunch. He agreed to meet me in half an hour.

We had a feast, consisting of a beer each, lots of rice, a few lentils, a little spinach, and for the first time in Nepal, meat. They were unrecognizable pieces of meat, hopefully beef, in thin gravy, served in a little stainless steel dish four inches in diameter and half an inch deep. The meat was so rubbery and laced with gristle that I couldn't eat it, but umbrella man could, and did. He sucked every shred of meat off the bones and gristle and then slurped down the gravy.

After lunch we parted, I to head for Manang and he to head for home four days away. His journey had been for nothing. His girlfriend was not in town, and no one knew how long she would be away.

16) Tea House

17) Distributing Rice, Besisahar

Chapter 8
The Letter Drop, Nepal

I stopped to rest in midafternoon where the thick brush hemming the trail higher than my head suddenly opened up to a wonderful view across the valley. Through the gap, I saw a confusion of mottled green ridges, sprouting ever higher as they reached an insurmountable barrier of snow-covered peaks that starkly contrasted a cobalt sky. I was more bored by the unexciting trail than tired, but I stopped anyway, sat in the shade, and sipped my safe, iodine-tainted water while drinking in that delightful view.

This part of the trail around Annapurna in Nepal was moderately steep, and it cut through heavy oppressive brush and a few scattered trees. With relief, I enjoyed my stop in an open area as much as I enjoyed the view. I was now in the fourth or was it the fifth day of my journey of about twenty-one days to complete the trip.

When I got up to leave, I saw a white post off to one side that I hadn't noticed before. Looking more closely, I saw it had something mounted on it about five feet off the ground. Curious, I looked at it more closely and suddenly realized that it was a mailbox. *What was it doing out here in the middle of nowhere?*

It stood alone with no signs or other trappings of civilization. It was made of cast iron with the body painted bright green, and the locked lid painted bright red. I lifted the hinged red flap on top of the lid and, sure enough, saw the slot used to drop letters into the box. Once in, they were gone because a heavy padlock prevented anyone from opening the top of the box. I touched the embossed Sanskrit characters on the surface of the lid, which I assumed said *mail. But who in their right mind would drop letters off here in the midst of this wilderness?*

I knew that in most countries the postal system was a function of government. If the government worked, the mail got delivered; if not, it didn't. I remembered the postal system of Zaire, now called the People's Republic of the Congo. Travelers were warned to buy and affix the stamp themselves, otherwise the agent might be tempted to pocket the money and forget the stamp. Then we continued to wait at the counter or desk until the agent canceled the stamp, because some wily agents tore the uncanceled stamps off the letter and sold them again. But beyond our control, a dutifully-stamped and posted letter might languish in the out-box for days, weeks maybe, or the ultimate horror never to leave the post office.

I thought about what I had seen so far in Nepal. Police and customs worked well, schools abounded, and people seemed fairly content and safe. I figured the Nepalese government functioned okay, so it probably delivered its mail. The white post and mail drop appeared newly painted and well-maintained. *But who in their right mind would take a chance of dropping off letters in the middle of nowhere. How would a letter get "out?"*

I visualized a Nepalese on his stubby horse carrying a sack for mail coming by this place to pick up letters on his weekly, or more lengthy schedule, or maybe no schedule at all. He would remove the contents of this mailbox, and then shove it in his sack along with mail he had already collected along the way. Then he had to ride out with his mail sack at least six days, or probably more, to a postal distribution point. Once there, I easily visualized the mail working its way through normal civilized and mechanized channels.

But the hard part of all this conjecture was to imagine a man eating, sleeping, and living with the mail and keeping it safe for days on end. "Neither snow nor rain nor heat nor gloom of night nor distance stopped the mail," came to mind.

Almost in slow motion, I went to my pack and took out three diary-type letters I had written to myself describing the events and my adventures in Nepal so far. I had pre-stamped them back in Katmandu, the capital, before beginning this trek. My original idea was to give them to a passing hiker going the other way, asking him to post the letters for me at the nearest post office. Even that was perilous, because I had to trust an unknown stranger to do me a favor.

I had no way of knowing for sure that such a person would be caring or careful enough in his volunteer job of delivering my mail. After all, we met by chance for only a few seconds on this trail. By the time he reached a post office, he wouldn't even remember me, and maybe even forget my mail. So far, I hadn't found anyone that I was willing to trust with such a favor. *So who in their right mind would drop off important letters in this out-of-the-way spot?* "I would," I said aloud, but no one heard that answer except me. I walked over to that mailbox inexorably, as if pushed by some unseen force. *What am I doing?* I carefully opened the bright red lid and deliberately slid my letters into the slot.

They immediately slid out of sight. I had no way of getting them back; they were gone forever. I looked at that benign-appearing mailbox a few seconds with mixed feelings of regret and daring. Then I shrugged into my pack and went on up the trail. Within a mile, the whole episode was washed from my mind. I didn't think about those letters again until I reached home several weeks later and found them all there waiting for me. Of course, they were. Nepal delivered its mail.

18) Postman or traveler?

Chapter 9
The Porter, Nepal

One afternoon, I think it was the sixth day of my trek around Annapurna, I was hurrying down the trail to get to the next village or find some sort of shelter. The thick black clouds overhead threatened rain, and by their looks, a downpour heavy enough to get my underwear wet. For me, most rainfall was not a great discomfort unless it penetrated my clothes enough to affect the underwear, and then I got cranky. Sometimes it happened fast, but other times it took all day. Today I figured the clouds would erupt in a fury of drenching rain quickly, getting me wet to the skin.

A man caught up to me and called out a cheery, *"kahAA jaane?"* as he passed me. Then he slowed to my pace for a few minutes to talk. One of the things he told me was that he was hurrying to meet a group of mountain climbers two days ahead. He hoped to get a job with them as a porter.

"So you climb these huge mountains?" I asked.

He laughed and shook his head. "No, I just haul supplies to the upper camps and come back down for another load.   Sometimes I see the same stretch of mountain over and over again."

"Up and down?" I asked.   "But that could add up to more elevation gain than the mountain itself."

"Well, maybe," he said thoughtfully, "I've never added it up. Perhaps I will this time, if I get hired."

"But some of the porters get to the top, don't they?" I asked.

"Very few, just some special men. Very few."

He talked on for a little while longer, and then with much apology, excused himself to hurry on ahead, because he, too, thought that heavy rain was coming. Maybe he didn't want to get his underwear wet either.

"I stop for the night in *Khudi* just ahead," he said, "and I will see you there."

Then he quickly disappeared, and I hiked on down the trail as fast as I could go. I finally saw *Khudi* across the river, a group of small buildings on either side of the path that had widened into a street. The buildings were made of rough-cut planks and thatched roofs. To get there, I had to cross over a raging river that roared its defiance as it crashed waves of water against large boulders littering the river bed.

A picturesque suspension bridge about twenty feet off the water spanned from bank to bank. The support cables made graceful arcs across the water, giving the bridge a peaceful stable feeling. However, when I strode out onto the bridge, it bucked up and down without warning, swaying from side to side in a twisting motion that threatened to pitch me off into the river. I grabbed a support cable and held on for dear life until the bridge settled down. I suppose for the sake of saving a little money the builders left each side completely open with no safety barriers, and I cringed to the center of the treads. I easily imagined slipping off into the river from one side or the other if the rolling of the bridge got too violent. That bridge swayed and bucked at the least motion I made, and I considered not trying to cross at all. But looking around, I saw no other way to get to Khudi, so I gritted my teeth and carefully balanced my way out toward the center of the bridge.

Then I came to a missing plank in the tread. *Great*, I thought, *don't they maintain these things?* I stopped, dead in my tracks, not moving an inch until the bridge stopped moving around under my feet. While waiting, I got excellent views of glassy, green waters, like twisted taffy, and white foaming spray pitched high in the air toward me, while the persistent, unremitting roar of falling water drowned all other senses except dread. When I thought the bridge was stable enough, I gingerly stepped across the gap and then moved on to the next opening caused by a missing plank. The planks were about twelve inches wide, but the gaps always seemed to be much wider.

Much worse than the missing planks were those that had major defective cracks across the center of them. They were harder to see than open gaps. I easily visualized stepping on one, having it break in half to plunge me and the plank onto the torrent below, so I stepped across those, too. Finally, I came to the ultimate obstacle where a cracked board lay next to a gap. In those cases, I used my engineering knowledge and some common sense to carefully step on the edge of the cracked board near its support before moving across the gap.

The rain came down hard and fast just before I reached the other side, and I got a little wet before I reached shelter under the eaves of a shop nearest the end of the bridge. My friend was under the eaves of another shop across the street that, by now, was a running river of water. He motioned for me to come over which I did when the rain let up a little. He said that he was staying there for the night. The owners had a place in the attic for travelers to sleep, and they fed us supper in their kitchen. We ate our supper of *daal bhaat*, lentils and rice, on benches by firelight. The village had no electricity, and my flashlight was in great demand.

After supper, we climbed a ladder to the attic that was about five feet high at the ridge and zero at the eaves. We spread out woven rice mats loaned to us by the host, took off our footgear, and went to bed by simply lying down on the mats. I used a sweater from my pack for a pillow. Rain still fell, and I heard it drumming on the roof above my head as it lulled me to sleep with a feeling of coziness in a dry, warm place. I woke before daylight and my friend from yesterday was already up. We went down to the kitchen for breakfast tea and the ubiquitous pancake-like bread, and then in predawn light we hit the trail together.

We traveled and talked for most of the morning in bright sunshine and cloudless skies, maintaining a rapid pace until we started up on a long slope around a large, open basin. The ridge we had to cross was about a thousand feet above, and I suggested that he go on ahead, because there was no way I could keep up unless he slowed way down. When I got to the small village of Bahundanda straddling the top of the ridge, I was surprised and flattered to see that the porter had waited there for me. He had rested and drunk some tea while waiting, but he had delayed going on to show me the proper route through the valley on the other side of the ridge. It was full of lush, green rice paddies flooded with water that glinted here and there with reflected sunlight.

"The trail is hard to follow," he said, "because it gets small where it wanders around the edges of the rice paddies. There are many choices of where to go."

He pointed out the landmarks for me to reach including the most important of all, a bridge far down the valley where it crossed a deep gorge on the river. Beyond that, barely visible, was a teahouse where he would wait for me. Because I went faster going downhill, I kept him in sight for a while, but he eventually disappeared. The trail became tangled in the cultivated fields where it split, and split again to go around the edges of the paddies. Several times, I had to retrace my steps where the path I followed dead-ended or was obviously going in the wrong direction. At last, I reached the bridge and the teahouse beyond. And there he was again, my friend, the would-be porter. This time he had eaten and rested, and was just leaving when I arrived. So I said goodbye again, thinking that I would surely never see him again.

Two days later, I was surprised to see the same man coming toward me. He stopped to talk, and I asked him about the job he was trying to get.

"No job," he said. "They filled all the positions before I arrived."

"But what are you going to do?" I asked, noticing how calm he seemed to be about this disturbing news. *I would have been distraught, more likely pissed off.*

"I go back home," he said.

"But you came all this way for nothing," I exclaimed, thinking about the effort and time he took to travel this trail for five days or more. I tried to express my sorrow at his misfortune.

He just shrugged, saying, "There will be other jobs, and I will get one sooner or later."

Then we said good-bye again. When he left me, I watched a few seconds until he disappeared down the trail toward home. Then I turned to travel in the opposite direction toward my goal, Manang. I never saw him again, but over the years, I've thought of him many times when plans didn't go as well as I thought they should. I'd smile to myself, and shrug, figuring something would come my way sooner or later.

19) A Porter's Workplace (note two climbers in right corner)

Chapter 10
Nepalese Hospitality, Nepal

By midafternoon, rain threatened and the wind gusted, picking up dust on the trail to make tiny whirlpools, which looked to me like miniature two-foot high baby tornados. The trail I traveled passed through Lower Pisang, which consisted of two guesthouses, already awash with other trekkers. The adjacent fields sprouted colorful tents as organized trekking groups made camp. The next village, Braga, was at least a half day's walk ahead, and I quickly found that I had no snug place to stay the night in Lower Pisang. Oh, I could flake out on a floor somewhere in an out-of-the-way spot, but my world suddenly seemed inhospitable, and I tried to think of what else I could do.

I looked up at Upper Pisang, the main village, which lay about five hundred feet above on a steep hillside. It appeared detached and remote from the bustle of tourists below, and I thought many travelers would not be willing to take the time and energy to climb up that far on the chance of getting a room. But I decided to take the risk to climb to the upper village and try to get a room there. After all, in the worst case, sleeping on a floor there wouldn't be much different than the floors down here.

Finding no trail to the upper village, I waded the stream on the valley floor and made my way cross-country toward the village. The route led upward, at first on moderate slopes that became steeper and steeper as I climbed higher. Thick grass and brambles covered the slopes about me, but disappeared higher up, replaced with bare, gray rock and large slopes consisting of *scree,* small pieces of loose grey rock. Still higher up, a solid cloud cover hid the immense white peaks I had come so far to see. I knew they were there, but I hadn't seen them yet. This was my tenth day of a trek that the guidebooks said should take about three weeks.

Traveling alone on the trail around the Annapurna massif, I carried a small pack with no camping gear other than a light sleeping bag. Thus I had to stay overnight in teahouses, inns, or private homes. At lower elevations, when traveling through the rice paddies, I could possibly bivouac when it was warm, but at higher elevations, the cold nights made it necessary to find shelter. Now, in late October, even the days were chilly higher in the mountains, and I wore a wool sweater and hat continuously.

Because of the altitude, about ten thousand feet, I had to stop climbing many times to catch my breath. At one of these stops, I saw that the village above me was made of rock with the houses joined together to form an uninterrupted exterior rock wall. From rooftops and walls, white banners fluttered on tall poles. The overall effect was that of a medieval castle with crenellated walls and battle flags flying. I found out later that those battle flags were actually prayer flags, white strips of cloth with prayers printed on them. The wind delivered those prayers to God, over and over, every time they flapped in a breeze. Eventually, the printing became too dim for even God to see and the villagers replaced them with new flags with freshly-printed prayers.

Reaching the village walls, I turned right and walked past the unbroken exteriors of walls, houses and buildings until I found an entry that passed me into the interior of the village. Inside, the streets were narrow and completely closed in by the rock walls of the structures and walls. In some places, buildings built over the street made them into tunnels, dark and mysterious with old beams and posts, doorways, and steps that led nowhere. I thought perhaps rats lurked in the shadows, but I didn't see any.

I came to a plaza-like opening where I encountered my first inhabitant. He was surprised to see me. I explained my need for a place to stay. This was hard to do for I knew only a few words of Nepalese. He was an older man and signed for me to wait while he conversed with some men, bare to the waist, who were working on the second floor in a storage building nearby. It was open to the weather on one side, and the men shoveled wheat into burlap sacks from a huge conical pile of the stuff spread out on the floor. As they shoveled, rats came to mind again, or at least the rat shit mixed with the grain did. I didn't dwell on that thought too long, but wondered how the grain got piled up inside on the second floor of that building?

When the old man came back, he beckoned me to follow him. We went deeper into the village with solid rock walls on each side of the street broken occasionally by a cross street or a doorway. I followed my guide through the twisting turns of the street and the occasional tunnel until he finally stopped and pounded his fist on one of the doors. In a short time, a Tibetan woman opened the door. She appeared to be about thirty-five years old. She listened to him and then the three of us dickered for the price of my room and board for the night. She spoke very little English, but the older man knew some English, and I knew a few words of Nepalese. We finally settled on a price, and she then invited me in, and the older man disappeared.

I passed through the gate into a level courtyard in front of her house, separated from other yards by six-foot high walls made of rocks laid without mortar. I followed her across about twenty feet of open yard to her house.

Under it and open to the courtyard was space for animals, hay, feed, and bulk storage. The animals were gone, but their presence was visible by the feeding troughs and droppings left here and there on the ground. Although never discussed, I assumed the area doubled as the bathroom.

We climbed to her house above the space for animals on a twelve-inch diameter log that had steps notched into it. With no handrails or handholds, it took good balance to climb up or down, and I made a mental note not to make any trips on that stairway in the dark.

Her house was only one room, about sixteen feet square with a covered balcony across the front. This balcony was continuous across other courtyards and connected the fronts of other living quarters. A few ladders connected the balcony to a common roof. The roof served as a place to store hay and firewood, and provided space to work and play. I found out later that, with careful navigation, a person could reach almost any part of the village without leaving the roof, and by this means, people visited each other without ever having to use the courtyards or streets below.

The roof also provided the best view of the surrounding area including the invisible massive Annapurrna, if only the clouds would move away. Tall poles with fluttering prayer flags sprouted from the roofs in every direction. As far as I could tell, the villagers had not yet invented railings or handrails, and edges of roofs and balconies remained unprotected.

My hostess invited me in for tea. As I dropped my pack and sat on a thin reed mat on the opposite side of the fire from her, I smelled an odor I couldn't identify. The fire was in a box of dirt on the floor located in the center of the left sidewall. The fuel consisted of wood sticks none larger than an inch in diameter, which indicated to me the scarcity of firewood in this part of the world. Light came only from the open door, from the fire, and from the small spaces between the rocks of the walls of her house laid without mortar.

The fire pit lacked a chimney, so smoke filled the room and drifted about until eventually escaping through the spaces and cracks in the walls. An open rack above the fire held meat, and clothing left there to dry. Hard-packed mud, or maybe it was cow dung, covered the floor to make a hard, smooth level surface. The wall next to the fire contained several built-in shelves, which held a pot, a frying pan, two spoons, a few stainless steel plates, and a few insulated stainless steel cups. Carefully displayed on a separate shelf were three decorative, delicate china cups and saucers which I assumed were her most precious items.

She made me tea and served it in one of the insulated stainless steel cups designed, hopefully, to keep the hot tea from getting too cold in the frigid air of this altitude. The room remained as cold inside as outside, and the fire was too small to make the place any warmer. She pointed with pride to the back corner of the room opposite the fire, where through the haze of the smoke, I saw two haunches of yak meat hanging from the rafters. I immediately recognized the meaty odor permeating the room which, until then, I had not identified. In respect to my hostess, I got up to take a closer look and admire her treasure. Nearby, two large baskets sat on the floor, filled with wheat. They were easily three feet high and three feet in diameter. I thought, *this lady is set for winter*, and shuddered at the prospect of spending a long time, winter or otherwise, in this primitive house.

After tea, I left to visit the *Gomba*, a holy building that was higher up and at the edge of the village. It was the only painted building in town, very white and very visible from anywhere in town. The three statues inside bordered on obscene, with grotesque faces and bodies covered with splotches of bright-colored paint. Piles of rubbish including rotting fruit and dead flowers lay scattered about. The general impression was that of forlornness and indifferent care. I felt uneasy and quickly left.

When I returned to my 'house,' it seemed like all the people of the village had gathered on each side of a street nearby and were waiting and watching. So I waited and watched with them. Soon, at the lower end of the street, I saw horses and riders galloping madly up the street toward me. Dust billowed up and dirt flew. On they came, on their short stubby horses, racing by me within arm's length. I flinched involuntarily and took a step back, hitting the rock wall behind me. The sound of hooves pounding the ground reverberated in the narrow street in a mounting crescendo, matching my excitement and I smelled the white frothing sweat of the horses. I saw bits of bright color on saddle blankets, and the clothes of the men as they passed. With wild shouts from riders and watchers alike, they turned into a street to my right and disappeared.

Still the crowd waited and no one left. Soon another bunch of riders came galloping up the street. Again came the shouts amid clouds of dust, flying dirt, and flailing hooves. When those horsemen disappeared, the crowd still waited, and just when I thought it was all over, two riders came racing by, accompanied by the shouts of the crowd. It appeared that the winners of the first two races were racing each other. When they passed, the crowd, including me, followed them into the street to my right which went up a slight rise to end in a small plaza enclosed on three sides by rock walls.

In one corner, the riders were sitting on their small horses dressed in dark hats and jackets highlighted with brightly colored patterns and designs. Their saddles consisted of homemade, tied wool blankets of beautiful, colorful designs. They sang songs that echoed off the walls of the enclosure, raising the hair on the back of my neck. The many men's voices sang the minor notes of music that I imagined came straight out of the lonely steppes of central Asia. Spellbound, I listened, not wanting it to stop. The women were in another corner of the plaza talking and laughing, and drinking *Rakshi,* a strong, homemade liquor. A few minutes later the songs ended, the spell was broken, and everyone left. I stayed a few seconds more, trying to prolong that fleeting moment and the feelings it generated--of unchecked wildness, melancholy, unrequited adventure, and joy of living.

When I returned to my lodgings, no one answered my knock, and when I opened the door, it came off its hinges. I tried to put it back in its proper place, but it was too heavy and I couldn't. People laughed as they passed by, but finally, one man stopped to help me. Together we managed to get the door back on its hinges, just as my hostess came home. It was getting dark as she ushered me up the log steps and into her house, where she quickly made a small fire for light and for cooking supper. I sat cross-legged on my mat opposite her with the fire pit between us and watched.

She made a large doughy 'pancake' with water and wheat flour and spread a little yak butter and malevolent-looking chili pepper on it for flavor. I washed it down with tea as she prepared the second 'pancake,' patting it into shape by hand. Suddenly she hawked and spit across the room. Then she pulled out a tiny mirror and, looking at herself, found a dirt spot on her cheek which she rubbed off with a little spit on her finger.

I was getting a little nervous eating the doughy cake anyway and, after that performance, I declined seconds. She shrugged looking a little surprised and flipped the second cake over in her pan, but it slipped off into the ashes where she retrieved it. She brushed the dirt off with her hand, and placed it back in the pan. It was misshapen, bedraggled, and dirty, but she ate it anyway when cooked. I had definitely made a good decision to refuse seconds.

After she had finished eating, I got hard candies from my pack to share. Then she brought out her *Rakshi* to share. *Rakshi* was a clear, homemade liquor, usually made from millet or rice, that ran from fourty to one hundred proof depending on who made it. It was very cheap to buy and many times the container it came in was worth more than the *Rakshi*. I found out later that if not prepared properly, the liquor could cause blindness. *Ignorance is bliss came to mind.*

A few sips into the *Rakshi*, the door flew open without warning. A little man who obviously knew his way around came and sat down by the fire, now not much more than a few embers. My hostess threw a few twigs on the fire to provide a little more light. The newcomer did his best to assure me with his meager English that he was not staying the night and would go in a few minutes. I found that a puzzling reassurance.

But *Rakshi* wrapped me in a blissful cocoon, and I watched my lady friend and the newcomer as they laughed and talked. She was definitely more handsome now than I had remembered earlier. She was dressed head to toe in a dark cloak, doubled across the front and held closed by a brightly-colored, woven sash around her waist. The two became more boisterous and soon she and the stranger were locked together wrestling and rolling about on the floor with much laughter. I was a little surprised, but it appeared to be just playful tussling. In the flickering light of the fire, sipping my *Rakshi* with the smoke curling about forming hazy tendrils and shapes in the twilight of that strange place, it all seemed quite natural.

I found myself admiring the woman; she was nice looking with high cheekbones and golden skin. She was bigger and stronger than the little man, so I figured she wouldn't be wrestling about on the floor if she didn't really want to. As I contemplated that hazy, boozy thought, the roughhousing suddenly stopped. Abruptly, the man stood up, said goodbye to me, and darted out the door. My hostess straightened her clothes and hair and sat primly again across the fire from me.

After the recent noise and bustle, the room seemed quieter and got darker as the fire died to embers. Outside I heard an occasional muffled laugh or shout, and running footsteps across the roof from a few late evening merrymakers. These noises made the room seem even more remote and still. For the first time, I felt the frigid night air as it seeped into the room, and my body shivered involuntarily.

The *Rakshi* was gone and still we sat. Suddenly, she uttered a single word, *sutnu*, which I thought meant sleep. I asked *"kahAA,"* where? She pointed to the corner behind her where I'd seen some forlorn looking blankets lying in a heap on the floor. I pointed behind me and began to lay out my sleeping bag. She got up, came around the fire, and stood watching me.

As I lay out my sleeping bag, she undid her hair, which fell in thick, black coils nearly to her waist. I was

113

beginning to get a little uneasy, but I took off my shoes. She kicked off her sandals to one side and I mentally thought, *what in hell's going on?* I crawled into the sack, removed my trousers, and rolled them up for a pillow. Meanwhile, she undid her colorful sash and took off her long, sleeveless outer cloak.

Under the cloak, she wore a white, high-necked, long-sleeved blouse and dark trousers. Her clothes were practical and sensible, and she was completely covered and chaste, but in my befuddled state of mind, very alluring. She stood looking down at me for at least a minute before picking up her cloak and sandals to stomp off to her corner beyond the fire.

A little while later she got up and went out, slamming the door shut behind her. I knew that she was angry, and I couldn't sleep, wondering what I should have done. In about half an hour, she came back with a woman friend. I heard their low voices and giggles as they prepared to bed down together in the cold room. Apparently, her culture expected overnight guests to sleep huddled with their hosts for warmth. My culture expected me to sleep alone in a warm sleeping bag.

Later in my trip, an English speaking Nepalese assured me that village elders often placed male travelers with a single woman or one whose husband was away. They did this for mutual benefit. The man got a warm fire, a meal, and a cozy house for the night. The woman got money for room and board, had protection of a man, and perhaps gained a little warmth during a cold night.

. 20) Nepalese dwellings near Tibet

Chapter 11
Paradise, Nepal

When I awoke in the morning, the woman who had taken my place to sleep close to my hostess and share a little extra body heat throughout the cold night had already left. I never did see who she was, but I mentally thanked her for getting me off the hook for that chore. Of course, a man and woman could sleep huddled together for warmth without the desire for sex, couldn't they? But my hostess was so different and came from such a different culture that I wondered what snuggling together with her might be like. Now I might never have that experience, and had to come to grips with a lost opportunity. I always hated losing an opportunity.

My hostess had a fire going and was boiling water for tea. She sat at her place across the open fire from me, primly dressed in her outer cloak and sandals with her hair neatly done up for the day. In the morning light, and without *Rakshi* cluttering my mind, she wasn't nearly as alluring as the night before.

Smoke curled about the room, but the door was wide open, allowing some light to enter and some of the smoke to leave. I put away my sleeping bag and lounged against my pack, in no hurry to leave. I had come so far and exerted myself greatly to get to this place to see Annapurna, which I knew filled the sky across the valley. So far, I hadn't seen much because of the persistent, dense, white cloud cover that extended almost to the valley floor. *Why rush off*, I thought. *I'm here, close to my goal, and only need to wait it out until the clouds lift.* After all, I doubted that I would ever get back to this out-of-the-way place again, and I made a tentative decision to stay in this village one or two more days if necessary, or until the mountain finally appeared.

I got my tea served in an insulated stainless steel cup. These cups and stainless steel plates were used everywhere in Nepal, manufactured and imported from India, and easily available in every local market. The cup had an inner and outer wall enclosing a small space for insulation. I thought that maybe the insulation was only the air sealed between the layers of steel, but I never cut one open to find out. The air would work as insulation for a little while until the hot tea heated the sealed-in air and then the cold would win out, quickly wicking away the heat. Drinking tea was a frustrating process. The tea was almost always too hot for me to drink immediately, but if I waited too long, it rapidly turned to iced tea before I could get it all down. As far as I could tell, only people with cast iron mouths and throats managed to get hot tea down before it turned to iced tea.

I walked out on the balcony and climbed one of the ladders to the roof. God heard no prayers on this windless morning as the prayer flags hung listlessly, unmoving on their poles. Around me, smoke from the small cooking fires from each dwelling drifted through the cracks and holes in the rock walls of the houses to create a man-made haze that covered the roofs. It appeared as if the whole village was on fire. I peered through the smoke looking for Annapurna across the valley. Dense, white clouds still covered the mountain, but I now saw that the clouds were rapidly lifting and thinning.

Without loitering about any longer, I went back to my room and packed up. I told my hostess that I would be leaving immediately, and paid the bill for room and board. She seemed surprised, especially when I refused her offer for breakfast. I tried to assure her that my stay had been pleasant, but I was anxious to see the mountains that I had come so far to see. I don't think she understood me, and when I said goodbye, she had already turned her attention to other things, without once glancing out the door at the spectacle of Annapurna.

When I stepped out on the balcony again with my pack, the view across the valley was staggering. With the clouds almost gone, I was not prepared for the sight of such a huge, white mountain filling the sky and extending across my line of sight for as far as I could see. The morning sun shone fully on the pristine snowfields and hanging glaciers, making them brilliant white in contrast to the gray, rocky crags. Fascinated, I could not move.

The four summits of Annapurna, together, formed a massive ridge stretching across the horizon. At thirty-four miles long, it formed a continuous panorama of one immense, unbroken mountain. It was the tenth highest peak on earth at 26,700 feet, and the trail around it took people an average of twenty-one days to walk. It took me nineteen days to do the trip, but now years later, I wished I had taken at least another week. How was I to know I would never get back to Nepal?

Eventually, I climbed to the roof and slowly made my way through the village, trying to walk and look at the mountain at the same time. That was hard to do since the view was off my left shoulder away from the general direction of my travel. I finally hit upon the stop-and-go method of travel, stopping to drink in the view and then going a little farther. Near the edge of the village, I dropped to the street level and went through the outer walls. I didn't go back down into the valley bottom but instead, took the high trail out of Upper Pisang that went toward Manang, my destination for that day.

Down below, trekkers were leaving Lower Pisang, like ants leaving a disturbed nest. I stayed on the higher trail and spent the whole morning slowly walking toward Manang, and stopping frequently to admire Annapurna. I soon lost sight of the other trekkers on the lower trail, and I never met a trekker, either in Upper Pisang or on the high trail until it joined the lower trail several miles beyond Upper Pisang.

At times, the trail turned away from the view of Annapurna, only to turn again to show in dramatic detail, right there in front of me, the crags and upper snow slopes. Magically, the cliffs and snowfields seemed magnified by some giant lens, and they appeared so close I thought that maybe I could reach out and touch them. I was intoxicated with the views and just couldn't get enough of wandering alone through paradise.

I slowed down to watch when passing a pasture where five men surrounded a yak, holding it steady with just their hands. It didn't run away or make a sound, but stood trembling while one man maneuvered a stiff wire into a vein in its neck. I wasn't sure, but I thought the wire ran into the animal's heart, and it was dying as I passed by. The yak's eyes were mostly white as the pupils rolled upward and back, almost disappearing into the eye sockets giving it a wild frantic look. Still it didn't run away or protest, but just stood there trembling, docile, held by the men's hands.

I don't think any pain was involved since my veins and arteries didn't feel pain when a catheter was inserted into them. Surely, my meat at home that came wrapped in cellophane was from an animal kill, too. But here in paradise, I felt dismay and betrayal that animals had to be killed, and I hurried on without watching the process any more.

In a little while, I stopped to look over at the mountain and revive my spirits brought low by the killing fields of paradise. The sun had swung further south and west toward the back of Annapurna, and the brilliant white of the snowfields and glaciers had lost a little of their luster. In several places, the exposed ice of the glaciers had a distinctly blue shadow on them. Near the top of the peak, a few dark shadows formed where the sun was no longer high enough in the sky to shine directly on those slopes.

Around noon, a woman asked me into her house for tea and *chapaati*, a flat, unleavened wheat bread, made a little more palatable with a few crumbles of cheese and chili on top. The woman's rock house was at ground level, and I sat at a real table and bench in a small open room devoid of any other furnishings. After I had eaten, the woman's husband went into a second room and brought out their little boy for me to see.

He was about two years old and not well. Large, open sores covered the top of his head extending to his face and neck, and he was listless. The sores were runny white spots, many of them two inches in diameter or more, and made the healthy skin at their edges inflamed and red. They were obviously spreading. The parents were desperate and thought that I could help them in some way. Their faith in me was painful to see, and I felt totally inadequate. I gave them some antiseptic soap with the suggestion that they wash the boy thoroughly with the soap. I gave them some Neosporin and showed them how to apply it after washing. But that's all I had or could think of doing for the poor boy.

I didn't think my efforts were going to help much, and I suggested that they take the boy to a doctor. They told me that the nearest doctor was five walking days away, and they were unable to make the ten-day round trip journey. I had never felt so helpless. When I left, they would not take my money for the food I had eaten, but instead bowed several times with their hands pressed together as if in prayer and said repeatedly, "namaste, namaste."

I left them there in the doorway of their house and felt horrible for there was nothing more I could do for them. Reaching the trail, I turned and repeated that they should somehow get their boy to a doctor. As I walked away, I thought, *trouble comes here, even to a place I think is paradise.* And I began to have niggling doubts about my definition of paradise.

I was satiated with views of Annapurna, and the sun had just winked out behind that massive mountain, leaving my view of it in complete shadow. The day had been hot, but now the shadow of Annapurna was racing across the valley and a chill was in the air. Manang lay not too far ahead, and I hurried forward to get there before dark.

The trail I followed joined the main trail coming up the valley from Lower Pisang, and shortly after that, I came to a junction of a trail leading to the village of Braga about a one-quarter mile to the right. A three-story *Gomba* painted white, stood out very visibly above the unpainted gray rock houses of the village. My guidebook said it was an inviting place to stay and visit, but I had been traveling toward Manang now for almost two weeks and refused to make a side trip when I was so close to my objective, which I figured was less than an hour away.

As I turned toward Manang, a man I had noted sitting on a large rock slid off his perch and stood on the trail in front of me. I think he had been waiting for me to make up my mind, which trail to take. Would it be Braga or Manang? He could have slid off his rock to confront me on the Braga trail just as easily. He bowed and gave me a "Namaste." Then with a broad grin, he told me his name, which to me was unpronounceable.

I smiled and shook my head, and he said, "Don't worry, just call me Ahmad. That's what all my English friends call me."

"I'm American."

"Well, Americans call me that, too. What are you doing out here alone? Where are all your friends?"

"My friends are behind me," I said. Not telling him, they were way, way behind me, in the United States.

"I saw you in Katmandu, remember? You were walking on the street, and I invited you to visit my shop, but you were too busy then and suggested another time."

Of course, I didn't remember any such meeting, but he went on.

"Now I meet you again and have brought some of my best merchandise along with me for you to see." He made it sound like he had brought his wares out here for me only, fully expecting to find me again.

Then he hoisted out a large suitcase, which I hadn't noticed before. Its handle was gone, and he had an awkward moment handling it and setting it down on a flat rock nearby. He opened it, and sure enough, he had a multitude of items neatly displayed, including jewelry, brightly-colored cloth, some medicines, belts, purses, and a few knives. But most of the items were jewelry.

I thought it amazing that all this stuff was out here, carried on foot, twelve days away from Katmandu. I realized then I was in the presence of a real, honest-to-god traveling salesman. He had nothing I really needed or wanted, but the opportunity to purchase something from him in this manner was too good to pass up.

I pretended to like a necklace made of large, red coral beads while surreptitiously looking over some bracelets that I thought were pretty neat. With disdain, I turned down his price for the beads as being way too extravagant, and in an offhand manner, asked about the bracelets as a possible consolation for his loss of the sale of the more expensive necklace.

"What will you pay for them?" he asked, picking up several and displaying them over three of his fingers.

I named a ridiculously low price, and he pretended to be horrified.

"Look closely," he said. "They are made from jade, in one piece. See, no joints. Jade is a costly gemstone, but I give you these at a good price. A low price."

His price was twice what I had offered. I mentioned something about plastic and repeated my initial price.

"No, no, no. Not plastic." And he rubbed one of the bracelets vigorously on his cheek and then placed on my cheek. "See, it's not plastic, but I give you my lowest price."

He named a price somewhere between his high and my low. I never did figure out how rubbing the bracelet on a cheek proved it wasn't made of plastic, but I believed him. Somehow glass was mentioned, but I don't remember if he or I said that nasty word. I gave him my second price only a little above the initial price, and got ready to go on to Manang.

"Wait," he said, before I could walk away. "You promise to come to my store, and I give you these bracelets at your price. That is a very good bargain."

"Okay."

I paid him the money and asked, "Are you going to Braga or Manang?"

"Neither," he said, getting his suitcase into a makeshift pack of strings, cord, light rope, and the ubiquitous trump line. "I'm going out to the road and return to Katmandu."

He planned to do in a week what had taken me twelve days to do. On the way to Manang, I forgot all about my promise to visit his store. Besides, what were the chances of ever seeing him again? Miniscule. But fate is a funny thing. When I finished my trek around Annapurna, one of the first people I met on the streets of Katmandu was my friend, the walking peddler, with his suitcase on his back. Oh well, promises are promises, and I followed him to his store. 'His store' was owned by another person who gave Ahmad, the traveling salesman, a commission for getting me through the door of his shop. Ahmad left immediately and I never saw him again.

When I reached the outskirts of Manang, majestic Annapurna was simply a shadow across the darkened sky. I began a search for a place to stay the night, and after several tries, found an inn that had room for me. The owner took me to the roof where he had added a dorm room large enough for six beds, and I took the last bed he had. Outside I pointed over at the darkened mountain and bubbled on about how much I enjoyed traveling through paradise.

"You mean Annapurna?" he asked. "That worthless piece of land? We can't grow crops on it or raise animals on it, and it sure blocks out the warm, afternoon sun. I would gladly give it away." Then he thought a moment, and said with a smile, "or better yet, sell it to some rich, confused American like yourself."

As he turned to leave, he reminded me that supper was ready and that I had better hurry down to get some before it was gone. After he left, I thought, *okay, maybe* paradise *isn't necessarily a place, or beautiful scenery on a bright sunny day.* I knew firsthand that this paradise had killing fields, sickness, and people out to make a buck. Was paradise just a state of mind, an attitude? If so, I realized I could, with a little effort, be in paradise anytime, anywhere in the world I happened to be. Even in Kansas.

Taking my host's advice, I hurried down into the dark bowels of the inn now lit by a few electric bulbs scattered here and there. The effect was like that of a classic dungeon with rough-cut rock walls, dimly-lit passageways, small rooms with shadows that lurked in the corners, and disembodied voices and noises coming out of nowhere. I saw shapes of men looking deformed, their faces hidden in the unshapely folds of blankets or cloaks.

I finally found the local hell on earth, the kitchen. The fire made it a hot place, made even hotter by the vast cold outside. Thick, acrid smoke filled the room making my eyes water and putting a bad taste in my mouth. Without a chimney the smoke drifted through the door, dissipating some of its heat into the next room, and on into the next and the next until it all disappeared among the outer rooms.

I got a plate piled high with *bhaat*, rice, and a small dish of runny *daal*, lentils, and hurried out of that hellish room looking for a compromise of minimum smoke and maximum heat. The warmer a room, the smokier it was. I found neither, in choosing a room lit by a few extra bulbs where several other men sat on benches hunched over their plates slurping down their meal with sucking noises and smacking of lips on fingers.

I joined them, noisily eating my own meal in a frenzy of speed to get the rice down before it congealed in that freezing room into a lumpy, gummy mass of cold, mealy mush. I smiled involuntarily, as tears streamed down my face from irritation of the smoke and thought, *this too is paradise.*

21) *Gomba* at Braga

22) Annapurna

Chapter 12
A Layover Day in Manang, Nepal

In the morning, hell in the kitchen was tolerable when compared to the night before. In the early morning cold, I welcomed the heat from the cooking fire, and the smoke hadn't yet become dense enough to be intolerable. Later on, with the lack of a chimney, the smoke thickened to a pervasive dark cloud of bluish-black haze coating eyes and lungs, undoubtedly causing cataracts and tuberculosis to those who defied the thick smoke and stayed close to the fire for long periods. In the meantime, the Black Death was already spreading its tentacles through open doors to dissipate in the clean, clear, crisp air of the rooms beyond the kitchen.

Breakfast varied a little from dinner the night before. I got some green, spicy hot spinach instead of brown, spicy hot lentils to mix with my mountain of rice. I took my plate and sat in the next room, which was a little more pleasant than the kitchen. I was making good headway into my rice mountain, the right hand coated with pieces of rice and wet with green goo of spinach, when the innkeeper came over and formally introduced himself. By mutual consent, we didn't shake hands, but instead nodded a sanitary "namaste." Now that I think about it, I don't ever remember shaking hands with a Nepalese.

"I'm Daman," he said. "I own this place, and I was the one who showed you to your room last night."

"I remember you," I said, smiling. "I thought about you when I saw Annapurna this morning. That worthless piece of real estate is still out there, bright and white in the morning sun. I guess you didn't get a chance to sell it or give it away yet."

Daman laughed and said, "I guess I was a little harsh last night, but we permanent residents can get a little testy at times with all these people hanging around town. Too many of them in such a small place put demands on us that we find hard to meet."

"So why is the town so crowded?"

"Haven't you heard? The pass is closed and people can't get through. They are stacked up here in town all over the place."

I sobered quickly at this news. No more fun and games, as I thought about having to retrace my steps all the way back to Katmandu, twelve days away.

"What's wrong?" I asked.

"The first snowstorm of the year came through and dumped enough snow to make crossing of the pass dangerous, so they closed it."

I didn't ask who "they" were, but assumed it was the police.

"Don't look so worried," said Daman. "It's only the first snow, and the pass should be open in the next day or so. Even now the snow is melting. Just relax here in town, and take a day off from trekking."

A layover day, I thought, *how novel.*

"Do you have any shops in town?" I asked.

"Umm, not too many," he said, "but we do have a lot of traders around willing to sell you their mother if they thought it could make them some money. What are you looking for?" he asked nonchalantly. "I have a lot of friends."

I bet he did, I thought, *all of them ready to sell me the proverbial Brooklyn Bridge.*

I told him about the horse races I had seen back in Pisang and how much I admired the blankets the riders used for saddles. "Maybe I could buy one and take it home with me."

"You ride horses?" he asked.

"Oh no, I just thought it would look nice on my floor at home."

"A carpet?" he asked in astonishment. Daman's forehead creased in a deep furrow, and his mouth turned down at the corners in disbelief. His expression was priceless as I imagined him thinking of something as a useful as a saddle blanket degraded to just a floor rug to walk on—with shoes.

He recovered quickly and left, saying that he would be right back. I had time to wash off morsels of rice and green goo from my fingers before he returned to display two beautiful saddle blankets.

"These are gorgeous," I gushed. "Are they for sale?" I asked too eagerly, much too eagerly. *Not a good way to start the bargaining process,* I thought.

"No, these are for my personal use for when I travel to Southeast Asia on trading trips. I thought you might like to see them up close."

And perhaps change my mind about using them for carpets?

"But you have two. Couldn't you sell me one of them?" I pleaded.

God, I hated to hear myself beg.

"No, my wife has told me she cannot make saddle blankets anymore, so these will have to last me for a long time."

Why can't she make more? I thought, but I didn't ask Daman such a rude question and instead asked, "How do you ride a horse with just these blankets? They have no stirrups, so how do you stay on the horse?"

"You haven't really looked at me, have you?" he asked. Then he stood in the doorway, and I saw his legs silhouetted in the light, bowed apart like two great arcs. He laughed when he saw my face, open mouthed with astonishment. "We hang on with our legs," he said gleefully.

Then he got serious. "I tell you what. I'll write out what you want to buy on a piece of paper, so you can show it to people in town. Maybe someone will have one to sell. But remember, these are not made to be sold. They're generally made as needed for personal use by someone in the family."

I took his offer and accepted a scrap of paper showing incomprehensible Sanskrit markings on it. Maybe it said *saddle blankets*.

Before we parted, I asked, "How come you know English so well?"

"I'm a trader," he said with a big grin. "I travel a lot, and the people I deal with know more English than Nepalese, so I've got to have good English whether I like it or not."

When I left the inn, I showed the paper to several people I met on the street. They all solemnly deliberated on the markings before slowly shaking their heads and returning the note. I finally found an old man who, after a lengthy deliberation, motioned for me to follow him. He led me to a house close to the center of town where I climbed a real stairway to the second floor living area.

The old man exchanged words with the host of the house and showed him my paper. A few seconds later, the host acknowledged me with a formal nod.

"Namaste," he said, and invited us to sit on reed mats at his fire which was nothing but smokeless embers. We talked about the weather, the closure of the pass, and the poor crops this year, while his wife served us tea that she brought out from a second room. We talked about everything except saddle blankets. Finally, the host spoke a few words to his wife in Nepalese. Her reaction seemed to be a protest, but she left the room and came back with a saddle blanket. "This is newly made," said the host proudly. "Never used. My wife just finished it."

I carefully looked it over, as if I were an expert at judging saddle blankets. The colors were bright reds, blues, and yellows in well-defined patterns on a black background. Turning the blanket over, I saw the same patterns and colors almost as distinct as on the front side. The blanket was stiff and heavy with a thick pile made by tying knots of wool yarn to a backing of cotton cords. I noted the tightness of the knots, and knew that the more knots per square inch meant better workmanship.

The blanket consisted of two separate pieces. The largest piece was about four by seven feet with about twelve inches of open cord backing, splitting the seven-foot length into halves of wool pile. The open part of the blanket went over the top of the horse's spine, and the two halves cascaded down the sides of the horse, exposing the bright colors and patterns of the blanket. The second piece was a heavier pile of similar colors and patterns about twenty-four by thirty inches, and when this piece was thrown over the horse, it became the seat for the rider.

The host must have noted the satisfaction on my face and asked, "How much do you wish to pay for it?"

Thus, the bargaining began. I was appalled at the high price he set and became even more dismayed by his refusal to come down much from his original amount during our battle of wits to achieve the final selling price. Unfortunately for me, I wanted the article far more than he wanted to give it up, so I ended up buying the blanket for much more than I had intended. When the host agreed to my final offer, the woman gasped and said a few words to her husband. I gathered that she was not pleased. *How much more money did she want?* I thought.

While I counted out the *rupees* to pay for my extravagant souvenir, the woman took the saddle blanket into the next room, rolled it up into a neat package, and tied it with string. When she came out, she formally handed over my saddle blanket without a word or a smile. That's when I noticed her gnarled fingers, perhaps deformed by arthritis.

I remembered watching young girls in India making tied knot carpets. With dazzling speed, their young flexible fingers tied knots with one hand and cut the knot from the skein with the other hand that hovered close by ready to cut off the next knot, and the next, and the next. They worked for hours in almost dungeon-like conditions until a few years later their fingers gave out, and younger girls replaced them. I realized that this woman didn't have the dexterity in her fingers to tie knots rapidly and, making a new saddle blanket meant days of frustrating work.

Still we men sat relaxing by the fire recovering from the intense hard labor of our negotiations while I heard the woman rummaging about in the next room. A few seconds later, she came out with yak butter tea, one of the most God-awful drinks I've ever had to swallow.

Serving yak butter tea was an honor of the house, almost a ritual. Good manners dictated that I had to get that first cup down no matter what, but I could refuse the offer of seconds without causing a breach of etiquette. It was made of tea, yak butter, and salt. The ingredients were thrown into a hollow section of bamboo and churned with a stick to create a homogenous mixture with the most vile taste. I often thought the butter was rancid, but I didn't know how rancid butter tasted.

In order to get it down without gagging or throwing up, I had to convince my mind that I was drinking soup. A hot, dishwater-like, super salty soup, swimming in puddles of grease. I found it best to gird my loins and slug a bunch of it down in a big gulp, rather than polite sips. This often confused the Nepalese hosts into thinking I loved the stuff, so they were always surprised when I refused a second "delicious" cup.

A short time later, the old man and I left with a bow and a "namaste." The woman didn't see us off and remained in the next room, perhaps starting another blanket. I figured that a few seconds after we were gone, the host would run smiling all the way to the bank with my money. When I turned to go to the inn where I was staying, the old man stopped me and insisted I follow him. Out of politeness, I did, and he led me to his house near the edge of town.

I climbed steps notched into a log to a balcony stretching across several adjacent living quarters. A few women were on the balcony talking while they worked at their chores. One kneeled over a flat rock slab grinding some sort of grain, while another sat weaving at a back strap loom. The old man spoke to a woman who disappeared inside and came out with a blanket or carpet in her arms. She laid it over a line and started beating the dust out of it with a stick. Good grief, was the old man going to try to sell me his saddle blanket? I already had one and didn't need two.

We sat in a room side by side with our backs against the wall facing out the door, which let in the only light. The cubicle was about six feet wide by ten feet long, and I figured it was his private sleeping area. Neither of us said much as I listened to the women talking above the beat of the carpet, and waited patiently for something to happen.

Suddenly, the carpet-beating woman appeared in the doorway with the carpet or the blanket rolled-up in her arms. She dramatically unrolled it through the door on the floor in front of me. It was thirty to thirty-six inches wide by about seven feet long. The colors and design were inferior to that of my new saddle blanket, and the background of black yarn prevailed. I didn't want it, but the old man sprang into action offering the carpet for sale.

He placed his head on his hands as if on a pillow and indicated that I should lay on it to try it out. He was selling me a sleeping mat, his bed. I politely declined, but he insisted that I make him an offer. The last thing I wanted was a used bed to cart around, so I gave him a ridiculously low offer, figuring he would refuse it in mock anger. I expected him to make a counter offer at a much higher price, and then I could reluctantly disengage from bidding any further. Instead, he placed the carpet in my hands, and signed that I had just bought his sleeping mat. *Suckered in again, I had just learned rule number one of trading; never bargain for something you don't want. You might get it.*

I carried my purchases under each arm back to my room at the inn. They got bulkier and heavier as I went, and I felt a niggling worry begin at the pit of my stomach. How was I going to get this stuff home? I still had about a week of walking to get out including climbing over a 17,600-foot pass. Finally, in my room, I tried rolling them tightly together, but they wouldn't fit in the pack. I tried folding them separately and tying them on the outside of the pack, but that didn't work either. Nothing I tried worked, and I had visions of leaving my expensive souvenirs behind right there in the room. How dumb of me to buy something I couldn't carry! But wait, this was Nepal, where men hired themselves out to carry anything, anywhere, anytime. With renewed hope, I went looking for a porter.

Most of the people I asked knew the word *porter*, and they waved me toward the edge of town where I had entered the day before. About the last building I came to was a tea house, now better described as a bar. Men filled the place, drinking, shouting, and laughing. Some spilled out the door, beer bottles in hand, and I asked one of these stragglers about hiring a porter. He said something in Nepalese, laughed, and shrugged, while pointing inside. The place was a bedlam of confusion and rowdiness, and I didn't want to go in. While I stood there, uneasy, debating whether to give up looking for a porter, a young man came over to me.

"I heard you asking for a porter," he said.

"Yes," I said eagerly. "Are you a porter?"

"No, but I want to get to Pokhara and could use some extra money. Are you going to Pokhara?"

"Yes, I am," I replied.

We discussed terms of employment, and I agreed to pay him $2.00 per day, plus his food and board each day. I figured the trip would take seven days. To cinch the deal I offered to loan him a wool sweater and hat to wear when crossing the high Thorung La Pass.

"What sort of pack do you have?" he asked.

"I have my personal day pack, but the items I need help in carrying won't fit in or on the pack. It's too small." Then I told him about my purchases.

"No pack or basket," he mused almost to himself. "I will have to see the load and figure out how to carry it, before I can agree to go with you."

Darn, maybe I don't have a deal after all.

"I will come by your hotel this afternoon to see if I can carry your goods."

We agreed to a time to meet, and I left to head back to my hotel feeling a little despondent in not knowing for sure what was going to happen. Porters apparently were more independent than I thought. I liked to have things neat and tidy with firm commitments. I hated vague maybes and open-ended plans. With my head down and bad thoughts churning through my mind, I almost missed the sound of chanting coming from an open doorway that I was passing.

Curious, I stopped to listen. Not able to see into the dark interior, I stepped through the doorway and waited a few seconds for my eyes to adjust from blinding white sunshine to the deep shadows of the room inside. In front of me were about twenty Lamas in sapphire robes sitting on stools at a high U-shaped table. They were chanting from books, and each Lama had a candle sitting on the table to light up the pages and a cup of something that they sipped from time to time.

Fascinated, I stood motionless until a woman came and tried to usher me to a seat on a log just inside the door. I was the only non-monk there and felt out of place, so I made a move to leave. She signed that it was okay for me to stay, and insisted that I sit on her log. *Okay*, I thought, *I'll stay a few minutes and then sneak out*. Then she went to the door and closed it. *Trapped.*

In the meantime, the chanting continued without missing a beat. When a monk stopped chanting to take in a breath or a sip of liquid, the others covered for him. I noticed that the monks turned the pages of their books in a staggered order so that the chanting never stopped-- ever. The pages of the books were bound in a loose-leaf manner with leather thongs. They were three-inches high by two feet long. I wondered if they chanted from the same book over and over. A book without end.

The woman replenished the monks' cups by ladling out liquid from a large pot and, at one point, brought me a cupful. I saw that it was *chaang*, a homemade beer usually brewed from millet. Normally, I had a hard time drinking the stuff. I remembered vividly the African ladies in Cameroon spitting into their bowls of millet mash to start the fermentation process. I sipped a little out of politeness, but aside from the thought of someone's saliva swimming about, the taste was mild and unappealing to me, and not very alcoholic.

I grew bored with the chanting. I was making plans to bolt out of the place, when suddenly two monks stood up and clashed large cymbals together making a frightful racket. That woke me up and boredom vanished. Shortly after, two other monks stood up and blasted out two baritone notes from a large horn. They played the same notes several times before all was quiet again except for the endless chanting. I ended up staying longer than planned just to hear those cymbal clashes and the two-note melodies. Perhaps anything sounded good after listening to chanting for a while.

I finally left, slipping out the door into brilliant sunshine. It took a few seconds for my eyes to readjust to the brightness outside, and I almost ran into Daman, my innkeeper.

"Well, you've had enough religion for the day," he said, after I had told him where I had just been. "Come with me. I'm going to visit my mother for a few minutes."

I started to decline, but he insisted, saying, "Come on, what else have you got to do on your layover day? Surely you don't want to be bored doing nothing."

So I dutifully followed him to his mother's house. She lived in a typical rock house on the second floor where a worn out fire kept the smoke level tolerable. We sat on reed mats around the fire pit and talked. She was about my age, small and sprightly, and I couldn't help thinking that *Daman must be the age of my son. Good grief.* She knew a lot more English than I knew of Nepalese, and Daman was very proficient at English. So the conversation was easy for me to follow and understand. Her knowledge of politics and world events surprised me. We also discussed such things as women's rights in Nepal, the state of the schools in the country, the problems of communication in Nepal, and the slow method of travel on the trails.

"We need roads," she said.

"When I started out on this trip, I followed a primitive road out of Dumre," I said. "It's a start."

"Yes, and if you come back in five years, it will still be a 'start,' still just a primitive track."

Then she excused herself for a few minutes and when she came back, served us with, what else, the inevitable yak butter tea. *Not another cup of that vile stuff,* I thought. *What were the chances of getting two shots in one day? Rats.* I think she recognized my discomfort at receiving her tea and, I swear, I saw a glint of humor on her face as she filed my cup only half-full. Daman and I left a little later after exchanging solemn *namastes* with his Mom.

"It was nice to talk to your mother," I said, as we walked back to his hotel. "She must travel a lot and meet a lot of people."

"She's never been out of this valley," he said. "She's lived here in Manang all her life and never traveled farther than Braga which, as you know is just down the trail an hour or so."

"How can a person live only in one spot all her life and know so much?" I asked in amazement. "She has no papers to read, no radio, or TV to hear newscasts, so where does she get all her information?"

"When I'm home, I visit her almost every day. I tell her about my trips abroad and what is happening in the world. Then, of course, there are lots of travelers like yourself who come by and love to talk and drink yak butter tea." He said this last part with a grin.

I shook my head, and he laughed. When we got back to his hotel, he came to my room to look at my new saddle blanket. He admired it and made suitable comments.

"But I paid way too much for it," I said. "It's not worth the cost."

He didn't ask me the price I had paid, but gave me advice that I have used since that day.

"When you get home, you will see this wonderful blanket every day and admire its beauty," he said. "In one month you will have forgotten what you paid for it. That will no longer matter."

It didn't take one month to forget its price; I forgot the price before I even got home. It's been like that with all of my purchases since that day. I always bargained hard, but when I consummated the deal, the price no longer mattered, and I forgot it.

Before he left on his inn keeping chores I asked, "Where can I buy some *Rakshi?* "I need to get fortified to endure the cold and smoke at supper time."

He laughed and pointed out a house that, from our vantage point on the roof, looked like it was on fire. "In there, they make *Rakshi*," he said. "You can tell by the smoke that they need lots of fire."

"Do you know approximately what I should pay?"

"The price is no concern," he said. "But you will need to bring your own container. When you're ready to go, stop by the kitchen, and the cook will give you an empty bottle."

A little later, my porter showed up. I was so relieved I could have hugged him, but that would have really turned him off. I almost didn't recognize him, he looked much younger than I remembered from that morning. He reminded me of high school kids back home.

He rolled each separate piece in a tight roll and fastened them with string. Then he reached into his pockets, brought out an assortment of strings, cord, and light rope and proceeded to fashion a rudimentary net bag to hold the rolls of fabric. He made a trump line that went around the bottom of the net bag and long enough to go over his forehead. When finished, he hoisted the makeshift pack to his back, adjusted the trump line, and walked around the room. He then jumped up and down a little to test the strength of his pack which held together, and he seemed pleased..

"Okay, I will go with you to Pokhara," he said, smiling. "Do we leave tomorrow?"

"We can't leave until the pass is open," I replied.

"But it is open now."

"How do you know that?" I asked.

"We Nepalese hear things from the wind," he said with a grin.

We agreed on a time to meet the next morning to go to Tengi, the last village before Thorung La Pass, where we would stay overnight before attempting the pass the next day. It was about half a day from Manang.

"Be sure to let me know what the wind tells you from time to time," I said when my porter finally left.

Before I went out on my errand to buy some *Rakshi*, I stopped by the kitchen to pick up an empty container. The cook was very reluctant to give it to me until I assured her that I would bring it back at suppertime. She finally handed over a bottle, a Coke bottle. Well, why not?

By now, the whole town was in the shadow of Annapurna, and the air was chilly. It seemed that in this high, thin air, the shadow of that mountain switched off the heat and immediately turned on the cold air. Maybe Daman was right about Annapurna being a worthless piece of real estate, and I smiled to myself. I found the *Rakshi* house easily, marked by all the smoke coming from every crack and pore in the walls. But even more telltale was the trail of men going in and out of the house. I could tell something was brewing there.

Inside, the room was dark, lit only by a robust fire. A knot of men stood around, watching a bubbling pot of mash sitting in the center of the fire. Above the pot was an inverted metal cone filled with water. As the steam rose from the boiling mixture, it condensed on the surface of the cone made cooler by the water inside. The condensation ran down the sides of the cone and dripped into an open channel that conveyed the stream of liquor to a container at one side of the fire. I was impressed by the simplicity of the working still. However, the primitive still was not very efficient, and I think the men were having fun breathing in air laced with *Rakshi*.

I asked a man who appeared to be in charge about buying some *Rakshi*. He frowned and gave me a quick shake of his head. I showed him my empty Coke bottle and he brightened up immediately. He took the bottle into the next room and came back with it filled with liquor, and had stuffed a rag into the open neck to keep the liquor from spilling out. The price was less than a bottle of Coke, and I realized the Coke bottle itself was more precious than whatever liquid it held. Then I remembered traveling in Zaire, Africa, when we traded empty cans and bottles for food. We had to hide and camouflage our garbage pits to keep the villagers from coming back after we left to dig up the pits to salvage useful items from our garbage.

That night I shared my *Rakshi* with other men waiting with me for supper. Each of us took a slug of the fiery liquor and passed it on. It was gone by the time we lined up for our usual mountain of rice. As promised, I gave the cook back her empty Coke bottle, and I swear she gave me a reward of just a smidge more rice on my plate That night we got a treat. In addition to rice and lentils, we each got a piece of roasted pumpkin. I squaffled that veggie down first.   As usual, I went to bed right after supper to stay warm. I could hardly wait for morning to get back on the trail again! What pleasure to look forward to the soothing routine of trail travel.   I decided that layover days were highly overrated and far too demanding.

23) A boy in Manang

Chapter 13
Over the Pass to Holy Places, Nepal

Finally, after all my worry and fears about getting over Thorung La Pass, I found it to be a "pussycat" once I learned how to walk at seventeen thousand feet elevation. I had already noticed that the higher I got the slower I hiked, yet at elevations above sixteen thousand feet, my legs hurt me so badly I had to stop every few minutes for the pain to go away. They recovered quickly, but I was surprised at how fast and excruciating the pain came back after each rest.

At first, I tried rest stepping which is the way I get to the top of most mountains. It's a mountaineering technique where after a step forward, I allowed my entire weight to rest on the back leg, thereby resting the forward leg since it had no weight on it. Then moving forward with a step, the rested leg took the brunt of my weight, and I allowed the second leg to rest. I always tried to move the back leg forward quickly to gain a little extra time for it to rest. By this method, I climbed for hours without stopping.

To people who had never seen the rest step, the gait probably looked awkward with its jerky movements, like Olympia, the wind-up mechanical doll portrayed by opera divas in the first act of the opera, "Tales of Hoffman." I remembered climbing Adams Peak in Sri Lanka where most of the way up was on stairways consisting of thousands of steps. At first, most people passed me with peculiar looks in my direction, giggles and words among themselves. But they weren't giggling when I passed them later, grinding up the hill at my jerky pace while they remained motionless, gasping, and regaining strength to move on.

I finally figured out that my legs weren't tired; they just couldn't get enough oxygen at that altitude to keep going. So I tried taking in two breaths of air at every rest step. That helped, but my legs worked best when I took three breaths at every step. I made a rhythm of breathing three times between each step and began enjoying the hike over the "rolling meadows" that was Thorung La Pass.

The pass was just that, a rolling meadow filled with snow. I followed the trail across the relatively flat pass made by hundreds of people before me plowing through about a foot of snow. At the top were two tall poles with prayer flags fluttering, each surrounded by a large pile of rocks made by people passing by through the ages. Each had carried a special rock with them to the top and left it there to mark their passing. I had a rock in my pack made special by carrying it all the way from Katmandu, and now

I stopped to toss it on the pile of rocks nearest the trail. Thus, I marked my presence at this spot for eternity.

The trail on the lower slopes going up to the pass was much steeper than at the top, but since it was at a lower elevation, I made good time going up despite the steepness of the trail. My porter had gone on up ahead of me, and I didn't see him again until I reached the top of the pass.

We had started out from Manang the day before, hiking an easy trail to the few scattered houses that made up the village of Tengi, the last settlement before Thorung La Pass. It was a short half-day trip, and I had received advice from other trekkers that this would be a good place to stay overnight to get more acclimated to the altitude for the big climb over the pass the next day.

The best technique to get acclimated to altitude was the old mountaineer adage "climb high and sleep low." And that's what I did at Tengi. I stopped for the night at a teahouse close to the trail, dropped off a few heavier items from my daypack, and hiked up the moderate slope of a mountain across from the teahouse. I went up at a good clip for about two hours and sat in the tall, fragrant, thick grass and rested in the warm sun. Way down below, I saw the teahouse, the trail passing by, and the few scattered houses that made up the village of Tengi.

Then I fell asleep. I don't remember ever falling asleep when climbing a mountain; there's usually just too much tension. But today was different. I was relaxed after my day off in Manang, and had absolutely nothing to do that afternoon. The warm sunshine, and quiet beauty of my surroundings combined to lull me to sleep. I awoke in a panic, first wondering where I was, and then wondering about the time since I never wore a watch. I was shocked to see the shadows of the mountain across the valley lapping at my feet.

Way below in the valley, the teahouse was almost lost in the gathering gloom and the smoke pouring out of its walls. Smoke meant fire, and that meant supper. I quickly gathered my stuff and strode down the slope at a rapid pace. I sure didn't want to miss supper. In two strides, shadows engulfed me, and I lost the heat of the sun. I felt the chill in the thin air at that altitude which was about fourteen thousand feet.

I was too excited to sleep well that night and was up early to start the climb over Thorung La Pass. At 17,650 feet, it was by far the highest point on my whole trip around Annapurna. From Tengi, I needed to climb a vertical mile to get over the pass, and I had worried about my ability to do that this whole trip. I don't recall taking time to eat, but I probably did, because my porter would not have missed out on his morning installment of food as per our agreement for payment of his services.

It was still dark when we finally hit the trail, and I used my flashlight to light the way. Daylight arrived, but the sun was not quite up when we came to a primitive hut built into the slope of the mountain. People were entering and leaving through a short entry so low I had to bend over to get through to the cave beyond. In the dim light of a fire, I saw the shapes of several other travelers like myself crammed into a small space getting warm and drinking tea. Smoke drifted about, and we sat on the floor of the cave with our backs against a wall. In the semi-dark with no way to identify anyone, the disembodied voices seemed to come from out of nowhere in a distorted rumble.

Two young women trekkers next to me were not feeling well, and a lively discussion in English was in progress about whether they should go on or not. The pass was still over four thousand feet up. My advice, if asked, would be based on the assumption that they were suffering from a mild case of altitude sickness. I'd have recommended that they return to Manang and wait a day or two to get more acclimated to the altitude before trying to cross the pass again. But I wasn't asked. Instead, my porter negotiated with them to carry their packs over the top. But first, he asked my permission. I agreed, reluctantly, because I was well aware that I might be aiding them in getting sicker.

I knew that, depending on the individual, altitude could cause very serious problems, even for experienced mountaineers. Mild symptoms of nausea, shortness of breath, and dizziness, could turn very serious in a short period, ultimately leading to pulmonary or cerebral edema. In those cases, the only remedy was to go down, fast. Lose altitude as quickly as possible. But if a person got too sick on the trail to walk, he or she had to be carried out, unless they were lucky to have an airstrip nearby. So who would carry those women out if they got too sick to walk?

Outside the cave, my porter rigged up a way to carry the girls' packs as well as my goods. I couldn't believe the outlandish mountain of gear he carried. I figured each girl's pack weighed forty-five pounds, and my stuff added another twenty-five pounds. He was a skinny guy and probably weighed only a few more pounds than what he carried. But he hoisted it up, carrying most of the weight on the trump line around his forehead, and started up the trail at a sort of shuffling gait, half walking and half trotting. The girls were long gone with their friends. I started to follow my porter, but a German man who had just arrived at the teahouse cave stopped me.

"Wait," he said to me. "Aren't you missing something?"

Puzzled, I recognized him as one of the people that shared my dorm the previous night. He was still asleep when I left early that morning.

"I don't think so," I replied. But I was vaguely disturbed by his urgency in confronting me since we had not talked at all before now.

"Do you have your passport?" he asked.

Aghast, I fumbled through the pocket where I normally kept that document, but it wasn't there. Frantically I looked elsewhere, but I knew where it should be, and it just wasn't there. Waves of despair, almost nausea, washed over me as I realized that I had to get back to last night's hotel to get my passport and hope that it was still there. Disaster loomed if I didn't get it back, and I had visions of retreating to Katmandu and wasting days to get it replaced. I looked up at the German man and he was smiling, holding his hand out with my passport

"I found it under your pillow before I left this morning," he said. Then seeing the confusion on my face, he went on. "I have this habit of searching my room each morning before I leave. I find some of the strangest things left behind by others. But never a passport," and he grinned at me.

I thanked him profusely. But what could I do for this angel? I thanked him again, but he waved me off and entered the tunnel leading to the subterranean teahouse. I never saw him again, and since then have never hidden my passport or anything else in a room. I never use closets, drawers, cabinets, or pillows, but leave everything out in the open. That way when I look around my room before leaving I can tell that everything is gone from the room. No need to ever look under my pillow again.

I met my porter at the top of the pass. He had shed his extra load of the two women's packs. Apparently, they had revived nicely walking up without their packs and had retrieved them at the top from my porter, before they pushed on downhill. I never saw them again. My porter was shivering and uncomfortable in the cool breeze at the top of the pass waiting for me, so I told him to go down, as fast he wanted in order to get to warmer air below. He went flying off downhill, promising to wait for me somewhere down below.

Down I went on moderate slopes, nothing difficult, just a hike in the park. I soon left the snow behind which was nice. People came crashing down passing me right and left as they raced to find rooms in the towns below. I caught up to my porter and sent him on ahead to save us each a bed in the next town, Muktinath. A mile or two before arriving there, the trail skirted two interesting holy areas, one a Hindu temple, and the other a miraculous place for Hindus and Buddhists alike. I wanted to stop and visit them, but was more anxious to find a place to sleep for the night, so I hurried on.

Arriving in Muktinath, I found the town strangely empty. My porter and I claimed two beds in an otherwise empty dorm. But where were all the people that had passed me earlier? I finally figured they must have hurried on down the mountain further and faster. Now that I had a place to stay for the night, I could relax, so I went back to see the holy places.

The first place I visited was a temple dedicated to the god Vishnu, who with Brahma and Shiva, made up the three gods at the top of that religion. The temple sat in a sunken, open courtyard about five feet deep. Little stone channels led water into 108 cast bronze cow heads mounted in the walls. From there, the water spurted from each cow's mouth in a watery arc to splash on the courtyard pavement. Pilgrims were supposed to bathe under each of the heads, but I figured a person would have to be masochistic to endure the pain of such freezing cold water out in the open. I didn't see any priests splashing or cavorting about in those grim holy waters. As a token gesture, I washed my hands under a few of the spouting cow's heads and figured that was good enough for the absolution of my few sins.

After spending some time with the cow's heads and listening to splashing waters, I went looking for the other holy place. It was in a cave with the entrance closed off by a ratty looking curtain. For a few rupees, the woman attendant pulled back the curtain for me to see the holy wonder hidden inside. Bending over, I peered through the entry into a rocky grotto. It took me a few seconds to see what made this place so holy.

On the back wall, about ten feet in front of me, a little stream of water about the size of three-quarter inch tubing gurgled out of the rock wall and splashed down the cliff face making the grotto floor damp. From the same aperture, a two-inch blue flame flickered and burned precariously, somewhat like a candle. *I could blow the darn thing out right from here*, I thought, and wondered who relit the gas when it did blow out. Then I realized that here, in this primitive place, was a miracle conjunction of the four elements of life, earth, air, fire, and water.   That idea came from many ancient civilizations, but I think the earliest writings about these elements came from Hindu philosophers thirty-five hundred years before I was born.

I almost laughed at such a puny, primitive display, but then I tried to remember where else in the world I had ever seen or even heard of a phenomena like this. In all of my travels, I couldn't think of another spot, but there were so many places in the world I hadn't seen or heard about yet that I figured somewhere in the world there must be another phenomenon like this one.

I did think of one place back home in Seattle where, for years hundreds of garbage trucks disgorged their loads along with loads of fill dirt into Lake Washington. In time, this produced a large, useful tract of land, which the University of Washington developed into a huge parking lot. The drainage waters ran off into the fill through perforated pipes and methane gas formed by the rotting garbage traveled back up the same pipes to reach the surface. The University built incinerators over each drain and burned off the gas night and day for years until it dissipated. So I suppose at that time, during rainy periods, a conjunction of earth, air, fire, and water was produced, but I didn't think anyone thought it was holy.

I gave the grotto one more glance, and said a short prayer to my god, just in case the place really was holy, then I left after paying the attendant a few more rupees for holding the curtain open for me.

By the time I returned to my inn, several other people had appropriated beds in the dorm by leaving their pack or other personal items on a bed. My porter was lying on his bed reading a book, and the only other person there was a young Tibetan woman tidying up the dorm. On a whim I showed her a hand-woven sash that I had bought in the market and pointed to the one she wore that held her long flowing cloak closed about her waist. She took it from me, examined it carefully, and then took off her sash and placed mine around her waist, all the while talking and laughing in high bell-like tones that I found very pleasing. *Uh oh*, I thought, *their goes my sash. She probably thinks it's a gift.*

Instead, she explained how to wear the sash. It had to be wrapped twice around the waist and tied off at the side. When finished, she giggled and pirouetted in a circle in front of me, so I could appreciate the whole appearance. Her high cheekbones, wide smile, and crinkled, almond-shaped eyes proclaimed her merriment which, I thought, was far more fun than a simple sash. I smiled and said something appropriate. Then she took the sash off her waist, and stepped close to me to put it around my waist. I tried to help, but she brushed my hands aside and reached around me with both arms. She stepped even closer and, for an instant, I felt her body touch mine.

Waves of confusion, pleasure, and alarm went through my mind until she stepped back, holding two ends of the sash too far apart to meet. Unable to tie it off, she laughed and patted my belly, and then held her arms wide apart to show me just how much longer my sash needed to be. I understood that she thought I was stout, and I was, when compared to the men who lived here who were invariably skinny as rails. I don't know why she thought it was so funny. I didn't think her waist line was that much slimmer than mine, but the sash did go around hers twice with extra to spare. But then I always was a poor judge of women's waistlines, especially when they wore flowing robes.

In the next few seconds, she folded up my sash and placed it in my hand. She looked me in the eyes and gave me a pretty smile with her head tilted up and to one side while holding my hand a moment with both of hers. Then abruptly she walked out of the room and left me alone holding my sash. The fun was over too soon, and I wished it could have lasted longer.

"What was all that about," I barked at my porter who was still studiously reading his book.

He deliberately put the book aside, and said, "Ah, Baabu. The girl, she likes you. She flirts with you."

"Okay, I got that, but what's this Baabu stuff?"

"Oh that. It means 'father,'" he said with a grin.

Good grief, does he think I'm old? Of course, I was easily old enough to be the girl's father, and that was not a pleasant thought. So was my porter poking fun at me for what he thought was foolish behavior by a silly old man?

24) Tea house at Tengi below Thorung La Pass

Chapter 14
Leaving Nepal Forever

I left Muktinath early in the morning eager to leave the 'high' country of over ten thousand feet, where I had been traveling for six days. I looked forward to reaching the town of Jomoson, over thirty-five hundred feet below on the main trade route between India and Tibet. Near this town, the Khola River had eroded a deep gash in the earth's surface separating two massive mountains, Annapurna at 26,700 feet and Dhaulagiri at 26,950 feet. Twenty-three miles separated the summits of these two giants, and the drop into the valley between them was over three miles deep. By comparison, the Grand Canyon's maximum width was about eighteen miles with the depth a little over one mile.

The lower I went, the warmer it got, and soon I shed my heavy wool sweater and hat, the uniform that I had practically lived in for the last six days. The trail finally leveled out on a broad valley floor and followed the base of the steep flanks of mountains jutting up from the valley floor. On the wide valley floor, the river braided itself into a myriad of streams, separating and coming together in a wild confusion of twisting shapes and channels that filled the valley. An uncomfortably cold wind blew up the valley hard enough to force me to bend forward to keep upright, and I soon put my uniform of warm sweater and hat back on.

I noted people traveling on a trail across the valley and convinced myself that it was a shorter route to Jomoson than the trail I was following, somewhat like "the grass is greener" elsewhere. I fought the urge to take that shortcut for a while, because it meant cutting across the valley and fording all those separate streams of water that made up the Khola River. But finally, I couldn't stand it and turned off my trail and headed across the valley to that shorter trail across the way. My porter was very surprised, but dutifully followed me into that watery maze.

The first few streams were shallow and easy to cross, and I congratulated myself on the choice I had made, but then the streams got wider and deeper and the waters more turbulent. Sounds of burbling and swishing water everywhere were disturbing and filled my mind with unease about whether I could make it across the next stream. It took me longer to find and convince myself of safe places to cross each stream. In some crossings, the current threatened to wash me away, and over the sounds of rushing water, I heard rocks tumbling on the bottom of the torrent I was crossing. A current that moved rocks frightened me.

At one point, I looked back to see if it would be better to retreat than to continue on. To me, it looked just as bad going back as going forward, and besides, I already knew what lay behind. It was a case where I felt better about facing the unknown rather than the known route behind me. This shortcut was taking a lot longer than I thought it would, but finally, the ordeal was over and I climbed up onto the trail on the other side of the valley. Now I would be able to make better time on this shorter route into Jomoson. After a few minutes of hiking, I looked across that valley of braided streams, and now it seemed that the shortest way to Jomoson was on the original trail I had just left. As is often the case, a shortcut ended up to be a "long cut."

Jomoson, on the main north-south trading route from Tibet, was a more organized town than those on the other side of Thorung La Pass. My dorm room bed had bedding and blankets on it, and the dining room had chairs and tables with tablecloths and menus. Best of all there was little smoke hanging about from the supper fires. But it was cold and central heating hadn't yet arrived. The town also boasted a short dirt runway where small planes serviced passengers flying to and from Pokhara and Katmandu.

Before supper, I talked a while with a Nepalese man who had recently retired from the army. He was very young when he joined the army under the British, and had witnessed the brutal partition of India and Pakistan when those countries were formed in 1947. He had been a sergeant and had fought in the high mountains on the borders of Pakistan and China. He had a wide, prominent mustache that bent down at the corners of his mouth and then turned upward to end in pointed tips near the center of his dark cheeks. His voice was gruff and booming, and reminded me of some first sergeants I had met in the United States Army.

"I'm walking home with my grandson," he said, pointing to a small boy playing in one corner of the dorm.

"How far do you have to go?" I asked.

"Oh, I think it will take us a week or more. Here, I'll show you where we live."

He pulled out a map that had been folded and creased too many times and was in the process of disintegration. I fumbled in a pocket and brought out my reading glasses. When he saw my glasses, he said, "those are very nice, may I try them on?"

I handed them over. He was obviously pleased and, after a thorough inspection and comments of awe, he carefully put them on and looked at his map.

When he saw that I couldn't see the map very well, he said, "I have glasses too, here try mine."

Then he pulled out his bedraggled pair of glasses. They were bent and crooked. The hinge pins on both sides were gone and the folding supports were held together with paper clips. Little strips of tape kept the lenses from falling out, and a chunk of heavy tape held the nose bridge together. I figured that without the tape and paper clips holding his contraption together, it would be in six separate pieces.

"Here, try them on," he said. "They work well."

Snookered again, I thought, *by these crafty Nepalese.*

We talked on for a while, laughing and trading stories about our lives in different worlds. He made no move to return my glasses. He invited me to visit him at his house when I got back to Pokhara.

"I'll show you around, and you will have a good visit," he said looking at me through my glasses.

Before leaving for supper, he said, "Look, let's trade glasses, you and me. Then we'll each have something to remember this time together."

What a terrible trade, I thought. But then, new reading glasses in my world were probably much easier to come by than in his world, and I really didn't care. So I traded glasses and went to supper.

The dining room was crowded, and I learned that the cause was because so many people were waiting in town for a plane ride out. For the past few days, the wind blowing up the valley was too strong for planes to land or take off, and some people had been waiting several days for a plane to arrive. But now the word was out that the weather forecast called for no wind in the morning, and I think a lot of people were starting to celebrate the possibility of getting out of town.

I went to bed early, tired out by the exertion of forcing a long, shortcut route across the valley. The sergeant's grandson was sleeping safe and peacefully in the dorm, and I fell asleep immediately amid the sounds of shouting and laughter coming from the hopeful celebrants in the dining room.

I left early in the morning before dawn while most of the people in the dorm were still asleep. Sure enough, just after sunrise the first of three or four planes came flying up the valley to land at Jomoson. They were all small, propeller-driven planes, and I guessed they would seat perhaps six to ten people. I hoped the would-be passengers were awake enough to catch their planes, because the system of seat assignments was on a first come, first served basis. It would be terrible to think of missing a plane ride out because of celebrating too intensely the night before. I still had almost a week to hike out to Pokhara, and felt a little sorry for myself when a little later the first loaded plane from Jomoson flew over my head and disappeared as a tiny speck way down the valley. What would take me six more days of hiking took them maybe an hour of flying.

In the next few days, I met a lot more travelers like myself coming and going on the trail. We traded stories and brief trail reports, and then slowly drifted apart. With his colorful load my porter attracted a lot of attention, like a living room conversation piece. The Nepalese women were particularly attracted, fingering the knotted rugs and inspecting the designs and colors. I didn't understand what they said, but it seemed that they were suitably impressed by the workmanship, and that made me feel good. Of course, they all wanted to know what I had traded for them. But by then I didn't remember what I had paid for them, so I shrugged and shook my head. They immediately lost interest in me, the dumb foreigner who didn't even know the value of his goods.

On my last night on the trail, I hurried through the town of Ulleri to find a hotel before nightfall. I could have stayed in a town a couple of hours before on the ridge behind me, but I had opted to push on.

Suddenly, from out of the gloom, a voice called out, "Hello, Frank King, come on over and have a beer."

I came to a screeching halt, wondering if I had heard right. How would anyone know my name out here in the middle of nowhere? Then I saw an arm wave.

"Come on over," it said, "before it gets too dark for us to see anything."

I told my porter to get us a couple beds at the first hotel he came to and turned toward the waving arm. I desperately tried to figure what this was all about. Someone knew me in Nepal? Impossible. When I got closer, I saw it was Dave Hanson, a Seattle Mountaineer, who had been with me on climbs in the Cascades two or three times recently. True to his word, he handed me a beer.

"What are you doing here?" I asked, still not quite believing that I knew this man. We had met casually together on climbs, but that was all..

"Same thing as you're doing here," he responded. "Trekking."

"Wow, meeting someone I know out here is hard to believe. What are the chances of that happening?"

"Not likely," he said, "but here we are."

"Where are you going? Or are you headed back?"

"We're going into the Annapurna Sanctuary," he said. "We've only been out a couple nights so far. But look, it's almost time for supper. Why don't you come over to our camp later on, and we can talk for awhile? We're loaded with lanterns and light, and maybe I can sneak a dessert for you." I agreed to come to his camp set up at the edge of town, which I must have passed when entering Ulleri.

When I got to the hotel, my porter was wolfing down the last of his supper. He pointed to the dorm and went on eating. I quickly ate some supper, left my pack on a bed to save it, and went off in the dark looking for Dave's camp.

"It's easy to find," he had said. "Even in the dark. We've got porters and cooks, camp gear, tables and chairs, and lights. You name it, we have it."

I found it easily, and Dave was sitting in the big dining tent with a couple friends hunched over some hot chocolate. They had just finished celebrating Halloween. *Today was Halloween? Just how does one go about celebrating that dubious holiday in the middle of Nepal?*

The camp was "dry," so I accepted a mug of the chocolate stuff although it was not my favorite drink. Smaller sleeping tents surrounded the big tent in an arc, and I saw several lit by lanterns inside that made the tents glow pastel red, yellow, or blue depending on the color of the tent fabric. They made a beautiful splash of color in the dark. I talked to Dave about my trip around Annapurna, and I think he might have been a little jealous.

"Well, I only had two weeks off," he said. "The best I could do was this short trip into the Annapurna Sanctuary, and then I have to get back to work.

We traded stories and caught up on our recent climbs in the Cascades. We laughed together over one climb we did of Three Fingers where the two of us were the only members of the climbing party to make the summit. Dave had a problem with his crampon straps and stopped to adjust them. I lingered behind to wait for him and, by the time we started on, the rest of the party was way out ahead of us and almost out of sight.

We followed them until Dave called out to me, "Wait, they're going the wrong way. We need to turn off here, go up, and traverse the ridge just below its crest. They'll never make it to the top the way they're going."

"Are you sure?" I asked.

"Absolutely, I've led this climb before."

"Well, they're out of sight and too far away to hear us yell."

"We might as well go ahead and climb the peak," he said. "By the time they realize their mistake, we'll be back down to meet them here. And if by chance they do find a way to get to the top, we'll meet them there."

The climb to the ridge was straight forward, but I almost froze up when I saw the steep rock cliff at the top of the ridge which we had to traverse. It was truly a knife-edge and I saw no way of walking across its top.

"It's easier than it looks," said Dave. "Grab a hold of the sharp fin of the rock ridge right at the top with your hands and lean out backwards. Bow your body so that your weight is transmitted through your legs to your feet. Hold the feet flat and perpendicular to the rock face for maximum friction, and just crab your way along sideways."

"But what if my boots slip?" I asked.

"No problem, just hold on with your hands until you get your feet back up perpendicular to the rock face."

"But what if I lose a handhold or a rock comes loose?" I asked.

"Whoops! That would be a problem. But don't worry; the knife edge of this cliff is as solid as a rock," he said with a big grin.

He crabbed his way out on the face of the cliff, and I followed. At first, I was sick with fear that one lost handhold or a loose rock would cause me to fall backward down the cliff with no possibility of gaining control. But the lay-back system worked, and I felt secure with all my weight holding my boots on the smooth vertical surface. *This is a snap*, I thought, *somewhat like walking on a vertical sidewalk.*

At the top, we took a couple minutes to look around and then, by mutual consent, headed back. We got back down to where we turned off from the route the main party had taken just in time to meet the party coming back from their mistake. They were a little pissed at having gone so far in the wrong direction and weren't happy when the leader determined it was now too late to make the climb to the top. Dave and I were unpopular for the rest of the trip, because we summated and they didn't.

I finally left the trekking camp after Dave and I agreed to see one another on a climb sometime back in Seattle. But fate is strange; I never saw Dave again. Our paths just never crossed, and I have only the memory of that chance meeting in Nepal. I should have gone back to Nepal, and maybe I would have met up with him again.

I never did get back to Nepal although I wanted to do another trek there. Trips in other parts of the world rose to a higher priority, and then one day I realized my health wouldn't allow me to hike at those high altitudes anyway.

I wanted once again to experience the small villages and the people who became friends along the way. I wanted to revisit the giant mountains, river gorges, and forests. And see the incredible sky on a clear night. I missed the wonder, delight, and surprise each day brought and I wanted it all to come back again. I always thought that someday I would go back and redo the trip. That someday never arrived.

After my heart attack, I thought someday I could do the lower part of the trail, Jomoson to Pokhara, for instance, where elevations don't get above ten thousand feet. That someday never arrived. Now, thirty years later, because of a deteriorating heart, I am quite sure I will never walk that trail again. Even if I could do so, one part of me knows that I would be doomed to disappointment for nothing stays the same, and magical moments are only memories. So the memories of those pleasant, carefree days on the trail in Nepal will have to last me for the rest of my life

25) "Fishtail Mountain," The last giant before leaving
the Annapurna area

Frank King

Route of truck travel across Africa

Chapter 15
Across Africa by truck

I don't know where the idea came from. Like most of my ideas, it started out small but got giant in the process of planning. In this case, I thought it would be fun to go on a little safari in Africa and see some wild animals. So I poured over the slick, colorful brochures touting African trips. They all sounded so good I wanted to go on all of them. My problem was that I want to see and do everything. Long ago, someone told me I was going to miss out on seeing some things and surely it was impossible to do everything, but I only half believed him and tried anyway.

Because of costs and my limited budget, I settled on going by truck, camping out, and cooking meals out on open fires, instead of local planes, air-conditioned buses and high priced hotels and restaurants. I traded comfort and spent extra time in exchange for seeing and doing more in Africa for less money. Somehow, the idea of crossing the whole African continent sounded exciting, and I chose the longest trip available. It would take at least fifteen weeks, a good three months of camping and sightseeing across Africa from the back of a truck, ending up in London, England.

Then a heart attack while on top of a mountain interrupted my plans six weeks before my scheduled departure. When my heart doctor heard about my African project, he objected a little.

"What!" he exploded. "You just had heart bypass surgery two weeks ago. I can't let you go traipsing off into the wilds of Africa until your heart mends."

"But this is such a cushy trip," I said, "nothing to do but ride the back of a truck and watch the scenery and animals roll by. What better way to recuperate from surgery? Probably lots better than messing around the house, bored to my eyeballs looking for something to do. Besides, I wouldn't go if I had any heart problems."

In the end, he agreed, pending his final okay of my heart just before I left.

Yeah, the trip was on!

I met the group of travelers going across Africa in a hotel lobby in Nairobi, Kenya. There we met the driver and the guide, both young women, and went over the details of the three-month long trip. The next day we embarked by truck for London, England. But what a neat truck. It was painted white with a bright orange stripe and the company's name, Dragoman, printed in large black letters down each side. Canvass curtains took the place of windows, and these were rolled up in good weather and rolled down in bad.

The safari company had customized the truck with bus-like seats all facing forward. The back end opened to a large storage compartment that took all of the passenger's personal gear and all the group gear such as tents, sleeping bags, and air mattresses. The safari company fitted the truck with oversized fuel tanks, a fifty-gallon water storage tank, a small refrigerator, lights for cooking after dark, and filled every extra space with cupboards and cubby holes for tables, folding stools, stove and fuel for cooking food and beverages away from an open fire, and for other miscellaneous gear.

One puzzling item was half a dozen garden trowels. I soon found out that these were used to excavate small "cat" holes for personal toilets. After burning the toilet paper, the holes were backfilled with dirt.

They stuffed the built-in storage cabinets under the seats with nonperishable food, such as canned fruit, veggies, and meat, mostly Spam®. That became a big incentive for us to try to find fresh meat in the local markets. In addition, there were jars and cans of jellies and jams, peanut butter, ketchup, mustard, coffee, tea, and butter. They also packed in pickles, olives, meat sauces, chutneys, and lots of pasta. All kinds of pasta. All we needed to buy at the local markets was fresh fruit, veggies, and meat.

And for those who had acquired a taste for it, there was Vegemite, a sticky chocolate-appearing concoction made from brewer's yeast that was slathered on toast at breakfast time. While some in the group might tolerate the God-awful stuff, I figured only the Australians actually enjoyed it, smacking their lips, and extolling its virtues.

Our group of truck passengers, nineteen total, came from all over the English-speaking world. We had two South Africans, some from New Zealand and Australia, two from America, one Irish man, and one Canadian, but most came from England. We all spoke English, sort of. But I had a terrible time trying to figure out what was said in the rapid give and take conversations around me. If they spoke slower and used "baby English," I did better. I was by far the oldest at sixty-two; the others ranged in age from their late twenties to forty-seven.

People from the London area spoke the worst, and their words were mostly incomprehensible. I had to ask many times over, "What? What did you say?" I learned some new English words from my cooking partner who was from Australia. For instance, she said "breed" when she meant "bread" in my language. I finally made closer ties to some of the people whose words I could understand the easiest.

Sometimes the other travelers didn't understand my American English which surprised me since I thought I spoke perfect English. I think that what confused the others was the use of idioms and colloquial sayings, such as strike while the iron is hot, mad as a wet hen, living high off the hog, you hit the nail on the head, it ain't over till it's over, etc. I never realized how many oblique colorful sayings we Americans use in the normal course of speaking.

We started the trip in Nairobi, Kenya, and went west following the equator across the great gash of the rift valley. We continued west across Uganda and Zaire, crossed the Congo River, and on through Central Africa Republic and Cameroon into Nigeria. We eventually got to Algeria, then Morocco, and took the ferry across the Straits of Gibraltar, and then on into Europe.

Unfortunately we had to cross some of the Sahara Desert by plane rather than drive. The Tuareg tribes living in that part of desert took out their anger at the government in Bamako, Mali by molesting people driving through their area. They robbed travelers of money, vehicles, and even the clothes on their back. The tourists were left helpless in the open desert until other travelers came by and rescued them. Our safari company refused to take the risk of driving and flew us over the conflict

Most of the roads had well maintained pavement or graveled surfaces, but the worst roads were in dirt or sand. In some places in Zaire, the road was nonexistent, marked by deep ruts and huge potholes filled with water and, in the desert, we sometimes followed dry ruts in the sand. On roads like that, we were lucky to travel ninety miles or so in a whole day's effort. On occasion, we got stuck in the mud or sand. But the safari company had foreseen this problem and had modified their truck so that the rear wheels could be locked to rotate together. When locked, if one wheel was stuck, the other would keep tracking and push us through the obstruction. I don't know what would happen if both wheels were stuck at the same time.

The truck also carried a dozen flat gratings about twelve inches wide and ten feet long. I think they were surplus landing ramps used by the troops in World War II to get vehicles from their beached landing craft to firm ground. When we encountered loose sand, we laid them out in two lines in front of the truck. The truck inched its way up onto the ramps and, as it slowly moved forward, we paying passengers grabbed the ramps no longer needed in back and ran around to the front to lay them out again ahead of the truck. This was a tedious and tiring job and the fun and laughter soon became grueling work. Fortunately, we rarely ran into loose sand and, when we did, it was in small patches.

When roads were really bad, especially in Zaire, our truck crawled along in its lowest gear, and we became the biggest event of the day for the local people. Women and children flocked to see up close the spectacle of white strangers from far off lands slowly passing by. The women wore colorful print dresses that covered them from head to foot. Their oversized headgear was made of folded and tied material that matched their dresses and made them appear taller and slimmer. They used their head covering as a sunshade as well as a decorative accessory to their apparel. And they put on a show for us, swaying from side to side with their arms in the air and singing. The children ran along beside the truck for a short distance laughing and screeching. The men sat in the skimpy shade of coffee trees and barely moved or glanced at us. The women were vivacious and engaging, and far more interested in us then their men.

Each of us was assigned camp chores, gathering wood and maintaining a fire for cooking, setting up tents, setting up the kitchen and folding stools, hauling out sleeping bags and personal gear, preparing the meal, and clean-up. Since I was still recovering from open heart surgery six weeks before, I was assigned to the cushy job of treating the drinking and cooking water. Whether it came from spigots, or wells, streams or rivers, it all was treated the same. I added the right amount of disinfectant tablets to the water and tested the mixture from time to time. I was known as the *water walla*, loosely translated as the water boy

If possible, we avoided taking water from lakes and other still waters, preferring to use moving water, the faster the better. Tiny snails and other tiny creatures lived in still waters, especially those places with reeds growing in them, and could ruin our day if ingested. The men waded into fast moving water and filled five-gallon cans, the ubiquitous "jerry cans" which we used only for water. When filled, the men carried them to the truck and dumped the water into our on-board storage tank. Then I would go about my duties as water walla.

The most important job was cooking meals for the gang of nineteen passengers plus driver and guide. Everyone had an assigned cooking partner, and the pair took turns cooking for one day in a rotating schedule. I think I ended up on cooking duty ten times for the whole trip. In addition, each cooking team had to provide help and support to the cooking team of the previous day. That way there were at least four people working in the kitchen at mealtime.

Usually there were plenty of additional helpers who volunteered to help cook when their own chores were finished. But it was the cooks of the day who planned the meal, shopped for food, figured out how to make it all come out right, and worried about having enough to feed twenty-one hungry people. I was lucky and had a cooking mate who was good at planning the meals and getting the job done, and I rarely disputed her decisions.

Hygiene rules were strict. After all, if someone got sick, where could we go for help camped in the middle of Africa? Besides if one person got sick, we would all probably come down with the same thing. The cooks made sure that basins of hot water were placed at the beginning of the lineup for food. One was for washing hands with soap, and the other was for rinsing hands. They provided no washcloths or towels since dirt and unseen vermin could contaminate them. Wet hands dried fast in the African heat, and air-drying them was considered more sanitary than with a towel or a shirttail.

Likewise all dishes, silverware and pots were air-dried, no towels ever used. At the end of a meal, using both hands, everyone grabbed dishes, cups, silverware, or whatever had been washed and rinsed, and walked about flapping their items in the air like a bird on wing until the items were dry, or at least dry enough. "Dry enough" was the operative words here and each individual made that decision based on his or her impatience or tolerance of flapping about the camp. I'm sure that much of the stuff put away for the next meal was wetter than dry. Flappers more dexterous than others dried four dishes or cups at a time. They were, of course, greatly admired, if not emulated by the rest of us. The flappers caught up silverware and utensils in small batches, never one at a time, and flipped them about until considered "dry enough."

All veggies slated to be eaten raw were immersed for at least fifteen minutes in water treated with potassium permanganate. This mixture killed any living critter or bacteria it came in contact with that could possibly live among the raw veggies. Too much of the chemical turned the water a bright red. It wasn't harmful, just a ghastly red color. Just the right amount of chemical caused no change of color in the disinfected water, but none of us were willing to trust a judgment of that exact amount of chemical. So to make sure we were safe, we stopped adding chemicals only after the water turned red. No one seemed to mind ingesting a little extra chemical to ensure safe eating of raw veggies. In proof that the system worked, no one ever got sick eating food, no matter how many fresh salads we ate. Of course, the insides of our bodies were probably as sanitized as the overtreated vegetables we ate.

Shopping for food was a treat. We stopped every two or three days and stocked up on the food we needed for the next few meals. This meant that several cooking groups were doing their required shopping at the same time for their turn as cooks. Almost every town we drove through had a large outdoor market where farmers, butchers, and craftsmen bargained away their wares. The markets were by far the most exciting and colorful spots in Africa, where people came from miles around, literally out of the woods. The women were always the most colorful with bright, flowered print blouses and long skirts balancing bundles of goods or large trays of food and wares on their heads. They were graceful and alluring, smiling and engaging. In contrast, the men wore drab Western clothing, sat around a lot, and hardly ever smiled.

Vegetables and nonperishable items were easy to buy, but purchasing meat took a little more thought. There were scrawny, anemic-looking chickens, obscene without their feathers, hanging by their long, disgusting, skinny necks in rows clad only in their yellow wrinkled skins. A few hunks of various meats---goat, pork, guinea pig, and other nameless meats---hung on hooks from the ceiling of the stalls. But the biggest meat source was beef which hung in great haunches against the wall.

There was no refrigeration anywhere, so the cooks debated and made judgments of how long the meat had been sitting out in the open and if it would keep from spoiling until needed. Were there many flies hovering about or worse, black spots where they hunkered down in colonies laying eggs in the meat? Was there a rotten smell in the air? We had a little refrigerator in the truck, but most of its space was used to keep our drinks cold, which by overwhelming consensus, took top priority. The cooks might be able to squeeze in some of the meat bought in advance, but generally, they had to cook it in the next day or so before it "went off" as the Brits would say.

Butchering of beef was not a refined art. The butchers simply chopped haunches of beef, bones and all, into small pieces with a bloody axe. They didn't provide sirloin steak, flank steak, T-bones, or roasts, only stew meat mixed from all parts of the animal's body. Piles of the stuff lay about in the open on their counters. And when that was sold, they laid another haunch of beef, if available, on the counter, and chopped it into piles of stew meat. They sold the meat by the handful, not by the pound. Each customer bargained for handfuls of meat, which the butcher plopped onto a piece of newspaper and gave to the customer without wrapping it any further. Sometimes the Spam® stored on the truck didn't look too bad by comparison to the piles of fresh, grisly meat offered up on bloody counters covered with flies.

For me, the best part of those wonderful, carefree days was at sundown. Almost every night I slept out on a plastic ground tarp, and as I prepared my bed, the sky went from yellow through orange and red, finally arriving at a deep vermillion that darkened as night approached. Someone told me that sand and dust blown high in the sky from the Sahara Desert still eight hundred miles away caused the abnormally brilliant red sunsets.

The trees appeared as black cutouts, each limb and leaf clearly etched against that deep red sky. In my sleeping bag, I watched the stars get brighter as the red sky turned dark. I listened to the rustle and sounds around me, feeling safe and cozy on my little plastic home turf. And, when it was quiet, I heard the distant throbbing of drums carried to me on the gentlest of winds and, sometimes, if I held my breath and listened very carefully, I heard faint wisps of laughter, and singing.

195

And then I felt that pang of loss when I was missing out on something, and wished I was there amid the drums and laughter, color, and excitement.

26) Bridge revisions

27) The truck, the guide, the driver

Frank King

28) African Teenagers

29) African children greeting our truck

Chapter 16
Gorillas and Volcanoes, Zaire

Suddenly, I was there in the center of a group of mountain gorillas, fatigue gone, and adrenaline pumping me up for "fight or flight." Minutes before I stumbled along through thick forest, sweat dripping off my nose, a little bored and almost comatose from the heat. I was tired of pushing through thick vegetation just to see a bunch of gorillas. All that changed in an instant. Stunned by the suddenness of the encounter, our group of eight people remained rigid and speechless, and I thought, *Wow! These big dangerous-looking animals aren't in cages.* I don't know why I didn't think of that before starting out to track gorillas. I had signed up to go along on the side trip with more curiosity than desire, and I hadn't known what to expect.

Government rules allowed a maximum of eight people to visit one band of gorillas for one hour each day. They established these rules in the hope that the great apes would not be adversely affected by contact with humans and would remain in a wild state. At that time, only two bands of gorillas were available for us to visit. So we ended up camping in a bean field at the head of a small valley for two days until everyone in our group had a chance to hike into the upland forests to track the gorillas.

The thought of finding gorillas in the wild had sounded like a little fun, but now face to face, I saw that these animals were big and not particularly cuddly or cute. And there were a lot of them, about twenty individuals dominated by one giant male. I tried to remember the instructions given to us by the guide before leaving to track the gorillas in case we encountered them. The main concern of the guide was that none of us do anything to challenge the authority of the dominant male gorilla. That gorilla was easy to recognize and impossible to ignore, and I had walked up to within eight feet of the giant before realizing it. He was twice the size of his female friends, and had a massive head that seemed attached to his shoulders without a neck. He sat eating his breakfast, or maybe it was lunch, which consisted of stalks of a bamboo-like plant.

As instructed, I hastily knelt down on the ground to get my head lower than his. This was supposed to keep me safe by implying a non-confrontational attitude on my part. You can bet there was no one in our group willing to confront that menacing mass of muscle. To get lower than his head, I sat on the ground amid thick ground cover still slightly damp from the morning dew. Earthy smells came up mixed with vague odors of rampant vegetation and decay. I looked over at the guard assigned to protect our group. He carried an old bolt-action rifle, and I didn't see how he would be of any effect if that huge gorilla got it in his head to show a dislike for our intrusion into his gorilla family. But nothing happened, and I breathed a big sigh of relief.

Our instructions also included not making eye contact with the big guy. Again, this bit of lore was an effort to keep us at a lower order of importance in the mind of the dominant male gorilla. I wondered if the experts really thought this would keep us safe, but I didn't need to worry. At no time did that huge gorilla ever look directly at any one of us. It was as if by not looking at us he could maintain the illusion that we weren't there, and therefore not have to do anything about our petty intrusion into his life.

The shock of my sudden encounter with the apes died a little when I saw them going on about their business of eating as if I wasn't there. I relaxed and began taking pictures. I watched different gorillas, but was drawn back again and again to the dominant male. He was huge with a massive barrel chest, broad shoulders, and arms longer than his legs. When he stood on his legs, he was five to six feet tall. His face was ugly with deep set eyes under heavy brows. He had a thick, hairy, black coat with a distinctive silvery sheen on the back of his shoulders and upper back. Most of the time, he sat and ate, but when necessary, he shifted among the stalks of vegetation with great agility, walking on his legs and shortening his arms by curling his hands to walk on the knuckles of his fingers. He broke off a stalk of vegetation, carefully peeled it, and then chomped it down like a giant piece of celery.

Another warning given to us prior to tracking the gorillas was never try to touch them. That was pretty easy advice to follow when it came to the bigger gorillas and especially the huge male. Who in their right mind was going to saunter over to pet that ugly giant? But the baby gorillas came unbidden to the women in our group and touched them. They would slowly climb into a woman's lap and wrap their arms around her neck. At first, the women were afraid and tried not to touch them, as instructed by the guide, but it was awkward and not a normal response. Soon, they were holding the babies in their arms as naturally as they would any human child. The gorilla babies never approached the men. They instinctively knew our gender and went unerringly to the ladies. After a few minutes, the babies left to find their real mothers who didn't seem to mind the impromptu babysitting.

The juveniles, like those of their human counterparts, tried to attract our attention. They lolled about on their backs, making faces at us or tussled with each other rolling about on the ground. Then, stretching out a hand or a foot, they grabbed an arm or leg of one or another of our group. One of them, apparently not attracting enough of my attention, stretched out a leg while lying on his back and without warning grabbed my arm with his foot. Startled, I almost jumped out of my skin. He sure had my attention now. His hand or paw, bare of fur and padded with firm soft flesh, felt cool on my skin. He held me in a firm grip long enough to attract my complete attention, and then rolled on to repeat the process with someone else in the group. So we couldn't touch the apes, but they sure had fun grabbing us.

Our allotted time of one hour with the apes quickly passed. Near the end of that time, almost as if the gorillas had timepieces, they disappeared into the surrounding forest. We still heard them chattering and eating nearby. The last to leave was the dominant male, showing off his beautiful, silvery coat when he left. An instant sense of loss and loneliness washed over me after he and the others went away. That surprised me. We still had some time left, and the guide offered to take us in close to see them again, but we decided not to go. The magic of the initial encounter had passed, and we thought we would gain nothing more in the few minutes left of our time.

That encounter happened almost twenty years ago, but I remember it today as vividly as if it happened just yesterday. It was such a short visit, a mere moment out of the lives of man and beast. In that brief time, I felt a kinship with those gentle apes, and it pleases me to know that we both share this big, beautiful planet called earth.

A few days after the encounter with the gorillas, our road crossed an area recently buried in hot ashes, cinders, and molten lava. The road was newly paved, and the surrounding area was still emitting steam and heat from the recent lava flow. About one-half mile away across the desolate field of hot black rocks and cinders was a bright ribbon of fire where the molten lava oozed out of a crack in the earth's surface. As it moved, the heat ignited everything in its way. Spouts of lava, hot cinders, and ash followed to complete the total desolation of the land. I figured it must have been moving away from us, but at a very slow pace. Even so, it was a disquieting scene of vast destruction, and I felt uneasy and glad to leave that spot.

We traveled on to reach a hostel for the night. Some of the group spent money for a room and adjacent bath, but I spread my tarp and sleeping bag out on the lush, green grass surrounding the buildings. During the night, I saw the faint red glow of spouting lava out of sight, but reflected in the sky.

The next day several of us went on an overnight excursion to see active lava forming new volcanic cones. We drove the safari truck to the closest village, still about five hours hike away from the eruptions that were completely out of sight. At the village, we hired porters to carry water, food, and camp gear into the area of new cones. We also had a guide and a guard armed with an old bolt-action rifle.

I asked about the need for a guard and was told that he was there in case a rhino or elephant were to attack us. Really? We spent most of the next five hours hiking through a dense maze of scruffy small trees and brush. No trail. I didn't see how anyone would have enough time to shoot a beast if one chose to attack us from such heavy cover. I worried about that problem for awhile, but finally forgot about it.

In the last hour of hiking, the brush and trees became less dense, and we walked on cinders and ashes and past occasional lava rocks strewn about. Finally, the way opened up, and I had views of small volcanic cones scattered across the landscape. I heard a faint, continuous roar, but in daylight, I couldn't see the lava or anything else spouting off. How disappointing after all the work to get there! The cones were all about the same size, and I guessed they were two to three hundred feet high. As we got closer, the roaring sounded more like the panting of giant steam engines, and I saw a few cinders and rocks thrown into the air from the one cone that was active. They cascaded down its slopes, slowly adding to the size of the cone. Here and there, I saw little specs of glowing lava cooling off on the sides of the cone. The site was not very impressive, just okay. I expected to see lava splash high in the air and cascade down over the cone.

The area was completely open to camping anywhere, no fences, no guards, and no signs. Everyone decided for himself where it was safe to camp, and if someone's gear burned up because of an errant hot cinder, it was his fault for not choosing a better site. I chose a spot about three hundred feet away from the volcanoes' base and made camp there. The others spread out wherever they wished. I noted the prevailing wind direction, away from me, and hoped it wouldn't change. In late afternoon, we climbed an adjacent, temporarily dormant cone in hopes we could see the bubbling lava in the active cone. Part way up the cinders got too hot to walk on. The bottom of one person's shoes began to melt, and the ground was too hot to sit on, so we got out of there.

The cinders around my sleeping bag were warm, and heat radiated from all sides so that a sleeping bag wasn't necessary. The ground shook constantly, and the roar from the volcano never let up. I found it hard to relax, expecting some calamity to occur in this inhospitable place. After supper as the sky darkened, I saw the hot lava spouting up out of the cone and breaking up into cinders and ashes that fell on the cone. Most of the time, the heavier globs of lava fell back into the cauldron. But there were times when the lava fell on the slope of the cone and washed down the slope with a splash of color and light. As it got darker, the fireworks became more pronounced and easier to see than in daylight. Now the show was worth the effort to get there, and I stayed up half the night watching the spectacle. Eventually I slept--a little--but woke up time and again to watch that incredible show of primeval forces producing a small mountain.

The next morning after breakfast we walked out the five miles to a calmer world, no harsh noises, heat, or molten lava. Near the end of our three month trip, the leader asked everyone to list the five top sights or experiences we had crossing Africa. Everyone's list included the gorillas or the volcanoes as the first or second choice for the best of all the things we had seen or done.

30) Gorilla with author

31) Gorilla Leader

32) Baby gorilla and baby sitter

Chapter 17
A Night Out with the Pygmies, Zaire

A man, about four feet tall, walked out of the jungle into our camp late one afternoon.   He was well proportioned, just small, a pygmy.   He brought trinkets made of seed pods strung on rawhide thongs to wear around the neck and wrists. After selling these items, he proceeded to barter away his knife, his belt, and his bow and arrows stored in a sewn bark quiver.   All were coarsely made and rudimentary, but he sold everything quickly. His price was perhaps too low, or his bargaining skills were not highly developed.   I marveled that he so easily gave up the necessities needed to maintain his lifestyle in the forest, and I was vaguely embarrassed that we paid so little for his tools.

We were in the northeast corner of Zaire now known as The Peoples Republic of Congo. I much preferred Zaire over the present name.   Our driver and guide had introduced the little man as the chief of a band of pygmies who were living nearby in the forest.   They were true nomads, living for six months or so in one spot, depleting the forest around them of animals and other food before moving to another location.   He had come to invite anyone in our group to go back with him the next morning, and spend a day and night as guests in his camp. About twelve of us signed up to go with the chief in the morning. We brought our sleeping bags, some food for supper and breakfast, and safe drinking water. He brought men from his tribe to carry all our stuff to their camp.

Early the next morning we trudged into the forest behind the chief, and I was immediately lost. I saw no trail or markings pointing the way to his camp or back to our camp. The porters quickly disappeared, going at a deceptively faster pace than we awkward big people. For three hours, he led and we followed closely, not wanting to be left behind, alone in the jungle.

At one point, he stopped beside a large Ceiba tree. It was one of the bigger species of trees in the forest with trunks two to three feet in diameter rising straight up without branches for a hundred-fifty feet. At its base, six roots above ground supported the massive tree. They formed large membranes a few inches thick and three to four feet high that flared out from the tree before entering the ground. I thought they looked like the legs of a giant coat tree.

Using his balled up fists, the chief hit the membrane of one of the roots in a pattern of strokes that resounded through the forest like a giant drum. Peter, a kindred spirit on the trip, and I tried to duplicate this feat, but my attempts were puny by comparison, and I ended up hurting my hands. Peter's attempts were just as bad. Like everything else, it took practice and technique to make that penetrating drum-like noise using hands only.

I got tired of tramping through endless trees and brush, and was bored by the unchanging, monotonous, flat jungle floor. I was hot and sweaty in the close, stuffy confines of the brush and numerous pesky flies tormented me. At one point, I smelled smoke, which provided some excitement as an unknown diversion to walking through endless brush. Then suddenly we were there. One minute we were stumbling about in suffocating jungle, and in the next, we were in the open area of a camp.

The camp had a central area devoid of vegetation, which had been trampled out of existence into the forest floor by the repetitive steps of many small bare feet. The number of open fires, all spewing smoke into the forest amazed me. The mystery of the source of smoke I had smelled earlier was solved. I felt like I was in a giant smokehouse where the whole tribe was slowly being cooked, dried, and preserved. A large fire pit marked the center of the camp, and that's where we met most of the people who lived there.

They were very friendly and curious, and I looked out upon a sea of heads upturned to see our faces. They packed closely around us, talking, laughing, and touching us. Of course, no one understood a word of the other's language, but we all got along anyway with pantomime and smiles. At first, I thought they were mostly all children until I realized that the height of an adult pygmy was that of a ten-year-old boy at home.

They brought out seats for us made of two sturdy, bowed branches tied at the center to form a cross. We sat on them where the branches crossed. The ends of the branches bent to the ground acted as legs to support the "chair" up off the ground a few inches. They were only marginally more comfortable than sitting on the ground and less comfortable than sitting on a large log. But large logs were scarce in the camp.

Except for the children, most of the people in camp soon lost interest in us and went back to their normal chores. I sat munching a little lunch and watched the activity. A man close by was beating a piece of bark laid over a log stripped of bark. He never stopped beating with his club-like rock in a monotonous cadence of thumps. As I watched, the piece of bark got thinner and its area increased in size. *Good grief, what was he doing,?* I wondered.

Scattered haphazardly throughout the camp and among the surrounding trees were crude shelters that looked like wickiups of our Southwest Indian tribes. They were about eight feet in diameter with domes about six feet high. They each had one arched, open doorway facing the communal area.

In each doorway was a place to keep a small fire burning. The fires lit the interior of the shelters, and at night, these glowed with a golden color like oversized Japanese lanterns. Absolutely beautiful. I learned later that only families, single women, and girls stayed in the shelters at night. The single men and boys lay out in the open around the central communal fire. Of course, that was where we guests were expected to sleep.

Across the camp in the first of a fringe of trees, two women were enclosing a shelter with large leaves about eight inches in diameter. They bent the stem of each green leaf over horizontal supporting ribs made of willow-like branches tied together to form parallel hoops set six inches apart. They carefully spaced each leaf individually to overlap the adjacent leaf and the leaves of the preceding row. I figured this slow, tedious method of placing the leaves was an effort to shed rainwater and keep the inside of the shelter dry. I saw that some of the older shelters had holes in their sides where the dried leaves, now a brown color, had disintegrated. Siding repairs with new green leaves were a continuous maintenance project in this camp.

That afternoon we went hunting with the men and older boys of the tribe. They led the way talking and laughing. As they walked, they taught us how to make loud clapping noises by slapping an open hand at an armpit. If done right, these claps made much louder noises than clapping hands. Of course, it only worked if bare-chested, which left the ladies in the group off the hook. We men practiced this technique as a sort of bonding to see who could make the loudest noise, kind of like seeing who could pee the farthest.

We finally arrived at a place in the jungle where the hunters strung out a rope fence between the trees and bushes. It was about sixty feet long and four feet high, made from the fibers of coconut hulls. The horizontal and vertical pieces of rope were tied together to form a fence with square patterns about eight inches square. Most of the hunters left us at the fence where we sat in the stifling heat waiting along with the pesky flies.

I wasn't sure why we waited there, but I guessed that the hunters who had gone off into the forest were going to drive game to us at the fence. We sat at the finish line where all the killing action would occur. I really wasn't sure I liked the idea of that or not. I had visions of bloody animal corpses piled here and there or, worse yet, squealing, helpless, wounded animals running amok desperately trying to get away.

The small group of hunters who sat with us showed off their prowess with bow and arrow by setting up a target on a tree and shooting at it. Their bows were rudimentary, made from natural branches.

"Those bows are way too limber to propel an arrow very far," said Peter.

"I think you're right," I said. "I bet the target tree is not over thirty feet away."

The arrows were about eighteen inches long, made from the straightest pieces of twigs available. They notched the back of the arrow and inserted a small leaf for stability when the arrow was in flight.

"Look here," I said, examining an arrow up close. "The tips of the arrows are carved to a sharp point and are charred. Why did they char them in a fire? It's a wonder they didn't burn them all up in the process."

"Charring wood gives it a little more strength," said Peter, who was turning out to be an expert in bow and arrow making.

"How did they know that?" I asked rhetorically. "I never heard of such a thing."

"Trial and error, I suppose." said Peter. "Over a long period of time--trial and error."

A few of the arrows had thin pieces of metal shaped to form an arrowhead tied to the front end of the shaft. Most of the arrows were so erratic they missed the target tree entirely, and those that did hit bounced off the bark without making a scratch. The metal tips of arrows that hit the tree crumpled and bent before bouncing harmlessly to the ground. Not one of the bows could propel an arrow forcefully enough to make it stick into the bark of the tree. None of this bothered the hunters. They simply retrieved their arrows, straightened out the leaf tail, and bent the metal tips back to normal. Good as new.

"Do you think these arrows can actually penetrate fur and flesh, or do any lethal damage to an animal?" I asked.

"I don't know," said Peter. "But they might be better off using clubs."

"Well, I think the prey will have to be moving very slowly or asleep for these hunters to make a kill with their bow and arrows."

Then from a distance, we heard faint clapping noises as the other hunters closed their human net, slowly tightening their noose around the game trapped inside. They drove the prey toward our rope barrier and the killer hunters who waited with us. Soon we heard shouts mixed with the clapping, but no animals rushed headlong into our rope barrier. All was quiet where we waited. In a few minutes, the first of the hunters beating the game toward us came into sight, but no furry varmints rustled or ran ahead of them. The forest was denuded of game and the human net remained empty.

The hunters greeted each other like long lost friends, and after a short break, they moved off, stealthily walking through the jungle looking for prey. We guests stumbled along behind trying to keep our not-so-stealthy noises quiet. We went past many small streams and pools of water looking for prey at their water holes, but the forest was empty. At first, I looked for prey as diligently as the hunters, but soon grew weary when not even the smallest of varmints showed itself.

Finally, the hunt ended and we went back to the village empty-handed. No meat for the pot that night, but not to worry. The women had saved the day. They had walked out into the forest too, when their men left camp to hunt for game. Carrying baskets instead of weapons, they dug up cassava roots, gathered edible plants, picked berries, and gathered papayas. No one in the camp would go hungry, at least not that night.

"Did you know that cassava roots originated in South America?" asked Peter. "And now they are one of the most plentiful of food supplies available in Africa."

"I wonder why we haven't had any cassava roots for our suppers." I asked. "We've been eating a lot of other native stuff along the way."

"They're laced with cyanide," said Peter with a cheery grin. "Haven't you heard the story about the cow that ate just one cassava and dropped dead?"

"Well, they look innocent enough," I said. "Just like oversized yams with a black skin. The insides look just like our white potatoes at home."

"Only they're full of cyanide," reminded Peter.

"So the women keep this tribe going by processing cassava roots to make them safe to eat?"

"Right," said Peter. "They peel the roots, cut them into pieces, and soak the pieces overnight to remove the cyanide. It's not scientific, so no one knows how much cyanide is removed. Then they wait until the pieces are thoroughly dried out in the sun before daring to cook them to eat. Do you think any of us would want to take the chance of properly preparing cassava roots for dinner?"

Not likely, I thought. *And I wondered if this little tribe of pygmies could survive without their women.*

As daylight faded, the camp was a busy place. Men and older boys brought in logs to stoke the many fires throughout camp. The man pounding bark that morning offered his beautiful bark cloth for sale. Women prepared dinners, and the young boys went looking for the chickens that were beginning to roost in the surrounding trees.

The chickens were free to peck about the camp all day foraging on anything they could pick up, no matter how disgusting it looked. They kept the camp spotlessly clean of garbage and other messes like children's poop. The toddlers wore no pants or diapers and their droppings were everywhere. In a way, little children and chickens had a symbiotic relationship, which relieved mothers of tedious chores. The villagers were afraid that wild animals would kill their chickens, so at the end of the day, boys found them and put them in cages close to the central fire.

Unfortunately, because of this system of chicken care, very few eggs were found. There must have been eggs somewhere, because the chicken population included little chicks and "spring" chickens along with probably the toughest old chickens on earth. Once in awhile one of those tough old birds made its way into a pot.

I thought their method of fire making was very efficient. The logs they used were four to eight inches in diameter, hardly the size for kindling a fire. The men and boys on fire duty continuously maintained four to five logs, up to eight feet in length in a circle, like spokes of a wheel. Only the tip of the log in the center of the fire pit burned. As they burned, the fire keepers shoved the logs into the center of the fire as needed for more fuel and a hotter fire. When a hot fire wasn't needed, they were pulled away from each other, but the smoldering ends were never pulled too far from each other to go out completely. When they needed a good fire again, they simply pushed the smoldering ends closer together. Just like turning up a thermostat. When a log was burned to oblivion, another was inserted into the ring of logs to take its place. The only downside was that everyone lived in a permanent blanket of smoke that hung over the entire camp

The chief's wife cooked our dinner, which was a one-pot dish that we had brought along with us. She squatted before the fire, duck-walking about to gather the items together she needed to prepare our supper. If I did that, I wouldn't be able to walk for hours.

After supper, most of the tribe gathered to stand, squat, or sit on logs or their branch-like seats around the central communal fire. They talked and laughed, and chewed on seeds, spitting out the hulls on the ground for the chickens to peck at in the morning. Suddenly, three skinny boys showed up covered in grey ashes and wearing white masks. They danced around the fire for a bit, and then participated in a strange ritual.

They stood rigidly erect in front of three men with whips. The men lashed out with the whips, and I winced at the thought of the inhuman pain they were about to inflict on such small helpless children. But the men were experts at using a whip, and they controlled the whip to curl harmlessly around a boy's skinny body without inflicting any pain whatsoever. Unfortunately, as the whips were passed on to others less experienced in using a whip, the control became more erratic. Several times the three children took painful licks from the end of the whip after it had made several curls around their skinny bodies.

The boys didn't cry out, but I saw tears running down their cheeks. The game ended abruptly when their fathers took them to one side out of the game and comforted them. I never understood the ritual or game played out that night using little children for whipping practice.

I had picked out a place to lay my sleeping bag near the center of the communal area. As a matter of courtesy, I had asked the chief's permission to sleep there, which he readily granted. The rest of our group lay scattered about the communal area wherever they felt comfortable to sleep through the night. For me, the downside of staying close to the center of camp was the smoldering, smothering smoke that engulfed the camp in a clinging blanket. I knew that if I didn't like that atmosphere, the animals of the jungle surely liked it even less and, therefore, I figured I was safe from them in my smoky environment. Otherwise, I might be just a piece of meat lying about on the ground.

I woke up several times in the night and saw a few men sitting around the central fire, and I heard them talking in low voices. The leaf shelters were no longer brightly lit up like lanterns and most of the fires in the camp were banked for the night, their thermostats turned to low. But the communal fire burned on continuously throughout the night, making me feel safe and cozy.

In the morning, our group ate a quick breakfast and got ready to leave. Some of the men and older boys were preparing for another hunt, and some of the women were ready for a day's foraging in the jungle. Two women continued their work on a shelter, and the man who made the bark cloth had sold it to a member of our group. We left the pygmy camp, and almost immediately, it was lost in the jungle, like Brigadoon, as if it didn't exist. I would never have found it again, and even if I could, they certainly would have moved on when the game stopped showing up in the hunters' net, and the women had to walk too far to dig up cassava roots. We modern travelers took the chance to peek in on them, but they weren't affected much by us, or by the rest of the world. They remained out of sight, a self-sufficient splinter of civilization existing in the middle of a jungle.

33) Pygmy Camp

34) Pigmies

Frank King

Chapter 18
Cameroon Charm, Cameroon

"Meet me, and we go up there. You see sunset. Beautiful. See you later."

Thus, my volunteer guide for the day coaxed me to see one more wonder in a day filled with interesting if not entirely wonder-filled experiences. "Up there" was the top of a small ridge just outside of the small village of Rumsiki, where our group, which was riding by truck from Nairobi to London was camped for the night. The campground lay right at the center of the village and was surrounded by a solid eight-foot high wood fence. Protection from thieves? Perhaps. Claustrophobic? For sure, but we were in Africa and this was northern Cameroon, only a few miles from Chad and about two miles, an easy walk from Nigeria.

Daniel, my guide for the day had attached himself to me that morning, and I could not persuade him to do otherwise. So I went along with him to visit his friends and neighbors in the village. We went in and out of houses, through backyards, and into walled compounds that enclosed several family dwellings, round mud huts with conical thatched roofs. At one point some ladies making millet beer dipped a gourd into a new batch of a

226

milky-looking liquid and asked me to taste it. I took a sip, but was squeamish at the thought that the fermentation process was probably started by the hostess spitting into her brew. It had a nondescript milky taste and virtually no alcohol yet.

We climbed Mt. Rumsiki, a five hundred foot high hill adjacent to the village, and he told me of bitter stories of raids during World War II when tribal enemies came from Nigeria to Rumsiki. The village men made their stand above their homes on the slopes of Mt. Rumsiki while their women and children hid in caves behind them. They were armed with spears and knives, but the raiders had rifles and killed many of the Rumsiki men. Those captured, along with the women and children, were marched away to Nigeria. The raiders destroyed the village, and I saw the ruins still there that day several hundred feet away. The new village, rebuilt years later, was located closer to the base of Mt. Rumsiki.

Back at camp, my friend Cathy decided to go with me to see the sunset. She was from Australia and one of the nineteen travelers crossing Africa on a truck. We were in our second month of the three-month long camping safari, which started in Nairobi and would end in London.

Cathy and I met Daniel, my self-designated guide, just outside the campground. As we walked up the road toward the ridge, we talked, but I had to make sure that Cathy was included. She cannot hear and has learned to read lips. In order to talk to her, we had to turn our heads toward her at least one-quarter turn. She was very good at reading lips, but when it got dark, she couldn't see well enough to "talk." She told me that sometimes she got lonely in the dark. In this part of Africa, daylight and dark were about twelve hours each all year round, so she probably was lonely a lot.

When we got to the top of the ridge, the sun was a red ball, fast disappearing, not setting, but disappearing into a gray haze caused by sand blown from the Sahara Desert five hundred miles away.

Daniel said, "The sky cloudy from Sahara sand. No be clear until rains come, maybe next month. Then beautiful sunset, you see."

But now, we saw the sun quickly disappear. Everything was over in a few seconds, and a gray twilight engulfed us. Daniel led us to some large, flat boulders nearby with lines chiseled in the top surface. The patterns were random, and he told us that villagers no longer knew what they meant. Some lines might indicate directions of the compass, and others might indicate the direction of the sun at its solstice. He showed us a pair of holy rocks about four feet across and knee height, one for men and one for women. Those also had chiseled lines on their surface, and several shallow depressions pocked the surface in a random pattern. He instructed us in the proper use of these rocks, first assuring us that he was himself Christian.

"Face the rock; line up with the chiseled lines. Then take out your sacred stone and place it on the rock."

"What is a sacred stone?" I asked.

He looked surprised, as if everyone had a sacred stone. "It's a special stone you keep. You know, a piece of quartz, or some volcanic rock, some special stone you found. You keep it with you always. After you place your sacred stone on the holy rock, you can talk directly to God."

Cathy wanted to do this, but decided that she couldn't, because she had no sacred stone.

I picked up a pretty pebble lying on the surface of one of the holy rocks and asked Daniel, "If I say this pebble was special, would you also consider it so?"

"Yes," he said without hesitation.

"Cathy, I give you this special stone I found at this holy place, and hope that you will use it as your sacred stone."

She placed her sacred stone on the female holy rock, and faced in the same direction as the chiseled lines. She then asked us to move away a short distance, so that she might talk to God in private.

We left the holy place and went back to camp. When we arrived, it was fully dark. I left Cathy at the gate, and followed Daniel in search of some homemade liquor. The town had no electricity, and the only light came from fires, candles, and the occasional kerosene lamp. We left the main street and entered a narrow twisting alley.

It was black as pitch and I had a hard time keeping Daniel in sight. We passed vague shapes of darkened houses jumbled together, and then abruptly entered an open doorway. At first, I saw nothing, not even the hand in front of my face. By now, I was feeling uneasy and would gladly have given up the quest.

Then suddenly there was bright light from several candles. I saw people sitting and moving about, cooking, eating, and talking, their long shadows making grotesque patterns on the walls and ceiling. They pretended not to notice me, but I stuck out like a great white beacon. They assured Daniel that they had no liquor, so we moved on through a bewildering complex of rooms and courts, some with people, light, menacing shadows, and others dark and empty.

At some place, long after I would have given up, we found some liquor. Daniel began negotiating with the distillers in the local tribal language, and I was forgotten as voices were raised in offer and counteroffer. The echoes off the bare walls magnified and distorted their voices, and in the poor light, the shadows of their gestures on the walls appeared wild and threatening. I was about to ask Daniel to give up and get me out of there back to the safety of an eight foot high fence. But suddenly, all talk ceased, three pint bottles were given to Daniel, and we left without another word spoken.

Outside it was only slightly less dark than inside, but I felt better, less hemmed in, freer. We had little chance to talk as we groped and stumbled our way toward the main road. There, in the reflected light from open doorways of stores and houses, and with people passing by, my spirits rose, and my uneasiness left. Daniel explained that no one wanted to sell me, a white stranger, liquor. So he purchased it himself, and I could buy it from him. He said that it was hard for him to buy liquor, because everyone knew that most of his family was Muslim, and Muslims were forbidden to drink liquor. In fact, a majority of the village was Muslim, and those that did drink were careful to do so very privately.

Daniel insisted that I visit his house after supper along with anyone else who wished to come. After supper, no one wanted to leave camp, and I didn't either. But Cathy and I finally did set out with gifts of beer and crackers. After some difficulty, we found his house. He was pleased that we had come and invited us to sit on woven mats on the ground outside with our backs against one of the walls of his house, He handed our gifts to his wife who, after acknowledging our greetings, disappeared inside the house; we never saw her again. Daniel brought out fruit and peanuts, some soft drinks, and beer immersed in a bucket of cool water.

Conversation was difficult as we sipped just-barely-cool beer, because Daniel's English was limited, and we spoke no African language. He told us he had worked for Americans in the Nigerian oil fields, and learned English there. He had just recently married and moved back to Rumsiki, and at present, had no work. He showed us his small treasure of mementoes and photos including pictures from the Nigerian days of him posing with American friends who were now long gone back home to America.

Just before we left, he brought out two amulets for us to examine. They were made of leather with some unknown substance sewed up inside them. They were strung with a leather thong to be hung around the neck. He told us these amulets were powerful protection and good luck and that his aunt and uncle wore them, but were now deceased. *Not powerful enough*, I thought. He wanted to sell them to us, and I thought his price was reasonable. He insisted that we wear them while he told us how to make the amulets even more powerful.

"You go to the market, and buy a chicken. You bring it home, and kill it. Then you roast it, and feed it to your children. By doing this, it makes the amulet stronger."

I couldn't figure out how that would work, but I reluctantly declined to purchase the amulet. I told Daniel that in my experience one could not purchase good luck, that if an amulet were to have any influence at all, it would certainly have to be a gift. Cathy agreed with me although I could tell that she, like me, would really like to keep them.

We reluctantly returned the amulets to Daniel and told him that we felt his price was quite fair and that he would probably have no trouble selling them. But for us, an amulet could not take on the meaning he described if purchased. He agreed with us and made no more effort to sell them to us. Shortly after, he escorted us back to camp, and we said good-bye. He asked me to intercede on his behalf to get a ride with us in the morning to the next village, twelve miles up the road. This I was able to do with great consequences for Cathy and me.

The next morning our camp came alive at daybreak. Breakfast was prepared while camp equipment was stowed and the truck prepared for the next increment of our journey. The last items were loaded on the truck, and the gates were opened to allow our departure. Outside the gate, Daniel was there with a small group of onlookers. I told him that he had a ride, and as I was about to turn away, he held out his hand to give me something. It was the smaller of the two amulets he had shown us the night before.

"Here, take this. I give it to you."

I was very surprised and thanked him.

There was no time for more conversation; everyone was moving to board the truck. On impulse, I went over to Cathy and briefly explained what happened and gave her the amulet. I told her that I knew she wanted this perhaps more than me, and now it should be a very good charm having been given twice in such a short time.

She was pleased, and immediately placed her good fortune about her neck for all the world to see. I sat near the back of the truck and could see both Daniel and Cathy. He glanced back at Cathy, noting the amulet several times during the short trip to the next village.

Meanwhile, I was feeling the grief of a loss. How could I feel so bad for giving up an item of absolutely no value?

A good luck charm? Good grief! Yet, I did grieve its loss and wished for its return. But at the same time, I felt a warm glow of pleasure that Cathy was so obviously happy with her good luck. Those conflicting emotions kept me occupied until we arrived at the next village.

Daniel got off and headed for the market without looking back. Just as we started to leave, I noticed the dramatic landscape about us. Volcanic plugs studded the hills around us, that hard rock pillar left after all else has eroded away from old volcanoes. I requested a photo stop, and several others got off with me to record the scene. As I turned away to walk back to the truck, Daniel came running from the market.

He came up to me with his hand outstretched and said, "Here, take this. Goodbye."

He left me as quickly as he had come. It was the second amulet. The truck horn blared to hurry my return to the truck; the others were already aboard. I tried to find him, to thank him, but he was lost in the market crowd, and I never saw him again.

I wore the amulet every day while in Africa, and on many occasions since. Each time I wore it, people came to look at it and touch my amulet. And many times I tell them how I got it, and what a powerful charm it is. I never made it more powerful by killing a chicken, roasting it, and feeding it to my children.

Cathy asked me once how those actions could possibly make an amulet stronger. I told her that it was symbolism of which we were ignorant.

"Suppose you told a person who was ignorant of Christian symbolism to break off little pieces of bread and feed it to their family. Then give them each a little sip of wine, By doing this, you and your family can be closer to God."

35) Traditional houses and storage shelter, Rumsiki

36) Traditional dwelling compound, Rumsiki

Chapter 19
Riding the Zambezi River Rapids, Zaire

All I heard was the roar of the rapids and the crashing of tons of water around us. The whole world was a raging, frothing, white water inside and outside our rubber boat, and there in front of us was a standing wave towering eight feet in the air. The eight of us in our little rubber raft paddled like crazy as if our Lilliputian efforts would make a difference in that awful maelstrom of boiling waters, spray, and noise.

We need a bigger boat, I mentally screamed, borrowing a line from the movie "Jaws." *What am I doing here?* I desperately wanted to turn around, start over, and certainly not be doing this. But the river had us in its grip, hurtling us into the base of that giant wave blotting out the sky, the river, and everything else except for its own solid wall of water that wreathed like a living thing, twisting, taffy-like, into immense sinewy shapes with an evil greenish-blue sheen.

"Look out," I yelled, but my voice was lost in the roar of crashing waters. "We'll be buried under tons of water," I screamed and braced myself for disaster as the bow of the boat dove into the wall of water.

Then I saw the bow flex and bend upward. Instead of burying itself in the wave, the rest of the flexible boat followed to shoot up and up, toward the top of the wave. Euphorically, I screamed my joy and exhilaration as the boat tilted ever more vertically riding the surface of the water. Now I thought the wave threatened to flip the boat and all its contents over backwards into the water. In a flash, my euphoria turned to fear again, and just as I was preparing for the worst, the bow crested the top of the wave and started down the other side. The flexible boat bent at the top of the wave, and I lost sight of the front part of the boat as it slid down the back of the wave. I, along with the rear of the boat, flipped up and over the top like a roller coaster. Then it was a wild ride almost straight down. Looking down, I saw disaster looming again; we would crash dive into the water at the base of the wave and drown, but the boat bent again with the front leveling out even as we in the rear continued the descent into hell.

The rapids continued with other similar but smaller waves, and we eventually got through to the quiet waters below. I was pleased we had made it through without disaster, and I guess it was kind of fun. There were many other boats around us resting in the quiet water with some waiting in line to go on down. Apparently, it was usual for one boat at a time to go through a rapid. The boat captain congratulated us and tried to encourage us to face the other rapids below. We had just navigated our first rapid of the day, known as rapid number eight. Our raft trip would end just below rapid number twenty-one. *Only thirteen more of these things to go*, I thought uneasily.

There were seven others paddling the boat, plus the captain who steered the boat using a rudder, and a boat boy whose function was not disclosed until later. The boat consisted of a two-foot diameter tube that formed the exterior of its shape. The bottom was a rubbery membrane fastened at several points to the tube. This was state of the art, manufacturing a boat that was self-bailing. It could never sink unless, of course, it was stabbed with a sharp knife or rock. Self-bailing meant that the boat always had water sloshing in it, even in the calmest of waters. What I noticed in the middle of the rapid was that water almost filled the boat most of the time; therefore, we were wet most of the time. The uniform of the day was swimsuit, sandals, hat, and most important of all, a life vest.

Before entering the boat, we lined up with our life vests on. The leaders of the trip went down the line and personally tightened up every vest to the point that I found it hard to breathe. Why, we complained, are you torturing us, and some started to fiddle with the fastenings to loosen their grip.

One of the leaders answered, "If you should by chance happen to get thrown into the river, the captain or the boat boy will lean over and grab your life vest at the bottom edge and pull it into the boat, hopefully, with you still in it. About two weeks ago we pulled in a life vest, but the woman in it slipped out, and we never saw her again."

I don't know if that story was true, but I noticed there were no more complaints, and people stopped fiddling with loosening their vests. Now, baptized by my first rapid, I surreptitiously tightened my vest even more as we got ready to head into the current and take on the next rapid.

I was in a grim mood as we rode through rapids nine and ten. But what's this? Was I smiling? We went through eleven and twelve, and hey, this was kind of fun. The boat bucked and jumped, and the water crashed all around, but we were paddling right through these babies with no apparent problem at all. Why, this wasn't so bad! "Zambezi, bring on your worst," I shouted. And it did.

In rapid thirteen, our captain made a mistake; at least I think he made a mistake. He didn't quite align the boat parallel to the current and took the first standing wave of the rapid on a slight diagonal rather than straight on. It flipped our boat upside down in a flash of a second. All of us went into the water, and I had no time to react, one second in the boat and the next in the water.

I came up under the boat where I gasped some precious air trapped there before frantically trying to get out from under the boat, Each time as I was about to make it, the outer tube of the boat hit me on the head, driving me under the boat again. *I'm going to die under this miserable boat*, I thought. I tried a couple more times before I finally got clear of the boat. When I did, there was no one in sight, and the boat too had disappeared. All I saw were big violent waves and the crashing of white waters surrounding me.

Unfortunately, rapid thirteen was really three rapids in one, designated as 13A, 13B, and 13C. So I floated through a lot of white water. I tried to remember what they told me about floating in the river, was the head supposed to be positioned downriver or upriver? In my panicky state of mind, I couldn't remember, so I chose to keep my head downriver which turned out to be wrong, because the water coming down the river kept washing over my nose and mouth. My life vest in frothy white water, which was half air and half water, couldn't keep my head above water as it should. Every breath came with a mouthful of water, and I went floating through the rapids halfway drowning.

I watched the bank sliding rapidly past, and made feeble efforts to swim to shore. I saw it was not going to be possible for me to make it to shore, and I began to have visions of ending up hundreds of miles downriver at the Kariba Dam. Of course, I figured the alligators or the hippos would get me before that, if the next rapids didn't. With these morbid thoughts, I came into the quiet waters below rapid thirteen, almost like a back eddy, and saw people and boats. They were clustered together helping our people out of the water. Just then, I bumped into a boat, and hands reached down to grab the bottom edge of my vest and haul me up on the boat.

There I gasped for breath on hands and knees on the bottom of my boat still upside down. I saw a couple other paddlers there also with our captain. But all I could do was to keep gasping, trying to get enough air, and thinking that if my heart doctor could see me now he would be pretty pissed. He had been keeping me going for seven years, and I was sure this would not be his idea of a heart-healthy adventure.

I was finally starting to breathe normally again, when the boat captain said, in an offhand manner, "Okay, everyone off the boat and into the water. We have to flip the boat right side up.

I groaned and made a half-hearted protest to allow us more time to recover, but one side of the boat was already in the air tilting the bottom. The side rose higher toward vertical, and I slid off ignominiously back into the water. In a panic, I thought I would be trapped under the boat again, but it didn't happen. Almost immediately, the boat boy hoisted me out of the water to safety in the bottom of our boat. There I huddled with the other survivors while other boats came alongside to offer us encouragement or congratulations and discharge members of our crew that they had picked up.

The official recorder came with his TV camera to take our pictures. He paddled about on the river in a kayak. He got us to wave and ham it up a little for his film of the disaster, but he missed getting a picture of our boat flipping in the rapid. But not to worry, when it came time to purchase copies of the VCR, he had spliced in pictures of other boats flipping in rapids. So I guessed getting thrown into the water was not too uncommon on these trips, and sold a lot of VCR copies.

Our crew was still not ready to go, and that gave me time to think of how I had gotten into this mess. I never intended to go on a raft trip. I always had a healthy respect for water and stayed away from water adventures like snorkeling and rafting, because I knew it was possible to drown. Water sports were just not my thing. However, a young woman in our traveling group got sick the night before, and asked me to buy her ticket for the rafting trip so she wouldn't lose her money. I gallantly agreed; after all, how bad could it be with all these boats and young people going? Our travel group contributed sixteen out of the seventy or so people riding the rapids that day. By unanimous choice, our group chose to paddle downriver in the only two self-bailing boats available. These were narrower versions of the great wide rafts with sweep oars manned by a captain. I found out later those boats very seldom flipped, and were far more stable in the water than our boats. Also, the crew on those boats didn't have to paddle; they just hung on and rode it out.

In order to paddle our boat, we had to sit on the round edge of the boat on top of the tube. There was nothing to hang on to, so I sat on one leg and clamped the other against the round tube, and jammed my foot between the bottom of the boat and the tube. It was a precarious seat at best, and took a lot of energy and balance just to hang on. Then we were supposed to paddle too. Before heading into the first rapid, we practiced a little with the captain calling out orders to right paddle, left paddle, and all paddle. And then, there were orders to left reverse, right reverse, and all reverse. In the melee of waves and roar of water in the rapids, we rarely heard what the captain ordered. And, riding that bucking seat, sometimes in the water and sometimes completely out of the water it was practically impossible to paddle anyway.

We had changed to swimsuits and suited up with life vests high above the river on a pleasant plateau under shade trees. We could look over the edge of the gorge and see the Zambezi River four hundred feet below. We were very close to Victoria Falls on the Zambia side of the river, and we heard its roar and saw the spray drifting above the edge of the gorge.

To get to the river, we climbed down an endless series of ladders made of two log runners and steps made of two to three-inch branches tied to the logs. They were steep, but they had enough of an angle so that the easiest way to go down was to face out like walking down a stairway. This took a little courage and confidence, and a heck of a lot of balance. If it got too scary, I simply turned around and went down facing inward like on a regular ladder. But it was a lot slower and used up more energy. Either way, the trip down was tiring, and after four hundred feet of ladders, my legs were giving out by the time I reached the river. The boats were already in the water. I don't know how they managed to get them down all those ladders.

Off to the right around a bend in the river just out of sight was Victoria Falls. The thunder of the falls echoed in the gorge, and spray shot out from around the bend in the river. People manned the boats with shouts and yells, and several boats were already in the water preparing to go down the river. The noise and excitement of the moment propelled me aboard without thinking of the consequences. And now here I was, not halfway through the trip, and fearful of going on. There was no way to go back, and no way to get out of the gorge at this place. I thought about jumping ship and hitching a ride on one of those wide boats with sweep oars, no paddles. But I couldn't let myself do that, so the only choice left for me was to keep on paddling.

At last, we resumed our seats and paddled tentatively out into the current. Almost immediately, the river caught us in its grip and propelled us downriver into the next rapid whether we wanted to or not. As we went through them one after the other, I lost track of their number, and how many were left to do. I gained back a little of the confidence in our boat and its captain, but never to that extent before being dunked in rapid thirteen. I kept paddling, but held on for dear life, not wanting to get thrown into the river again.

As luck would have it, a young woman and I, both of us sitting near the back of the boat were thrown once again into the river. When we crested a sharp wave in the rapid, the rear of the boat whipped up over the top of the wave and casually flipped us out. Once again in the water, I felt panicked, but this time my hand grazed the boat and I grabbed a rope fastened to the circumference of the boat for that very purpose. The woman was hauled in first, almost immediately, and it was one of the few times I have ever resented the maxim "women and children first." Before I could build up much resentment, I was hauled in too. But that was the end of my paddling for the day. From then on, I simply held on, praying for the end of this miserable fun.

The end did come, finally. We navigated the last rapid, and right there below it was the take-out point. It was a welcome sight, even for the diehard enthusiasts. We all had cramped legs, sunburn, and wrinkled skin from being immersed in water so long. Facing us was the climb out of the gorge, four hundred feet of log ladders. In time, we reached the top, changed into real clothes, and ate some food and drink provided by the trip's organizers.

The two boat crews from our camping group hung out together, and the subject of most of the conversation was the big upset of our boat and the dunking of our crew into the river. Everyone's story had to be told firsthand, and we were celebrities of a sort for a short time.

However, I was amazed that the other boat crew was jealous of our dubious adventure. They would have loved being thrown into the river in a struggle for their lives. It turned out that, by chance, every person in the other boat had some experience in river rafting, some with considerable experience, whereas, not one single person in my boat had ever gone river rafting before. The gods can be capricious.

37) Victoria Falls on the Zambezi River

Frank King

Places of interest traveling in Peru and Bolivia

Chapter 20
Adventures in Peru

I met Susan and her eighteen-year old daughter, Kathleen, in Lima where I had agreed to loiter in front of the Gran Hotel Bolivar at nine o'clock a.m. and six o'clock p.m. until we met. While I had been climbing in the Cordillera Blanca, they had been sightseeing in Ecuador. Susan and I had been married for about seven years before we obtained a mutual divorce. After that, we lived together for nineteen years, slowly growing apart to live separate lives. We did this trip to South America about five years into the divorce.

When Susan first arrived in Lima, she befriended a woman in the bathroom of the swanky Gran Hotel Bolivar. The woman was not from Peru and unaware that few bathrooms in that country supplied toilet paper, but Susan was a more savvy traveler and always had a roll of the stuff with her. So in exchange for a little toilet tissue, the woman told her where to find a nice spare room in the nice suburb of Mira Flores.

And that's where we went after we joined up. The room was just that, an outbuilding with a clean floor and a roof, but it had a door that locked and the price was cheap. We slept on the floor in our sleeping bags and went to the bathroom in the main house. We became good friends of the single woman who owned the place and lived in the main house. She took us to art fairs, markets, an operatic musical, and a play of "Don Quixote," in Spanish, of course. We took her out to dinners and she introduced us to many of the nicer restaurants in Mira Flores. All very cultured and genteel.

We went into Lima one night to buy some CDs of Peruvian music to take home. While at the record store, a mob of yelling people suddenly dashed down the street in front of the store, and we heard what sounded like gunfire from somewhere nearby. The shop owner immediately closed his heavy metal shutter that extended across the whole front of his store to keep the crowd from entering. Looking around, we saw that everyone in the store had magically disappeared, and we were all alone. Dumb Americans who didn't know what to do at a mob scene. The storeowner finally grabbed us and ushered us out the back door of his store into the alley where we had to fend for ourselves. We went down the alley, which ended at the plaza where we had gotten off the Mira Flores bus just an hour before.

But now there were no buses. Instead, two armored vehicles sat parked in the middle of the street with squads of soldiers lined up with their weapons ready for use. Down in one corner of the plaza came the shouts of an angry crowd, gunfire, and whiffs of tear gas. Looking around, I was scared because I saw no place for us to hide or get away. Just then, a cab came squealing around a corner and stopped beside us. It already had three passengers plus the driver, but they squeezed us in somehow and drove rapidly away from that place. They took us to a bus station where we caught a bus back to Mira Flores where peace and tranquility prevailed. The people there didn't know about the rioting in Lima, but they assured us that it was Thursday, the teacher's strike day.

That night I suggested leaving the coast, going into the high desert of the Altiplano, and on into Cuzco to see Machu Picchu. Susan and Kathleen agreed with little discussion. We left Lima by train early the next morning and were soon climbing the steep west escarpment of the Andes. The high point of the trip was well over fifteen thousand feet, and special conductors in white coats came down the aisles to dispense gulps of oxygen to people who needed it.

We stayed a couple days in Huancayo set in a shallow valley at 10,700 feet elevation, and visited cathedrals and other sites recommended in the guide book. One day we walked into the countryside on a little-used dirt road, and heard distinctive smacking sounds off to the right.

Leaving the road, we followed the sounds to a lake where women stood ankle deep in the water washing clothes. After soaking them in the cold water, they spread them out on flat rocks lying about two feet out of the water. Bending over the rocks, they rubbed soap into the fabric, and kneaded and twisted the apparel to form soap suds throughout. Then lifting the soapy fabric over their shoulders, they swung them in an arc to hit the flat rock hard, with a resounding smack that could be heard a long distance way.

After this torture they rinsed and twisted the material to remove excess water, and then laid the clothes flat on the grass or bushes to dry in the hot sun. What toil! We did the same thing at home with a push of button.

We went on to Ayacucho by train which was the end of the line, and stayed there for a couple of days to see the sights. The next leg of the journey was more difficult, because there were no trains or buses that traveled a direct route through the rough country between the cities of Ayacucho and Cuzco. We stayed in one of several one-room cabins with toilets in another building outside. Most of the people there were French tourists who could speak some English, but chose not to and they monopolized the toilets in the mornings. Very annoying.

We finally got a ride on a charter plane with the French people on tour going to Cuzco. It was a DC-3 with a lax pilot. He invited some of the prettier girls to ride in the co-pilot's seat or anywhere they could stand, sit, or kneel around him. The door of the pilot's cabin stayed open for most of the trip and from where I sat, it appeared that he spent more time cavorting with the girls than flying his machine. Worst of all, he called out various interesting sights along the way on one side or the other of the plane, and everyone but us ran to that side to see the interesting sight out of those small windows. I kept expecting the plane to roll over out of control, with all that shifting of weight from side to side.

From Cuzco we took the train to Aguas Calientes, the closest village to Machu Picchu, and stayed at a very rudimentary dormitory. The village was overrun with people, and we were lucky to get bunk beds in a room jammed with them. The village was a noisy, nasty place, and we wandered about the village waiting as long as possible before trying to sleep in that hellhole. The separate bathroom outside had so much water running over the floor, I refused to use it and peed in the bushes. I don't know what the women did.

I got a glimpse of the kitchen in the only restaurant in town, and immediately decided not to eat there. It was a filthy mess with food hanging off the counters and littering the floor. So we wandered about in the dark village lit by a few lanterns, and the occasional bare bulb powered by a private generator. We were looking for sanitized, prepackaged food, such as peanuts, candy bars, and cookies. Bananas and oranges fit that category too.

Normally, most visitors rode the train all the way to the station at Machu Picchu, took the shuttle bus up the mountain, stayed a few hours at the ruins, and returned to Cuzco for the night. But I wanted to see the ruins early in the morning before crowds of tourists could get there. The next morning while most of the people staying in the village slept in, we were up early walking the tracks to the Machu Picchu station. We caught one of the first buses making the trip up the mountain and had the ruins to ourselves for most of the morning. But we sure paid a price the night before for that luxury.

We caught the last train out of the Machu Picchu, and it was already dark by the time it started its long slow trip back to Cuzco. We couldn't get seats so we stood for awhile in the aisle, finally getting so tired we sat on the steps between the coaches. This was illegal, and we got roused out whenever the conductors came by.

Even the bathrooms were packed with bags and baskets. At times, looking out the open doorway, I saw pee water arcing out at open windows like miniature waterfalls. Several years later, I went back to Machu Picchu and found the trains to be much better and more numerous, so that everyone had seats and access to a bathroom. The word *luxurious* comes to mind. I never revisited Aguas Calientes.

We stayed in Cuzco several days, visiting its colorful markets and beautiful cathedrals. Of great interest to me was to see Inka temples completely intact that had been hidden under a more modern Christian cathedral for hundreds of years. An earthquake had destroyed part of the newer building, exposing the ancient temples. The Inka masons had constructed their buildings well and these were untouched by earthquakes.

Eventually, I suggested that we go on to La Paz in Bolivia, and Susan and Kathleen, agreed. There we visited museums, not my favorite pastime, markets, archeological sites, and *Peñas*. *Peñas* were a fun venue for Andean folk music put on by different groups of amateur singers, dancers, and musicians. Their programs generally started late in the evening and lasted into the early hours of the next day. They jammed lots of people in a small space at long, skinny tables wide enough for drinks only, leaving barely enough space in the center of the room for the performers.

The first drink was on the house to get everyone "oiled up." From then on, the liquor flowed like water, the room got hotter and hotter from all the people crammed in, and the foot stomping folk music went on nonstop for hours. By the end of the program, everyone was up dancing with or without partners. I invariably had a portly, young Bolivian girl pull me out of my chair to dance. At that altitude, twelve thousand feet, I had a lot of trouble keeping up with her and was out of breath before the dance was half over. I was happy when the ordeal was done and I could collapse back into my chair, catch my breath, and rest a bit. After a few days of these activities, I had my fill of hanging out in the big city.

"Let's go see the jungle," I suggested to Susan and Kathleen, thereby starting a lengthy discussion in which my sanity was questioned.

They were happy to monkey around in the big city, but now I was suggesting we descend into the jungle and journey by boat through a labyrinth of river tributaries that formed the mighty Amazon River.

"There is a new port built on the Ichilo River where it's possible to catch a freight boat down river to Trinidad," I said. "According to the guide book, it takes about five days on the river, and from there we can catch a plane back out."

I made it sound like a lot of fun, a piece of cake, making sure to also mention that it would be much warmer than our recent travels in the Altiplano. After a little more discussion, they agreed to go. The first leg of the journey was a night bus to Cochabamba. Still high in the Altiplano we arrived, cold and miserable just at daylight before the sun was up.

The bus to Puerto Villarroel left Cochabamba at about nine o'clock. So with four hours to wait, we took refuge in the only warm place we could find, a bar that was open all night. Not at all hungry, we toyed with some bar-type finger food, and fended off the boozy attentions of some men drinking at the next table. The drunken, friendly men insisted on ordering us a round of unwanted beers. Not wanting to rile them, we accepted their offer, and I drank a little of mine out of courtesy for their kind gesture, but Susan and Kathleen barely took a swig of the stuff. Beer at five in the morning was not our beverage of choice.

Shortly after leaving Cochabamba, our road twisted and turned on itself as it dropped thousands of feet to the flat jungle floor. At that point, the pavement changed to a graveled surface, and the road carved its way through the dense trees and brush in monotonous, long, straight stretches between rare bends. The bus got warmer the lower we went, and off came our excess clothes. Soon we were sweating in shirtsleeves with all the windows open and nothing left to remove. The day was already hot and it was not yet noon.

We passed a few lonely homesteads chopped from the jungle to form small, shallow enclaves of civilization adjacent to the road. The residents' daily living spilled out into the road rather than penetrate into the vast area of dense trees and brush that surrounded them for miles on every side. Chickens, pigs, dogs, and little children ran about on the road. The older people tended tiny plots of crops and sat along the road working their handicrafts. Our bus was the only traffic, and it came by twice each day, to and from Villarroel. Anyone needing a ride simply stood in the road and waved an arm for the bus to stop and pick them up.

The buildings in Villarroel were mostly open structures using natural tree trunks and branches to support a thatched roof. Floors were hard-packed dirt. Partitions needed for privacy were made of rough, un-planed, wide wooden boards, and when completed, had myriad of peek-a-boo holes in them due to the imperfections in the boards. It was so hot, no one cared.

Beds were hammocks with mosquito net coverings. I usually woke in the morning with dozens of mosquitoes humming and swirling about above my face just outside the net. We also had a powerful mosquito dope that kept them at bay, but nothing kept us from their relentless high-buzzing noises as they constantly probed our defenses.

That afternoon, Susan, Kathleen, and I walked through the ragtag wood buildings and houses of the small village to the port. It was simply a spot on a high, steep muddy bank of a very muddy river. We could tell it was the port because a small, one-room building at the edge of the river had a sign that read "port office." It was by far the most substantial building in town, built of concrete blocks with a tile roof. And to prove the spot was a port, several boats floating side by side were tied to the bank.

When the three of us entered the one room, all conversation ceased as the men inside looked us over, probably wondering what three *gringos* were doing in that remote place. Someone pointed out the man in charge of port traffic who sat at the only desk in the room, and I asked him about getting passage on a boat going down river to Trinidad. The room immediately burst into a buzz of conversation when the reason for our visit became evident. There was nothing private about this office, and I was sure the whole town would know about us by evening.

The official appeared very sorrowful as he shrugged with his hands held palm up, and rattled off some Spanish. It was way too much and too fast for my meager knowledge of Spanish. So then began a painful translation among the official, the men idling in the room, and me. The main idea that came across was that the river was *muy peligroso* and that hardly any boats were going down river. None right now, but maybe later on. I knew that *'muy'* meant very, but I couldn't figure out *peligroso*. What a disappointment that there were no boats available to take us to Trinidad. Just then, a big man with a fat belly, barely covered by his untucked shirt came in. The port official's face lit up with a smile.

"This man goes down river," he said. *"Mañana,* tomorrow. You should talk to him."

I didn't ask the official how no one was going down river, yet this man showed up and was leaving the next day. I presented my request to the big-bellied captain as best I could. He looked us over, thought about it, but in the end, slowly shook his head and refused to take us. What a disappointment.

"Muy peligroso," he said, and turned away.

That night we ate dinner with Kiren, from Bombay, India who shared our table. He spoke excellent English and was much better at Spanish than the three of us combined. We told him our sad tale about not getting passage downriver, and that's when I found out that *peligroso* meant dangerous. Great. Coupled with *muy*, the people here thought the river was very dangerous.

"But how can a slow moving, big muddy river be dangerous?" I complained.

"The water is very low," said Kiren. "This area has been in a drought for many weeks and some of the bigger boats can get stuck on unseen mud or sandbars lying in midstream."

"How do you know about this?" I asked.

"I arrived here just this morning after being on the river for two weeks with some local hunters. We came down river in dugouts, but still the men were very careful where they paddled when on the river. They were genuinely afraid of the river, even in their small shallow-draft boats."

"Well," I said, "we'll just have to go back to Cochabamba on tomorrow's bus and try something else."

263

"Maybe we should try asking the captain again," said Kiren thoughtfully. "I was hoping to get to Santa Ana which lies on downriver from Trinidad"

"But if the river is too dangerous--" I started to say.

"The river above Villarroel is truly dangerous, but here the river is joined by two tributaries that add more water to the river's volume. It should be safe enough to travel downriver, unless our captain has a truly big boat with a deep draft."

That night when we got ready for bed, we came face to face with the drought. The place we stayed was woefully low on water. Their well was dry, and they had collected water from the roofs into fifty-five gallon steel drums. We literally dipped water from the bottom of the barrel. When I asked the owner about the situation, he shrugged and stated that they would have to close up in a few days due to lack of water. Then he went on to say that the other places to stay in town were already closed. The whole town was suffering from lack of water.

"It's a good thing we have the river," he said, and I shuddered at the thought of using such muddy, dirty-looking water for anything.

In the morning, Kiren engaged a boatman and his dugout to take us to the other side of the river where the fat captain had parked his freight boat. Two boat boys appeared and held the dugout to the freighter while Kiren talked to the captain. He was on the upper deck leaning on a railing, looking down on us. A small, slim woman joined him, and she turned out to be his wife. She joined the conversation on occasion, and I got the impression that she helped us persuade the captain to take us on as passengers.

As a condition of our passage, we agreed to eat whatever was available to all the others aboard with no special considerations for us as passengers. They had no beds, and we agreed to sleep on the deck. The captain provided mosquito nets and enough space under the covered upper deck for us to set up a bedroom of sorts.

The all-inclusive cost was twelve dollars, and the trip was scheduled to take five days maximum. Luggage was no problem since all we carried were light packs, which doubled as pillows at night. I had convinced Susan and Kathleen that the trip would be a fun adventure. Certainly, we could stand a little hardship for the four or five days that it would take to get to Trinidad. How was I to know the trip would last three weeks?

Chapter 21
Travel On Jungle Rivers, Bolivia

With heady excitement and anticipation, I agreed to the captain's terms for our passage downriver to Trinidad. I would have agreed to anything at that point, and I guess Kiren felt the same way, because he decided to go too. We set a time to meet on board that afternoon with all our stuff to begin our voyage down the Ichilo River. When we left the captain and his wife, I noted the name of his freighter printed in big white letters on the bow, *Arca de Noah*.

Noah's Ark? I thought. *Well, why not?*

Back in town, Kiren went his own way while Susan, Kathleen, and I debated whether to buy some extra food and goodies for the trip. We decided it might be too complicated and impolite trying to hoard such things for ourselves or somehow share them fairly with the others on board. Other than buying three blankets to spread on the deck for a mattress, we decided to do the trip "cold turkey," with no special help or comforts not provided by the terms of our passage. After all, we could handle most anything for five days, couldn't we?

When we got back to *Noah's Ark* that afternoon, the captain's wife met us and showed us to the top deck, where we would eat, sleep, and spend countless hours until we reached Trinidad. Our quarters were an open, metal clad deck near the stern above the kitchen and engine room, which were located on the bottom deck. It was flat-roofed and had a railing around it. Unlike the rest of the boat, it was not crammed with cargo, and appeared to have no useful purpose except as a bedroom, for us, of course. To get to our bedroom, we went up a flight of open steps at the bow, went through the pilothouse where the captain stood next to his great steering wheel, and then through a room with two single beds, the only real beds on board.

At night, Susan, Kathleen, and I spread our blankets on the hard deck, and strung three mosquito nets above them, one for each of us. Using a portion of our packs for pillows, we crawled under our netting each night and waited for morning. Kiren ended up slinging a hammock and mosquito net in the pilothouse each night.

I discovered early on that sleeping under a mosquito net was stuffy. The fine mesh that kept the mosquitoes out also kept a lot of fresh air out. So many times, I lathered up with mosquito dope and left parts of my body outside the net, kind of like air conditioning. For me, the buzzing of mosquitoes was worse than their bites, and they never stopped buzzing until daylight when they mysteriously disappeared.

The captain and his brother David had built the *Arca de Noah* from scratch. It had a wood hull that was about fifty feet long by twelve feet wide at mid-ship. In addition, they had built two wooden barges, each about thirty feet long by ten feet wide to carry additional cargo. They lashed these to each side of the freighter, making the whole, unwieldy flotilla appear to be a large floating lobster. The barges tied on each side near the bow were the claws and *Arca de Noah* formed the body and tail.

Almost immediately after boarding, we started the journey downriver. We would follow the Ichilo River to where it flowed into the Mamoré River just before reaching Trinidad. The Mamoré went on to join the Madeira River at the border of Bolivia and Brazil, and that river went hundreds of miles across northern Brazil to join the Amazon. If we had the time, we could get all the way across South America to the Atlantic Ocean. Now that would really be a trip.

Our river, the Ichilo, twisted and turned in unending, convoluted loops flowing through uninhabited jungle near the geographic center of Bolivia. At every bend, the current eroded the banks on the outside of the curve, so that the jungle began in the river or at its edge. On the inside of every curve, the current deposited sand that formed large, pristine, crescent shaped beaches.

Almost immediately after leaving the mooring at Villarroel, we rounded two bends in the river and were traveling a short, straight section when we abruptly came face to face with another good reason to describe the river as *muy peligroso*, very dangerous. We had been told earlier that the water in the river was dangerously low, and we might get stuck on a sandbar in the middle of the river. Now we all heard a menacing thump, and felt a sickening shudder run through the entire boat. As the boat continued to move forward, we felt and heard something scrape the bottom of the boat from bow to stern, like some huge claw of a giant cat.

It couldn't be rocks, could it? Nah, the bottom of the river was sand or mud.

Amid shouts of alarm and panic from the entire crew, the captain immediately beached his flotilla and ordered his crew to unlash the barges. The captain's wife gave a shriek of alarm and began crying. Not understanding any of the rapid fire Spanish, I stayed out of the way, wondering what all the fuss was about. The captain sent some of his crew diving into the water to inspect the hulls for damage. Others looked for leaks inside the boat and the barges. They found no damage to hulls, but the captain stayed put through the rest of the day.

That was my first lesson on the menace of snags. The captain was deathly afraid of hitting a log snag that could easily punch a hole in one of his boats. The loss of the boat would be bad, but loss of the cargo would be disastrous. I was more worried about how we would ever get back to civilization if the boat sank.

From that time on, he was extremely cautious and moved his boat very slowly, most days for only a short time. We measured our progress by the number of bends traveled in a day. Many times, it was only two bends and out. The captain spent a lot of time with David and Julio, the oldest boat boy, out in the dugout scouting the river ahead for signs of snags, and the best way around them. Even so, we hit several more during the trip.

The snags were dead trees that floated downriver until their branches were caught and anchored in the mud or sand on the river bottom. The other end was almost always broken off to form a sharp, jagged, splintery point that faced upstream and floated unseen somewhere between the bottom of the river and its surface. Snags formed a perfect battering ram to stave a hole in the hull of a boat or worse, impaling the boat on the snag itself.

More common was damage to the rudder or propeller, which occurred to our boat in separate collisions with snags.

More water in the river meant more depth over the snags, and the safer it was to travel. So from that time on, the captain urged all of us to pray for rain. The captain pointed out that it didn't necessarily have to rain on us. Rain anywhere in the greater river basin would make the waters rise very quickly. I felt more comfortable praying for rain on a larger target, which I thought was a more reasonable request to God.

One night it did rain on us, by the bucketfuls, accompanied by gusts of high winds, and I thought the open barges might fill up and sink right there tied to the bank. The continuous, bright flashes of lightning followed almost immediately by ear splitting claps of thunder were truly awesome and far more than what I had prayed for. When it was finally over, I didn't notice any rise in the level of water in the river, and I wondered how big a rainstorm the captain needed to fill his river to a safe level.

The captain's wife left us the next day, and we didn't see her again until the end of the trip at Trinidad. She had to go to La Paz and endure tests for cancer. These were the days before cell phones were available, so the captain was out of touch with her until we reached Trinidad. We did have a two-way radio aboard, but communication to the outside world was difficult.

The captain loved to tease, laugh, and poke fun at everyone on board, even us, his first class passengers. Most of the time I didn't think he was the least bit funny. I figured he had a mean streak in him about as wide as his belly. Susan and Kathleen remained wary of him throughout the trip, but he was always polite to them. He was merciless in his taunting of Kiren, who was probably half the captain's weight and size. He did this with impunity, because he was God aboard that boat. Kiren believed the captain would easily abandon anyone he didn't like on shore in the middle of nowhere. That threat kept me in line, and I stayed out of the captain's way as much as possible.

The captain's uniform invariably consisted of shorts and sandals. An expansive beer belly eclipsed any other attributes I might have remembered. Dotted across that vast belly and chest were mosquito bites in various stages of infection, and these formed a part of his uniform too. New bites appeared each day to take the place of those that healed and he unconsciously scratched at them all day.

David was the next in command. He was the captain's brother and was nice to everyone he met and, thus, we all liked him. They both slept in the bedroom between the pilothouse and our quarters. David was the all-around handyman and trouble shooter, but his main job was maintaining and operating the diesel engine that propelled the boat. He started the engine easily with a large battery brought on board for that purpose, but it was usually disconnected and used on other projects. So instead, he marshaled the boat boys to pull on a rope wrapped around the flywheel to turn over the engine.

Many mornings I awoke with the shout of *"uno, dos, tres,"* and heard the engine cough and sputter. They always got it going by the fourth or fifth try, but it seemed like a lot of work when a perfectly good battery was at hand. I never got used to the idea of hand cranking a diesel engine. My engineering mind said it couldn't be done, so I continued to be surprised every time the engine finally hiccupped and sputtered to life.

David was also the captain of the dugout, which was a canoe-like boat carved from a single log. At about thirty feet long, it was the largest dugout I saw on the river, and the workmanship of its carving was far superior to most. It could be paddled, but it was usually powered by an outboard engine mounted at the stern of the dugout on one side or the other.

Besides the captain and David, the crew consisted of four young men, boat boys, ranging in age from fourteen to twenty-one years old. They were a cheerful group, full of fun. They slept among the cargo wherever they could find a place to nest. By the end of the trip, each one had asked Kathleen to marry them at least once, but she declined all offers. The oldest young man, Julio, offered her a dowry of three cows if she would reconsider, but still she refused, holding out for more cows no doubt.

We came aboard as first class passengers along with Kiren, the man from India. He was a skinny, little guy and wore a piece of cloth wrapped around his lower body and tucked in at the waist. All day long, he skillfully unfastened and rewrapped that skirt never once revealing what he had underneath. He spoke Spanish and English, and we thought this would be a great help to us since we spoke very little Spanish and understood even less when it was spoken. But he was a quiet man and talked very little to us. I figured he must be from a high caste, for he translated on only a few occasions when the captain demanded it or when we begged him enough.

A family, including their three-year-old daughter, Marie, came aboard as second class passengers. Packing all their possessions in two suitcases, they were going to Trinidad to "seek their fortune." Husband and wife were both accountants and had seen advertisements for the need of accountants way out here in the wilds of Bolivia. They camped out on top of the cargo on the lower deck under the pilothouse. They were never allowed on the top deck, the private preserve of the captain and his first class passengers. They paid less money, but ironically, they slept on a part of the cargo made up of soft mattresses, compared to our hard, unyielding deck.

Kathleen, using the meager Spanish she had gained in high school, spent her time talking endlessly to the parents and playing with Marie. She claimed that she could easily understand Marie's baby Spanish.

At one point in the journey, when we were tied to shore, Marie fell overboard and disappeared under the muddy waters. Her father dove into the water time and again desperately trying to find her. The mother screeched an alarm, and all the boat boys dove into the river. Time after time, they disappeared under the surface feeling about for Marie, because they couldn't see in such muddy water. The father had finally given up, and was trying to comfort his wife. The boat boys returned to the boat quietly shaking their heads.

Then the cook, looking out the galley door at the stern of the boat, saw a little hand appear in the murky water. She reached down and scooped Marie out of the river, dripping wet and very much alive. The current had dragged her under the boat and carried her from near the bow to that exact spot by the galley door at the stern where the cook stood. A few seconds more, or a few feet to one side or the other, Marie would have been lost forever. She didn't fuss or cry as her father snuggled her in his arms and suggested that she had had a nice, little swim. *Wow*, I thought, *what a minute difference between life and death*.

Altogether, we numbered fifteen people on board, eating the cook out of house and home. The cook had a ten-year-old son with her and he spent hours playing amid the cargo and fishing. She and her son slept on a bench in the galley.

I asked about the drinking water supply and was informed that it all came from the river, but not to worry, the cook boiled it first. She delivered a small pail of fresh water to the top deck each morning, covered with a cloth to keep out the dust and varmints during the day. The river was a murky brown mixture of mud and water looking like coffee with cream. I couldn't see my own hand two inches below the surface much less any creature that might be lurking below.

We discovered early on board that the toilet at the stern was simply a box to sit on over a hole in the deck. I saw the river gurgling at the bottom of the box, and sometimes at night, I saw the moon reflected in the opening of the toilet seat. *Rather romantic*, I thought. It was located about five feet away from the rear door to the galley where the cook reached down to fill her buckets with river water for cooking and drinking.

Knowing that it took at least ten minutes of hard-boiling to kill all the bugs in untreated water, I was skeptical that her boiled water was safe to drink. With no argument or discussion, the three of us grimly laced our "boiled" drinking water with an iodine solution the entire trip.

We made the solution from iodine crystals, which we placed in a two-ounce bottle and filled with water. In a short time, the crystals saturated the water in the little bottle with a percentage of iodine that didn't change no matter how long the crystals sat in that bottle. Adding a capful or two of this solution to a liter of water did the job. Our water always had a nasty taste of iodine, but it was safe to drink, and we never had to worry about thyroid problems. It must have worked because the three of us never got sick, but then no one else on board did either, and they never once put iodine in their water.

One day a boat boy, Roberto, who was about sixteen, teased the cook's son too much, and in return, got stabbed in the arm with the ten-year-old's nasty-looking fishing knife. We disinfected the wound with our iodine solution and bandaged Roberto's arm. As a precaution, we started him on a cycle of antibiotics, but he healed fast and never came back to our "clinic" for more medicine. He told Kathleen that life was so bad that he would not live to age twenty-one anyway.

The captain was furious that one of his crew was hurt. He ranted and stomped about the boat while everyone tried to stay out of his way. He lashed out at the cook for not controlling her son, and they came very close to banishment on shore to be left behind.

Then a day or so later, Kathleen cut her hand open with a nasty gash from the careless use of a knife. Out came the iodine solution again, but we had no way to stitch the wound to keep it closed. I stretched Band-Aides tightly over the edge of the wound, and that worked pretty good. Then we wrapped the whole mess up in bandages and started a cycle of antibiotics. I always carried extra antibiotics with me when traveling, for use in controlling high body temperatures caused by infections. In this case, I hoped they would work to stop any infection before it started.

Susan worried a lot about her daughter, using worst case scenarios to fuel her fears for Kathleen's future, like how would we transport her to a hospital if necessary. I didn't have answers to those kinds of questions and tried to ignore or change the subject when worst case scenario fears surfaced. My theory was not to worry about stuff until you had to. But Kathleen was a healthy young woman and healed rapidly. She was soon frolicking in that awful, murky-looking river along with the boat boys, all thoughts of her badly cut hand forgotten. Maybe the river had unknown medicinal qualities.

Almost every day, the boat boys played and frolicked in the water and usually the others on board would join them. Holding back on that first day, I had vowed not to immerse my pristine body into those murky waters. But heat and boredom broke down my resolve, and I was soon splashing about in the cool, refreshing water, fully dressed, of course. Susan and Kathleen wore bathing suits, but complained that unseen creatures would come to nibble at their legs if they stood still too long. *What a good idea*, I thought, *to wear my trousers for a swimsuit*.

The boat boys warned us not to step on stingrays swimming on the bottom because they were dangerous and could hurt us. I heartily agreed not to step on them, but they never told me how to see a stingray under those muddy waters. The thought of stepping on one of their sharp spines gave me the shivers. We generally stayed close to the splashing, active boat boys under the theory that they probably scared away anything dangerous.

Swim time was also bathing time, and everyone took advantage of using soap and the plentiful waters to suds up and wash thoroughly. Bathing was a lengthy process, almost a ritual, sometimes performed twice a day. So everyone aboard stayed squeaky clean. Fortunately, the mud in the river didn't collect on the skin or in the hair, but it did in my bathing suit trousers. The soap had to be a floating type or it sank out of sight almost immediately, never to be found again. Also we couldn't leave floating soap unattended, because little fishes nibbled on the bar and would eventually eat it all up.

The barges and the lower deck of the freighter were crammed full of cargo with no place to walk. The only free space was in the galley, the area around the engine, and a small portion of the front deck left open to access the barges on each side, and the stairway to the upper deck. A trip to the galley or the toilet entailed walking a six-inch wide gunwale almost the entire length of the boat. The cook made this trip back and forth several times a day with food and water. The rest of us made the trip only when necessary, and I always concentrated that if a fall were imminent, it would be to the inside of the boat rather than into the river.

We had no electricity when the engine was down which was most of the time. After dark, the cook provided us with candles, but a visit to the toilet was a trip never taken lightly at anytime. In a kind gesture, she always left a candle burning on a barrel in her kitchen, so we could see where to dismount from the six-inch gunwale to the deck.

The days passed, mostly motionless, tied to shore in stifling heat. At least when moving, even slowly, we had a slight breeze. Luckily, Susan had acquired a huge batch of paperback books in English, before we came aboard, and she spent hours rotting away her mind, reading "bodice rippers." Those are the kind of books showing a distraught woman on the cover, half out of her white, diaphanous dress, running away from a sinister-looking house. I learned how to shoot pesky yellow flies dead with a rubber band. No matter how many carcasses I piled up, still others would ignore their dead brothers and fly in to take their place.

I watched with envy as other boats passed by at full speed on their way down river, apparently not concerned about potential snags. I thought that maybe our captain was a little too cautious, even "chicken," perhaps. I was bored and frustrated and might have jumped ship, except Susan and Kathleen wouldn't leave the *Arca de Noah*. They had adapted their lives to the boat's routine and were now nested comfortably for the duration, however long that might be.

Many times the captain decided that the bend in the river was too sharp to get his entire flotilla around the curve. So he left one barge behind tied to the bank, and came back for it after getting the first barge safely around the sharp curve. On one of these occasions, Kiren and I stayed alone with the parked barge, just to get a feel for being in the jungle alone. When we walked a short distance away from the river, we quickly lost the comforting sight and sound of the water, and I was depressed by the immense solitude of the vegetation pressing in so tightly on all sides. Perhaps Kiren felt the same way, because he didn't object when I turned to walk back to the river.

Then I panicked, a little. Was I walking toward the river or away from it? I had no way of knowing. We had no landmarks, the vegetation all looked the same, and we couldn't see or hear the river. My panic grew, and I stopped walking. I dared not turn in other directions for fear of losing any orientation I still had that the river lay directly ahead. We could be within just a few feet of the river and never know it, lost. We should have brought some breadcrumbs to mark our way.

I told Kiren my fears and asked him to move on ahead, keeping me in sight. My idea was to stay put at a fixed point and have Kiren cast about side to side for signs of the river. It worked almost immediately, Kiren saw the river, and without words, we walked nonchalantly back to the parked barge. But I never did that again, and was satisfied to stay on the boat or at least in sight of the river, no matter how bored I got.

When we first boarded the boat, I had asked about camping at night on one of those beautiful beaches. Every curve of the river had one. No one on board would do it, and when the captain heard about my neat idea, he forbid any of us to sleep on the beach away from the safety of his boat. He mentioned something about bad spirits moving around in the jungle at night, and that it was *muy peligroso*. I mentally scoffed at that response and suggested he was superstitious.

"I am Roman Catholic," he said, "and do not believe in ghostly spirits or superstitions, but the jungle is dangerous at night, and you must sleep on the boat."

After my experience alone in the jungle that day, in broad daylight, I was now inclined to agree that the jungle might be a dangerous place at night, and I never asked about camping on the beach again.

I relished any deviation to the daily routine that destroyed the peaceful boredom of the ride downriver, like the occasional stabbings, swimming in a murky river with unseen varmints nibbling and swimming about, and the occasional snags that we hit. One of them hit the rudder and twisted its shaft, so that the captain had to turn his big steering wheel hard to the right in order to go straight ahead. It was not a life-threatening event, but it sure made steering the boat awkward.

He beached his flotilla, and then David, with the help of Julio, disconnected the rudder assembly from the rear of the boat. This took endless dives into the water to feel about, find the bolts holding the assembly on, and then ratchet each of them loose, all the while holding their breath under water. They carefully lined the bolts on the deck, out of the way, so they wouldn't get lost. *Good idea*, I thought. *Where was the hardware store to buy others if these got lost?*

They finally dragged the rudder assembly aboard. A one-and-one-half inch steel shaft about fifteen feet long supported a piece of flat metal at one end, the rudder, and at the other end was a four-inch square piece of metal two feet long, the tiller. I noted the bent shaft near the middle where no bend was supposed to be, but worse, the twist in the shaft was very evident. The rudder and the tiller were about ninety degrees off alignment from each other. *Wow! How do you fix that?*

While David and Julio worked getting the rudder assembly off, the boat boys frolicked and horsed about gathering a great pile of wood on the beach. Then they dug a large fire pit in the sand. *They're going to fix this over a campfire?* I thought. *That can't be done. You might get a fire hot enough to straighten the bend, but how do you get it hot enough to twist a one-and-one-half inch steel shaft?* But of course, the captain, David, Julio, and the rest of them didn't know that it couldn't be done, so they went ahead and did it anyway.

The fire burned for hours, creating a thick bed of coals. At last, they placed the bent part of the shaft in the fire, and in a relatively short time, heated it to a dull reddish color. Then they took the shaft off the fire, wedged the bend over a fulcrum of rocks, and pushed on the rudder and tiller at each end to straighten the shaft, easily. *Well okay*, I thought, *now comes the hard part. How are they going to twist the shaft?*

They did it so easily, I almost laughed out loud at my so called engineering superiority. They put the middle of the shaft in the fire and built up the fire to a tremendous size. It was a super bonfire that singed anyone that got too close and eventually made the steel turn white in its heat. Then some boat boys, laughing and shoving, balanced themselves on the flat rudder, while David and Julio grabbed the tiller and simply twisted the shaft to align it with the rudder. Oh, for sure, it wasn't an exact alignment, but close enough, and the shaft probably still had a slight bend in it, but it was good enough. Then without thinking about it, they allowed the white-hot shaft to slowly cool in the dying fire. Actually, they all went swimming after such a hard day's work.

At long last our river, the Ichilo, joined the bigger, wider Mamore River, and the boat boys happily informed us that Trinidad was only one week away. Still we loitered our way down river even though the threat from snags or getting stuck on the bottom was almost nil. We no longer had to take one barge at a time to get around sharp curves, and our flotilla majestically floated downriver on the wide waters past scattered small homestead clearings chopped from the jungle.

Three weeks later to the day after starting the trip, we tied up to the bank with other freighters, which were being unloaded. A string of men carried the freight on their shoulders up the mud bank to pickup trucks waiting to carry the freight into town. Trinidad was about fifteen miles away across the flat flood plain, out of sight. Aside from a single-track road, the jungle pressed down to the edge of the riverbank, and our view of the shore from the river was just as primitive as the day we left Villarroel.

The next morning we packed up to go to the town of Trinidad where we planed to stay a couple of days and then catch a plane back to civilization. We said our good-byes and paid the captain who had raised the charges for passage to $20, because, he said, the trip took a little longer than expected. *A little longer?* I thought. *A trip that took twenty-one days instead of four or five days was a lot longer in my measurement of time.*

I negotiated a ride for us to Trinidad in the back of a pickup, and loaded in our packs. But when I went to get Susan and Kathleen, they didn't want to leave. They sat huddled on the upper deck, weeping, mourning the end of their fun adventure and loss of their familiar nest. Through tears, Susan said it was like being on a Disney ride through a giant theme park, escorted by the Boy Scouts of South America. *Not a bad description,* I thought, *but it had all been very real.*

287

Chapter 22
Finding Food in the Jungle, Bolivia

Pity the poor cook who has no food to cook. The captain of *Arca de Noah* had packed enough provisions for a week-long journey downriver from the new port of Villarroel to the town of Trinidad, which normally took four to five days. Now, after a week on the river and nearly out of food, we were nowhere near our destination. Our passage downriver had been painfully slow, and the boat boys couldn't even guess how much longer the trip would take. No matter how efficient she was, the cook couldn't possibly manage to eke out food to last for the whole trip.

In desperation, she baked a dough from the last of the flour and fed us all two hamburger-sized buns at each meal. To wash them down, she gave us a choice of tea or a hot purple corn drink. For three days, breakfast, lunch, and dinner, we ate the proverbial menu of bread and water. At first, the novelty of fresh baked buns was welcome, but that wore off about as fast as they got stale. It might have helped if she had any butter, or jam, or even peanut butter, which I hate. Anything to slather on the rolls to make them tastier, but all we got were bare buns.

I liked the corn drink and easily downed that every day. It was a deep purple color and tasted somewhat like cider. It came in a powder form, just add hot water, and stir thoroughly. I had no idea how the powder was made; it came pre-packaged.

Prior to our menu of bread and water, Susan and I went night fishing with David a couple times in the dugout, and watched as he attracted the fish with a spotlight hooked to the ship's battery. In the bright light, he harpooned black and white zebra-striped fish at least three feet long. Their heads, with a great wide mouth and long feelers on each side, made up one-third of their bodies' length. David brought them in, thrashing and twisting until he could dispatch each of them by bending the great head back to break their spine at the base of the head.

For several meals, we ate fresh fish and rice, while the excess fish were salted, and left to dry in the hot sun. At night, the cook took in the drying fish like taking in the laundry, and in the morning, she spread them back out again to continue drying. We eventually ate up all the dried fish too.

The answer to lack of food was simple, just get on downriver to the town of Trinidad where they had lots of food. I thought the captain was too cautious, and spending way too much time tied to the riverbank worried about hitting snags. He and David spent hours in the dugout with the oldest boat boy, Julio, scouting the river ahead for snags. The river was so full of mud; no one could see more than two inches below the surface anyway. Scouting a river that murky made no sense, and I itched to get going. Something like "damn the snags and full speed ahead" came to mind.

Almost immediately, the river answered my thoughts, and we hit another snag. It was such a slight bump that I think, normally, no one would have noticed, except the boat began to vibrate and shake. *What could make a boat this size shake so badly?* I mused. When the captain slowed the boat, the shaking decreased, and he finally stopped to find the cause of the shaking. David and the boat boys began a series of dives to inspect the hull, rudder, anything the captain could think of that would make the boat shake as it did. At last, they found that the snag had bent the propeller blades out of alignment making the propeller unbalanced as it turned. *Well, that's an easy fix*, I thought. *They can just change to a new propeller.*

Wrong again. My mind hadn't yet grasped that these people didn't have the luxury of carrying new parts around with them wherever they went. They patched the old part some way, made do without it, or stopped dead in the water. An appropriate phrase at this point, I thought. But not to worry. The boat boys gathered firewood once more, while David and Julio dove repeatedly into the murky water feeling about for the bolts to remove the propeller.

When it came up out of the water, I almost laughed out loud. No way were they going to bend the three blades of that propeller back to the precise alignment necessary to produce a balanced rotating propeller. Fortunately, they didn't know that and proceeded to make a fire and build up a small bed of hot coals. While waiting, they all frolicked and played in the river, taking time occasionally to keep the fire burning. Someone set a big rock near the fire to use as an anvil, and David brought out his hammer. After heating the propeller, he began to hammer the blades back to what he considered was the proper shape and alignment for the propeller. It took a lot of time and advice from the captain to repair the propeller to a point where they both thought it would be adequate.

When they finally agreed the propeller was as good as it was ever going to get, the captain got a wicked smile on his face and threw the propeller over his shoulder into the river. Everyone stood still, shocked by his action, and I saw it splash the water and disappear. *Idiot,* I thought.

*How are you going to get your boat downriver now? Float
down on the current perhaps?*

David was the first to recover and sent the boat boys
diving into the river time after time to find the propeller.
Since they couldn't see, they had to feel for it on the
bottom of the river. David took the dugout and anchored
it above where he thought the propeller had disappeared.
The boat boys used it to catch their breath and rest
between dives. One of them found it about an hour later,
and he was hailed as a hero. To this day, I don't know
why the captain threw his propeller away, unless he was
just showing off in some weird way.

The propeller looked great, but I knew the difficulty of
getting each blade to a precise alignment and shape with
the others. I was pretty sure it wouldn't work very well.
But I was wrong again. When installed the boat did shake
a little, but not too badly. The captain quickly found the
optimum speed he could use with a minimum of shaking,
and we went merrily on our way.

If only we could fix hunger as easily. All of us were
losing weight fast. One desultory afternoon sitting
around almost comatose from the heat, a boat boy
spotted an animal on shore and spread the alarm.
Immediately, everyone on board galvanized into action
to hunt the creature down. The animal, identified as a

joche, had come out of the jungle to drink water from the river. The boat boys ran along the shore to cut it off from the jungle and drive it into the water. Susan and I joined David and Julio in the dugout to cut it off from swimming across the river. With great whooping and laughter, the boat boys flailed away with clubs until a lucky blow put an end to the animal's struggles before any of them were clubbed accidentally.

The cook cleaned and dressed the joche, and it fit very nicely into her blue plastic pan. She used the same pan to cart around dried fish, laundry, garbage, and anything else requiring a large, blue, plastic pan. On the way to roasting it over an open fire on shore, she showed it to us for our approval. We made the appropriate sounds of appreciation, although it was the ugliest animal I'd ever seen. The joche had the appearance of a rat's head and tail with the body of a small pig. She had curled the tail to lie alongside the body and stuffed its mouth with a withered lemon. Its snout was propped up on the edge of the pan, and its blank unseeing eyes stared up at me. But the meat was delicious, and most of it was gone in one day.

After the smaller Ichilo River joined the larger Mamore River we saw a lot more river traffic. It seemed that every other captain was going faster than ours. I gritted my teeth and fretted, but didn't complain. One afternoon a smaller freighter than ours stopped next to us and tied up for the night. The two captains knew each other and spent the rest of the day and evening talking. I thought maybe the other boat might have a few extra provisions to spare, but I don't remember seeing any transfer of food from the other boat to ours.

They had a big parrot that sat on its roost at the rear of the boat, preened its feathers, and called out words in mangled Spanish. It apparently didn't "speak" any English. Susan, Kathleen, and Marie spent the afternoon teaching it to say words back to them with varying success. During supper that night, Kathleen happened to look into the water and saw bright colored feathers floating by. We glanced over at the other boat, but the parrot was gone, and the roost was empty. Was the parrot in a pot of stew? Unthinkable. Then a parrot head floated by with a dead beady eye staring up at us reproachfully. Was this evidence that other boats were low on food too? Or did the people in this part of the country simply like parrot meat? Kathleen was appalled, but I thought of it as a large piece of useless meat that sat there on a roost all day trying to look beautiful.

On rare occasions, we came to a farm or homestead and stopped to obtain food. At one of these stops, we were invited to the house to visit the with the farmer's wife while the farmer and David gathered the food. We sat in stifling heat on a covered porch of a one-room house set high on top of ten-foot posts. *They must have pretty big floods here*, I thought. Later I found out that the river flooded acres of land for weeks at a time. During those times, the only way to get around was by boat, and the farmer evacuated his livestock to higher ground.

The house was made of unfinished wood planks that had many imperfections such as open knotholes and cracks. The roof was made of thatch, and the homemaker kept her floors clean by simply sweeping the dirt and garbage through the cracks in the floor planks onto the ground below. Dogs, pigs, chickens, and other farm animals ran loose below the house scavenging the garbage and keeping the ground clean, thereby forming a symbiotic relationship with the humans living above.

At one point, our hostess served us drinks made from the fruit of a tamarind tree, a large shade tree with evergreen leaves. The fruit was encased in pods like lima beans, and the juice had a reddish tan color that tasted a lot like lemonade. But it was barely cooler than the day. With no electricity available, there was no ice. Susan took a sip, but refused to drink more, because the water used to make the drink was probably untreated, right out of the river. After thinking about it, I surreptitiously dumped my drink into a potted plant nearby when I thought no one was looking. We worried a lot about drinking impure water. When we said good-byes to our hostess, David and the farmer were loading papayas, yucca root, and plantains into the boat.

The papayas were huge, twelve to eighteen inches in diameter, and David scored the outside skin of the fruit in concentric circles about two to three inches apart and let them set for a day or two. They bled a white milky substance and only David could tell when each fruit was ready to eat. The yucca root was my favorite. The cook boiled and served them like potatoes. Their consistency reminded me of parsnips, but the flavor was mild and much better tasting.

We always knew ahead of time when the cook would serve plantains. They came aboard in large bunches like bananas and were hard as rocks and just as tasteless. To make them palatable, the cook boiled them the night before. In the early morning, she woke us up with the noise of her pounding them into submission resounding through the boat. She would finish the process by cooking the mashed plantains in a frying pan. The result of all that work looked like mashed potatoes piled high on our plates, but instead, it was an absolutely tasteless mass of starch. Toward the end, when almost gone, they became riper and acquired a faint taste of green bananas.

One day, Roberto saw a turtle swim by the boat. He sounded the alarm and we watched as David harpooned the turtle. The point of the harpoon stuck into the shell about one-quarter inch, but that was enough. David swung the turtle aboard in a great arc from the water to deck. It was about two-and-one-half feet in diameter, very much alive and kicking when it hit the deck. It went scrabbling about and hissing while fifteen people tripped over each other, laughing and ducking out of its way until someone flipped him over and mercifully sent him to turtle heaven. Susan, Kathleen, and I thought of the turtle as unusual and cute, but the others saw it as fresh red meat and were excited.

Roberto went after the bottom shell armor with an ax amid much laughter and shouting from everyone on board. He tried to hold the turtle steady on its curved back with his bare foot while chopping at the turtle's breastplate. As he chopped, the turtle slipped about the deck, and Roberto's fellow crew made bets whether his foot would get chopped off before the turtle's breastplate came off. Roberto's luck held; the breastplate came off, and we had before us a large bowl-like shell of red turtle meat, bone, and guts. Then we found an egg and, thereafter, the turtle was a she.

To my surprise, Susan joined in helping to extract turtle eggs from the interior of that bloody mess. Could this be the same woman who read happy little stories about *Yurtle the Turtle* to her kindergarten classes? With a grin from ear to ear and blood up to her elbows, she helped until all the eggs, eighteen of them, were found and given over to a joyful cook. Hunger apparently made Susan able to do unusual things.

That night, she and I joined David and two of the crew on a turtle hunt. We paddled out on the river in the dugout. In the pitch black of night, I lost sight of the little freighter almost immediately and wondered how we would ever get back. The air felt like velvet on my skin, and inky blackness swallowed me in its cocoon. Without an engine on the dugout, the night noises from the jungle sounded louder out on the river, and we heard the swishing of water against the hull of the dugout. Close by, frightening us at first, fresh water dolphins came to the surface to blow. Their first puff was loud as they expelled air, and we jumped involuntarily. After that, they took several human-like breaths, then silence.

David hooked up a light to the ship's battery and lit up the surface of the river. What appeared to be a lot of submerged sticks with a knot floating at the surface were actually the head and eye of a lot of turtles. Like an iceberg, only the tip, in this case the head, could be seen. As Julio maneuvered the dugout alongside each turtle, David harpooned it, and brought it into the boat with one swift movement.

Susan and I had to keep them immobilized, upside down, while the hunt continued. They were all about two feet in diameter, and looked like oversized army helmets rocking slightly on their curved backs.

As time went by, the turtles became bolder and stuck their heads, legs, and tails out of their shells.   They strained, arching head and tail to reach the deck and form pivot points to tip one edge of their bodies toward the deck.   The legs on that side scrabbled wildly to gain enough purchase to swing their whole bodies right side up. I thought the energy required for that maneuver was at least equal to a climber making a crux move on a steep rock face. We tapped their shells, legs, and heads to try to keep them from turning over.

One finally got loose, and scrabbling and hissing, he came charging straight toward Susan. She retreated with a yelp, and I gallantly moved to one side to let them by.

The boat boys were yelling and laughing, busy flipping and intimidating the other turtles who were inspired by their rogue friend. The turtle chased Susan to the bow of the boat where she prepared to throw herself overboard, but David came to her rescue by flipping the turtle on its back.

After that melee, the turtles seemed resigned to their fate, and were much less active. We found our way back to the freighter; I don't know how in all that watery blackness. The turtles were dumped into the hold of the boat where we heard them moving and clanking about all night.

Now we had turtle meat, turtle eggs, and turtle soup. One night we went out to gather turtle eggs. It was easy. The turtle left her tracks in the sand, and at the end of the trail were at least a dozen eggs buried about six-inches deep. We must have gathered a hundred eggs that night. The cook hard-boiled them, and anyone could have an egg snack whenever they pleased.

Susan consulted the cook about making rice pudding using fresh turtle eggs. The cook agreed, but their recipe called for milk. They needed milk. As it turned out, a major portion of our cargo was cases of condensed milk given to the government of Bolivia from the United States Department of Agriculture. I didn't ask, and the captain never said how our foreign aid ended up as cargo on a boat headed downriver to the remote settlement of Santa Ana, deep in the Bolivian jungle.   But he graciously contributed one can of condensed milk to the project.

Susan did fine getting the ingredients together for the rice pudding, but when she tried to add the turtle eggs to the mix, she ran into a problem. Turtle eggs weren't hard shelled, but had a tough, leathery skin, and she didn't know how to crack them open. The cook gave her a hint by pantomiming a pinching movement of her fingers. But when Susan pinched the egg open, the contents squirted up into her face. She had quite an audience at the time, and everyone had a good laugh. Then the cook showed her how to pinch the eggs open to spew the contents down into the rice mixture, and Susan had no trouble from then on.

When first cooked, the rice pudding was a sensation, and the captain thought it was so good that he decreed it could not be eaten until supper. It was fine when freshly made, but it lost a lot of its flavor and good consistency sitting around in the heat all day. For me, it was a disappointment trying to eat the stuff that night.

By the next day, we had passed through turtle country and were back to dreaming of food. About that time, the cook's son who was fishing brought in a small colorful fish, which David identified as a piranha. It had a small mouth with lots of little sharp teeth, but it was so skinny and small, about ten inches long, that it was hardly worth catching for food. I had heard stories about Piranhas, how they could strip the meat off a cow's bones in two minutes. With such a small mouth, this could only be possible if they attacked in huge numbers. I wondered how long it would take for them to eat me, and just what in Hell were we doing swimming out there in the same water?

The captain assured us that it was still safe to swim, because there were lots of other fish left in the river. Was he suggesting they preferred fish to me? He went on to say that no one swam below Trinidad because of the greater numbers of piranha, but it was still safe to swim above Trinidad. *And just how does a piranha know where Trinidad is located?* I saw great flaws in his theory, yet all of us went swimming once more when we finally did reach Trinidad, our long-awaited goal.

Surprisingly, it was the increase of piranha in the river that provided us with fish dinners the rest of the way. They chased large schools of food fish with such frenzy that those fish leaped out of the water in desperate attempts to get away. They launched themselves into the air landing on our decks, into the dugout, and even through the back door of the galley. The cook finally had to cover the door opening to keep them from cluttering up her floor with fish. I thought maybe she should just open the oven door and let them leap into the fire, bypassing the frying pan.

Exactly twenty-one days after boarding *Arca de Noah* we arrived at Trinidad's primitive port. The settlement of Trinidad was still fifteen miles inland from the port. I was very happy to be off the boat, very healthy, and a lot thinner. *A good way to lose weight*, I thought, *just hitch a ride on a Bolivian freighter, and try to live off the land.*

Throughout the entire trip, Susan refused to throw any garbage into the river, so she collected all our trash in two large green garbage sacks. Arriving at Trinidad, she could find no garbage cans, no trash barrels, and no dumpsters. No place where she could dump the accumulated garbage. People she asked about it smiled and simply pointed to the river. In the end, she had to dump the sacks into the river right there at Trinidad. Thus, she concentrated pollution at that point rather than spreading it out over a long distance. Creatures in the river ate the garbage and paper rotted away, but plastics remained forever. The river looked trashy with

Frank King

accumulated plastic garbage that, before modern times must have looked reasonably pristine.

That night the captain dressed up in a shirt and invited his first class passengers to dinner ashore with him. We ate out in the open under a thatched roof in the only place serving food. Pigs, dogs, and chickens ran about among the diners feet eating up stray food and garbage dropped on the ground. In the shadowy light of kerosene lanterns, we ate with a crowd of rough-looking characters, and I was glad our captain appeared big enough to protect us all.

The owner of the restaurant announced that in honor of our arrival his cook had prepared us a surprise, a very special delicacy for us to enjoy. Susan, Kathleen, and I exchanged glances, worried that the exotic dish might not be edible by our standards. After all, we had been eating strange food for awhile which was considered ordinary by the local people. A delicacy presumed something out of the ordinary, and for us, that might be really strange. For some reason, monkey brains crossed my mind.

But not to worry, the delicacy in this case was a plate of sliced tomatoes. How ridiculous, I thought, that plain ordinary food at home could be a delicacy out here in the jungles of Bolivia. Yet, the local people ate turtles and their eggs, and thought nothing of it. At home, the closest thing to that would be mock turtle soup which, by its name, implied that real turtles weren't used. And I'd never heard of anyone eating turtle eggs back home.

****

During our trip down river, we were hungry at times, so we did what the locals did and ate what they ate, and everyone survived just fine. But what about the poor turtles? Are there any still left? Maybe eating the turtles might not have been so bad, but destroying all those eggs certainly was. The worst is that our boat was only one of dozens plying the river, killing turtles and harvesting eggs for food. I saw several dugouts piled high with eggs going to market for profit.

We were told that twenty years before our visit, every beach along that stretch of river had crocodiles. There were so many crocodiles the beaches were black with them. But people were hungry and ate them. They exported their skins for cash. As a result, the crocodiles disappeared, and not a single one has survived. In the years since our visit, I think the people there are still poor and hungry, and I fear that the turtles too have disappeared.

Chapter 23
The Killer Mountain, Switzerland

"Why do you want to climb that mountain?" asked the proprietor of the hotel I was staying at in Zermatt, Switzerland. "It's a killer mountain."

"But it's the Matterhorn," I replied, as if that should explain it all.

It seemed obvious to me. After all, it was a very prominent peak, easily seen from the town of Zermatt, and its silhouette was well known throughout the world. What mountain climber wouldn't want the chance to climb its summit?

"But surely you're not going unguided," she continued. "That's a very dangerous mountain. Half of the graves in Zermatt are filled with climbers who died on the Matterhorn."

"Oh, I think we'll be all right. Our party has quite a bit of climbing experience."

"You shouldn't be without a guide," she persisted. "You could easily get into trouble, and there would be no one to help you. It is groups like yours that have the accidents."

I discounted the proprietor as a grump and went off to meet my friends to complete our plans to make the climb.

Seven of us had gathered in Switzerland from different parts of the United States for a climbing vacation. Our main goal was to climb the Matterhorn, but we had spent a week in the Zermatt area climbing other peaks first. Based on the experiences of those climbs, we decided that only four of us would be capable of doing the long, grueling rock climb of ten hours or more required to make the summit of the Matterhorn and return.

Talking to other climbers and using our own observations of the mountain while swilling beer in the comfort of street cafes in Zermatt, we saw that the weather on the Matterhorn appeared to follow a five-day cycle. First day, heavy clouds appeared. Second day, snow fell and some of it might get as far as Zermatt in the form of light rain. Third day, the clouds cleared off, and the mountain appeared in bright sunshine sheathed in brilliant white snow. Fourth day, the mountain slowly lost its white sheath under sunny skies. Fifth day, the skies were mostly clear and the snow almost gone. A small, stationary, harmless-looking cloud touched the peak on the windward side of the summit and formed in the same spot almost every afternoon. Based on these amateur observations and with great confidence, we left Zermatt on the fourth day of the Matterhorn weather cycle to put ourselves at the base of the mountain to climb it on the fifth day.

As predicted, we had a beautiful, clear day to hike to the base of the Matterhorn. Silently and smoothly, we floated up from Zermatt across a valley on a cable car to the high, open meadows below snow-covered peaks. Here the air was cooler than down below, and the peaks stood out, crisp and clean in the bright sunshine. The Matterhorn dominated the view appearing beautifully aloof and fearfully steep and unclimbable. I had read somewhere that the Matterhorn, first climbed in 1865, was one of the last major peaks to be climbed, because the early alpinists actually thought it was unclimbable, and would remain so forever. A shiver went up my spine. And I was going to climb that? Shaking off those misgivings, I started up the trail to the *Hörnlihüttte,* the jumping off place of the climb, and the hut where we would stay overnight.

About three hours later, I saw the bright red shutters that identified the hut, still a good distance away on a flat piece of ridge. A little distance away the ridge met the steep flanks of the Matterhorn itself. When closer, I saw that the hut was two buildings, not one, connected by a large patio in front. Several groups of people sat at tables on the patio conversing while drinking tea and nibbling pastries. Some gazed out at the magnificent view of the Matterhorn, now so close that I saw the details of glacier and rock slopes that now looked even more fearful and much steeper. Still others peered through binoculars in hopes of spotting climber friends and family on the rock slopes above.

The first building included a restaurant and gift shop; the second building was the actual climbing hut. A hut master ruled this building, and he assigned us numbered sleeping spaces, two feet wide, located on a communal sleeping platform. Upper and lower sleeping platforms filled the room on each side of a narrow, central aisle with the entry at one end of the aisle and a window at the other. Each person's gear had to be stowed in the allotted two feet of sleeping area. In addition to the sleeping rooms were a dining room, kitchen, a small store, and the bathroom. Boots were banned everywhere in the hut, and were stowed on racks near the entrance to the hut, so everyone walked around in socks, slippers, or barefoot.

Each person received one blanket for the night. The two women in our group expressed grave doubts about staying warm through the night with only one blanket. But we discovered that the forty bodies filling our room gave off so much heat that, for some of us, blankets weren't needed at all, and the only window in the room stayed open all night.

Too excited to sleep, I lay still and dozed through the long night. Then suddenly, a little past three o'clock, it was time to get up. People stirred with more purpose, the lights came on, and the four of us who were going to climb got up and got dressed. It was then we found out that Dick, our leader was not going.

"I'm sick," he said. "I've been up all night going back and forth to the bathroom, throwing up everything I've eaten over the last ten weeks. I want to go, I really do, but I don't think I can make it."

He had been designated our leader by virtue of having once climbed the Matterhorn with a guide. That left Norm, Rick, and me, the Seattle contingent, to carry on having never been on the mountain before.

"Don't worry," Dick said in an offhand manner. "The route is pretty straightforward, and there's probably a hundred climbers out to make the climb today. You can just follow along with them."

In the dining room, climbers and guides were eating and drinking coffee. Guides were with their clients, one on one, talking earnestly to them and going over equipment. Many climbers like us had no guides. I was too excited to eat, and since I didn't drink coffee, I was ready to go, right now.

"Come on you guys let's get going," I said. "All the guides are leaving, and we're going to be left behind. We should stop wasting time and get going too."

"You bet, Frank, right after I finish this coffee," said Norm, completely unperturbed by my comments.

"Yeah Frank, we've only been up a little over half an hour so far," said Rick. "Give us a break. We're not wasting any time yet; besides, It's only 4:30.

Of course, not everyone had left yet, and other climbers putting on boots and gathering their gear for the day joined us. It was pitch-black outside and we turned on headlamps to make our way across the short distance of flat ridge to a twenty-foot high cliff. This was the place that separated the hikers from the climbers. The cliff was steep, and most hikers turned back here rather than trying to go on. We had scouted this part of the route the day before, and decided there would be no problems for us the next morning. But the cliff was a lot harder to climb in the dark. We couldn't find the foot holds and hand holds that were so easy to see in the daylight. Above the cliff, we walked along the ridge on one or another of the numerous climbing trails. There were so many of them converging and diverging that we weren't sure which trail was the right one.

"What a bad way to start a major climb," I protested. "Where are those one hundred climbers we were told would be climbing today? Where's everybody else? We should at least see which way some of them went."

Suddenly, fifty feet above us on another trail, came a taunting cry, "What are you people doing down there? Are you out to climb the mountain today, or just out for an early morning stroll?" Without waiting for an answer, he went on, "If you want to climb the mountain today, I suggest you get up on this trail. You'll never get there on that trail."

Upon climbing to the upper trail, we found ourselves among other climbers who had also been confused by so many trails. They were following a client with his sarcastic guide. We fell in at the end of the line, and in this way, reached the face of a steep rock chute where the trail ended abruptly. This was the start of the four thousand foot rock climb to the summit by way of the *Hörnli* Ridge, considered the easiest route to the summit. We stood in line and waited impatiently for our turn to climb. While we waited, other climbers arrived to take their turn to climb behind us. Meanwhile, we turned off headlamps to conserve their batteries.

"My Lord," I gasped. "Look at the lights up on the mountain."

Starting from where we stood, we saw a line of twinkling lights from climber's headlamps strung out up the mountain for hundreds of feet. The climbers were invisible. Like a giant incandescent shape from some alien world, it twisted and turned and slowly inched its way ever upward.

"This has to be the most climbers I've ever seen on a mountain at one time," said Rick.

"I've seen it only once before on a mass climb of Mt. Adams," I said.

"Well, you folks should consider there are another thirty people or so waiting here on the trail to join that line of lights," said Norm.

We knew that most of the climb consisted of class four rock with a few pitches of low class five. Theoretically, that meant we could climb most of the way without a rope. Pitches of class five rock normally required ropes and perhaps pitons or other protective hardware, and each person climbed one at a time roped-up with a belay. Climbing that way took up a lot more time than climbing without a rope. However, determining the class of a rock climb was not an exact science, and most climbers relied on how comfortable they felt when climbing before deciding to use a rope or not. At this stage of the climb, no one was using a rope.

At last it was our turn to start up. Because of the press of so many climbers wanting to start out, it was a disorderly mob scene at the bottom of the rock face, and we had to exert ourselves to stay together. Once started on the face of the cliff, the pace was fast and the fun of climbing the Matterhorn soon wore off, as the climb became hard work. The climber's foothold above me became my handhold, and my foothold below became the next climber's handhold. Like a giant centipede, we formed a line where handhold followed foothold, and no one would stop. I was beginning to tire and my breathing became more labored, yet I didn't dare step aside to rest. I was afraid I wouldn't get my place back in that line of climbers.

My world diminished to a small circle of light from my headlamp. I saw the rock in front of my face, and no one except for the climber's boot above me as it moved from hold to hold. Generally, it was quiet except for hard breathing and the scuffling of boots on rock. Once in awhile one of us would call out to the others to check that all was well or to give a word of encouragement. I could tell the others were hurting too, but still we would not stop and give up our place in the line.

An hour passed and then another. The dark began to dissipate with the predawn light. The pace slackened, and soon we were going too slowly. Pent-up conversations broke out up and down the line. Dawn came, bathing us in warm sunshine. A little later, we all came to a complete stop. Still no one moved out of line, and we rested as best we could where we were. About two hundred feet above us, we saw a guide trying to maneuver his client up over down-sloping rock slabs. They were roped up and going very slowly. The client appeared tired and was having difficulty moving. He was the cause of our backup, because we saw no other climbers on the route above them.

When it was dark, it was easy to pick out the location of climbers by their lights, but in the daylight, they faded into the background of jumbled up boulders, slabs, and scree. High up the steep slope, I made out several figures clustered around a small stone building, the Solvay hut. But beyond that, nothing.

A few climbers tried to go around the bottleneck, but as soon as they deviated left or right from the prescribed route, they found themselves in trouble on higher-class rock. We found that if the climbing got more difficult than class four, we were off route. No one wanted to use up time to protect a route on class five rock that lay on either side of the relatively easy guide's route. So we all stayed put and rested.

Finally, the guide and his client moved off, the climbing jamb broke, and our part of the line of climbers followed up to the Solvay Hut. The hut was an emergency shelter located about halfway up the mountain. It was about ten feet by sixteen feet, built on a flat rock shelf just big enough to hold it. We didn't stay there long. We had already rested down below.

Frank King

The route above the Solvay Hut led steeply up a knife ridge. The day was warm, and we climbed in bright sunshine. As we climbed higher, the drop-offs on each side of the route became steeper and farther down. A fall here could be disastrous. We had beautiful views, but I was very uncomfortable, and I thought of our ropes still tucked away in the packs. Sometimes I planted one foot on each side of the knife ridge, hoping to straddle the ridge if one or the other of my feet slipped, and I went down. No one asked for a rope, and we carried on.

We finally went left away from the knife ridge onto easier slopes. Almost immediately, we ran into another bottleneck. We came to a series of class five cliffs with climbers strewn up and down each cliff, climbing with the protection of ropes. The guides had anchored one-and-a-half inch fixed ropes up each cliff, and we saw several parties using these ropes to climb the cliffs without belaying each other.

"Shall we break out the ropes?" asked Rick.

"I don't want to waste the time using them if it's not necessary," said Norm.

I said, "It seems obvious to me that the guides don't bother to rope up here. After all, they went to a lot of trouble placing these fixed ropes to use in order to save time. What's good for them should be good for us too."

Without another word, Norm grabbed the rope and started to climb. I followed a short distance after him, and Rick came up a few feet behind me. By the time we reached the third band of cliffs, my hands were hurting from hanging onto the rope. It was far harder to climb that way than I thought it would be. With my hands painful from gripping the rope and cramping badly, I tried to rest them by holding the rope in the crook of my elbow, alternately using each arm. This meant if my feet slipped, I would be hanging by one hand, not good. After the third band of rock, I saw with relief that we had only one more cliff to go, and I willed my hands to keep gripping the rope.

We caught and passed several teams who were playing it safe by belaying each other up. They moved quite slowly and took a lot of time since they had to set and reset anchors and belay each of their members up one at a time. We ducked under and over their ropes trying not to step on them, grab them, or fall off the cliff. On the third band of cliffs, we met a guide and his client coming down from the summit. At first, I couldn't believe it, since it was only 10:30. How could they have gotten all the way to the summit and back down so fast?

We kept encountering others coming down, and at times three teams were trying to occupy the same space on the cliff. There was our team going up, a parallel roped team going up, and a guide with his client going down. In a few places, I clung to the fixed rope in desperation as the guide and his client climbed down past me using the same fixed rope. The guides wouldn't wait for us to get clear. They urged their clients to go, go, go. They came crashing down through our position with their boots and ice axes flailing, and I thought I was in danger of falling off. I was furious.

At one particularly bad spot, I was in a precarious position clinging to the fixed rope with cramped hands and my feet on a poor foothold. About ten feet above my head, a young woman peered down at me as her guide urged her to get on down. I yelled to her to wait while I climbed up to her position, which was a wide, safe ledge at the top of the cliff. I continued yelling at her to wait even as the guide urged her on. Fortunately, she understood English, because I told her I was prepared to push her off the mountain if necessary to save myself. I quickly scrambled over the lip of the ledge, but when I turned to thank her, she and the guide were already gone.

We learned that most guides got their clients started on the mountain by 4:00 a. m. They knew every minute feature of the route, and hauled and cajoled their clients up as fast as they could. The clients got minimal rest breaks going up and were allowed ten to fifteen minutes on top before the guide rushed them back down. I thought this was terrible treatment by the guides, but later, I wasn't so sure.

The fixed ropes ended where the rock slope became a little less steep. In a short distance, we climbed over the edge of the steeper slopes onto the moderate slopes leading to the summit which came into sight just ahead.

"It's a walk-up from here," I gloated. "We've got it made."

The last portion of the route was on moderate slopes covered in snow, and we saw many parties going up and some coming down. With so many climbers on the summit slopes, a trail had been worn in the snow that led all the way to the top. We arrived at the summit at about 11:30, where with great glee, we photographed each other, fingers in 'V' for victory signs and ice axes raised on high.

The summit was a short, narrow ridge covered with patchy snow. Here and there, several spots were wide enough and clear of snow to sit comfortably by the trail and allow people to pass unimpeded. Of interest to me were several large, ornate crosses, six to eight feet high, made of iron mesh placed along the summit ridge. We ate a leisurely lunch in bright sunshine and looked down into Italy on our left and the valleys and mountains of Switzerland on the right. Far off to the north we saw Mont

Blanc and the French Alps and to the south, much closer the snow covered summit of Mt. Rosa.

Rick finished his lunch and said, "I think we should get ready to go back. It's a long way down from here."

But Norm and I waved him off contented to continue our rest.

"After all," I said, "We'll probably never get back here again, so let's enjoy this as long as we can."

Our lunch was finished, but still we sat in serenity with a great sense of accomplishment. Finally, Rick could stand it no longer and got ready to go.

"We need to leave now," he said. "Come on, let's get going. Take a look around. The sun is not nearly as bright as it was and most of the people have left the summit."

I did look around and what Rick had said was true. I saw wispy clouds forming and a niggling doubt intruded into my happy thoughts. Had we stayed too long?

Going down, we found that the firm snow of morning was now soft and melted through in places. One or the other of us would suddenly punch clear through the soft snow to slip on a slab of smooth rock, or almost lose our balance on a loose rock beneath the snow. It was slower going down than going up, and when we got above the upper cliff band with its fixed rope, the slope was steep enough to be truly dangerous. Now a fall or slipping on a rock below the snow could cause any one of us to lose control and slide over the cliff. I shuddered at the thought.

By mutual consent, we brought out the rope for the first time and rappelled one pitch and belayed a second pitch down to the start of the fixed rope. The last few feet down to the fixed rope was on a smooth, open slab that got steeper the farther down we went. I felt very uneasy and doubtful that I could down climb without slipping. So I called for tension on the rope to help support me on the last few steps to the five foot iron rod embedded in the rock that provided the anchor for the first of the fixed ropes. I grabbed that iron bar and held on for dear life until I clipped into it with a sling. Now safely tied to the anchor, I went off belay and Rick came down to join me. He was grateful to hang on to that solid iron bar, too. Norm came last and I belayed him down, but he had the more dangerous assignment, down climbing without an overhead belay.

Now we noticed that the wispy clouds had changed to substantial clouds. But not to worry. Didn't clouds form on one side of the Matterhorn every afternoon? Even so, they seemed a little heavier and more widespread than they should be. Without wasting any time, we grabbed the big rope and started walking and climbing down the cliff backwards, hanging on tightly to the rope. In a short time, my hands began to tire from gripping the rope.

Once started down, there was no way of relaxing them until the cliff ended. There were three more bands of rock with fixed ropes to descend, and we debated setting up anchors to repel down.

But now thick clouds filled the sky and were following us down the mountain. If we didn't move fast enough, they would soon engulf us, so we opted to continue as we were. By the bottom of each cliff, my hands were so painful I had to will them to keep a grip on the rope. Between each cliff band, I tried to relax my hands and prepare them for the next ordeal, but there was never enough time. On the last cliff, all of my energy and thoughts were concentrated on trying to ignore the pain in my hands and keep a grip on the rope.

By the end of the last fixed rope, we saw no other climbers. We had passed a few who were taking time to rope up. But below the cliffs, we were alone and never saw another climber. The clouds had long since blotted out the sun and were now a dark shade of gray. I felt uneasy, as if I was in a race to get away from the mountain before the clouds and their contents engulfed me.

We went down the knife ridge carefully. What had appeared so pleasant in bright sunshine and the freshness of early morning was now cold and menacing. I tried not to look down at the steep drop-offs on either side of our route, concentrating instead on my balance and placing my feet properly. We arrived at the Solvay hut, but hurried on without stopping until we reached the top of the down-sloping Moseley Slabs. These were much easier going up than coming down, and no one questioned the use of ropes here.

We broke out the ropes again and set a repel anchor. The first person repelled down with our second rope. While he set up the next repel, the other two repelled down to join him and bring down the upper rope. This procedure was repeated again and again as we raced the clouds down the mountain.

At many places, the guides had set thick steel bars into the solid rock to use as repel anchors. Using these saved us a lot of time. They were located where natural anchors were hard to find or use, but more importantly, they helped us find our way down through the jumble of slabs. Several times we had to cast from side to side to find the right route, and were always relieved to stumble across one of those anchor bars.

As the clouds got lower and darker, we gave up repelling as too slow, and took the risk of a fall by down climbing the rock without the rope. We caught distant glimpses of the Hörnlihütte far below, and a little while later, turned a rock rib and saw it very clearly. All the lights in the hut were on, and it appeared as a beacon beckoning us to its safe haven.

We realized that we had about an hour to go before it got dark. So we pressed on, down climbing the rock with an abandonment that comes only with great confidence or desperation. When we came to the last twenty foot cliff, our four friends left behind that morning were there to greet us with congratulations and to escort us the short distance to the hut, bright with lights in the early twilight.

We were just in time for supper. But it was a subdued meal. We received word that two climbers had fallen to their deaths. Many climbing parties had not yet returned. Most were probably sheltered in the Solvay Hut, but I was sure many others were out on the mountain bivouacking where darkness found them.

We went to bed tired and happy. In the night, snow fell quietly, and by morning had covered the ground four inches deep. It would be much deeper higher on the mountain. Later in the morning, the hut master informed us that three other climbers had died in the night from hypothermia.

The snow stopped falling by noon, and we packed up to return to Zermatt. Just as we were leaving, a party came in loudly expressing its happiness at getting back safely to the *Hörnlihütte*. They had spent the night sheltered in the Solvay Hut. At daybreak, they had left their shelter and carefully made their way down through the Moseley Slabs covered with twelve inches of new snow. It was a long, tiring, treacherous descent for them, and they were extremely happy to be back down.

As we hiked down the trail to catch the gondola for the ride down to Zermatt, the sun came out, and the snow melted rapidly. The last of the clouds disappeared and a magnificent Matterhorn filled the sky. It was incredibly white and beautiful in its mantle of new snow. But it was also a killer. The guides knew this, and they made sure they got their clients back down as soon as possible. We knew it now too, because five climbers were killed in the same time period as our happy-go-lucky climb. The mountain had capriciously compressed its five-day weather pattern to only four days.

Back at the hotel, my landlady asked, "Did you climb the Matterhorn?"

"Oh, yes," I said. "It was a good climb, and we made it to the top. But five climbers lost their lives yesterday."

With a disparaging toss of her arm and a shrug, she said, "Oh, that happens all the time. My husband died up there fifteen years ago. He was trying to rescue a party that had no guide, people like yourselves."

Frank King

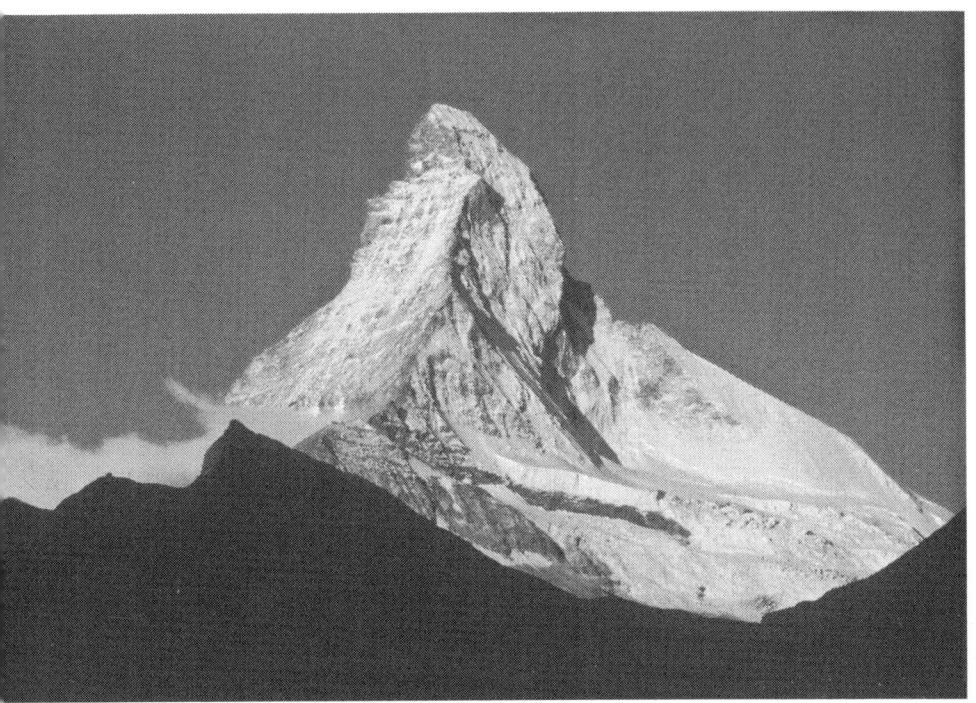

38) The Matterhorn

Chapter 24
In the Back Country, Guatemala

"Okay, we got this far," said Josh, my traveling partner for two weeks in Mexico and Guatemala. "But now what? We're stuck here at the end of the road, our bus has gone back to Palenque, and we have no place to sleep."

In just a few words, Josh had summed up our predicament. We had left Palenque, Mexico, the site of impressive Mayan ruins, early that morning in a mini-bus expecting to reach the largest town in the area, Flores, Guatemala to stay the night. But we arrived at the end of the road on the banks of a very muddy Usumacinta River in late afternoon instead of at noon which was the time we had expected to get there.

We still had to go upstream by boat to Guatemala to catch the bus to Flores, which now seemed impossible to do, even to me, the eternal optimist. The dirt and gravel roads from Palenque were full of ruts and potholes formed by recent rains and travel was slow. Very slow. At one point, the driver had stopped to give his twelve-year old-son some instructions on how to drive and then let him drive for a while. Since the driver had no schedule to keep, time just slipped by.

"Let's go find a boat to take us upriver to where the road continues into Guatemala" I said to Josh. "The village there, Bethel, is a little bigger than this place, and should have a place to stay."

We hooked up with a man that said he would take us upriver, but he wouldn't go until morning.

"Too late now," he said. "Better in the morning."

"Okay," I said. "But where can we spend the night?"

He signed for us to follow him, and we walked about five minutes to a little hardware store set off by itself on a dirt street. He talked to the owner in rapid-fire Spanish, and they reached an agreement which our boatman explained to us. The owner of the store would provide us a place to stay overnight in his storage room and feed us for a few pesos. We agreed without further discussion. Then the storeowner, with the help of the boatman, cleared a little space in the storage room and slung two hammocks.

The boatman left, promising to return in the morning, and we followed the owner to his two-room house that sat behind the store a few steps away. The larger room included a living area and the kitchen. The second room was for sleeping. He introduced us to his wife and two children before inviting us to sit at the family table in the kitchen for supper. The wife served us tortillas sprinkled with cheese and a few pieces of chicken, topped with a dab of hot salsa. She also had the inevitable beans and hot tea. We tried to make conversation, but it was difficult. We weren't fluent in Spanish and the others knew only a few words of English, so we made do with a lot of gestures and smiles punctuated by periods of quiet eating.

After supper, I asked about the bathroom facilities, and the owner pointed to a stand of small trees off to one side of his yard. They had no outhouse, just the screening cover of the trees. I spent a long night trying to sleep in the hammock, a strange sort of bed, in a strange place. In the morning, the wife fed us tortillas topped with a sprinkle of hot peppers, and tea.

The boatman arrived in time for the last of the tea, and then we were off to board his boat. It was a small open boat, perhaps thirty feet long, with an outboard engine in the rear. We spent the next hour traveling upriver to the small village of Bethel on the Guatemalan side of the river. The boatman ran the bow of his boat up on the mud bank, and then jumped out to rearrange a couple of twelve-inch boards so we could disembark without getting our feet too muddy. He pointed to a path that led up the mud bank toward the village.

At the top, a contingent of the Guatemalan army greeted us. I hadn't expected that and looked back at the river, but our boatman had already left. *Now what?* I thought. *And how did they know we were coming?* The welcoming group consisted of six soldiers lined up in a row with weapons held at the ready across their chests. A captain who spoke good English led them.

He politely requested our passports, then escorted us through the small village of Bethel to their fortified base camp, which consisted of some ragtag buildings, and an open parade area, all surrounded by a fence. At each corner of the enclosed square, a soldier stood guard in a tiny shelter. In one of the buildings, we were asked the standard traveler's questions. "Where were we going and for how long? Where did we come from?" Then, he dutifully stamped our passports into Guatemala and we were now in the country legally.

I asked about bus service to Flores, and the captain pointed his finger at an empty desk in another corner of the building, which served as a bus ticket office. After a short wait, a man came by and sold us two tickets on the afternoon bus. Not knowing the bus schedule, we waited outside in plain sight of the terminal. At about noon, a bus came rattling down the road from Flores and drove by without stopping. We thought it went on to pick up passengers in town first, before picking us up on the way out. But we really didn't know.

After waiting an hour, we went looking for the man who sold us the tickets to Flores. We finally found him in the village eating a leisurely lunch with the driver, who told us to go back and wait at the terminal. He picked us up, finally, and soon we were bouncing along the road to Flores which we found out was supposed to be a two-hour ride from Bethel.

About an hour later, the police stopped all traffic with a blockade where our side road from Bethel met the main north-south road in northern Guatemala. The police lined up everyone from our bus, scrutinized all travel documents, and pawed through private bundles, packs, and parcels.

I didn't know what they were looking for, but as people got their stuff together and started to board the bus, I turned to Josh and said, "Let's get away from this madhouse and head south, away from the tourists and crowds of people."

"Gee, Frank, I wasn't aware we were in the middle of a big crowd of people. Where do you want to go?"

"Let's go south from here," I said. "The main road has lots of oil trucks, so we should be able to get a ride on one of those."

"But where to?" asked Josh.

"The road is designated as Route Five on my little guide map and that should get us to Sayaxché where we could stay overnight and see a few Mayan ruins nearby, the next day."

"So you want to charge off to the right and head back into the jungle, just like that?" and he snapped his fingers.

"Sure," I said. "What else have you got to do? We can get to Flores anytime we want. This might be fun."

We got a ride easily on one of the many oil trucks passing through, which I guessed made up about ninety percent of the traffic on the road. They were small compared to the monster oil carriers at home, and I think they were full when they left the capital, Guatemala City, way in the south, and came back from Flores, empty. So I figured we were riding an empty truck. We tried to carry on a conversation, but we knew only a few words of Spanish and the driver knew only a few words of English, and we sat in silence most of the way.

Sayaxché lay across the Rio la Pasion on its south bank, and the main road did not go through the village. The truck dropped us off at a little ferry landing and then went on. We had a short wait until the ferry picked us up along with a few other passengers and a couple of pickups. The main part of the village lay out of sight behind the raised banks of the river, but we stayed at a hotel on the riverbank with views of the river and road activity from its large shady patio with comfortable chairs and full bar services close by.

Josh went off to explore the village and came back with three pretty, very blonde Danish girls in tow. Anything blonde in Guatemala was a novelty, but these women were beautiful, too. They wanted to go to the Mayan ruins at Parque Nacional Ceibal which was about ten miles east of Sayaxché. They had a ride set up for the next day in a pickup truck, and wanted us to go with them for safety. I looked over at Josh, who appeared to have swallowed the canary and was beside himself with excitement, to see the ruins, of course. I readily agreed to go, but thought the safety of the mission was more like locking two granddaddy foxes in the hen house and throwing away the key.

We met the Danish women and their driver the next day, and drove to his farm, at least he said it was his farm. It was on the edge of the park and after letting us out promised to pick us up later in the day. We never saw him again. Maybe those Danish women were smarter than I thought.

The park grounds were beautiful and well-kept with many of the ruins rebuilt. None was large or grandiose. We met a park guard who attached himself to us for the rest of our visit, making sure that we saw all the ruins whether we wanted to or not, including the stelae. These were solid rock pillars twelve feet high covered in carvings of animals, flowers, and Mayan hieroglyphics.

By midafternoon, I was done with ruins and was happy to leave the park and head back to Sayaxché. We stopped and waited awhile at the house of the man who drove us there in the morning, but finally left when no one came. We got another ride back to Sayaxché, where Josh walked the women to their hotel.

Back at our hotel, I realized my time for taking a shower had passed when the hot water remained cool. I had a hard time remembering that the village ran its generators for only a few hours each day, or if I did remember, I had forgotten what those hours were. It was much easier to remember at night when lights were needed, and my stomach told me it was suppertime.

In this case, I found a comfortable chair on the patio and spent the rest of the afternoon sipping cold beer until the electricity came on again for the evening hours.

Power was turned off again promptly at nine o'clock. After that, candles and lanterns had to make do until the power came on at eight o'clock the next morning.

The lack of power didn't seem to hamper the operations of the late night bars, and Josh was able to maintain his nightly schedule without hardship. He woke me up about one o'clock when it was still black outside to tell me that he and his Danish blondes had taken a wild swan that someone in the village had trapped. In a humane gesture, they planned to release it back into the jungle and wanted to know if I wished to join them. I passed up that adventure and went back to sleep, wondering if they realized that they had just stolen someone's dinner. It was not a thing to be taken lightly in this part of the world. The next morning Josh confirmed the success of releasing the wild swan back into the jungle.

"It was easy," he said. "We opened the door to its cage and it just flew away."

That's when I suggested we leave town and go to Flores. Now! As soon as the next bus arrived. Josh and I caught the early morning bus, but the girls stayed behind.

The police remained out of sight, and nothing marred our two-hour trip. The modern town of Flores was built over the Mayan ceremonial site of Tayasal, on a one-mile, rectangular-shaped island in a large lake. It was now connected to the mainland with a fifteen hundred foot long causeway.

At the time of the Spanish conquest, Tayasal was full of temples, pyramids, and idols, but not a trace of those remained today. God-fearing Spanish soldiers tore them down to build the modern town of Flores. In a rare example of the continuity of history, the town was finally brought under Spanish control just seventy-five years before the American Revolution.

We stayed in Flores for a couple days before taking the bus to Tikal, a large site of many Mayan ruins, including temples, pyramids, palaces, and dwellings. The giant pyramids made a great impression on me, many of them rising to one hundred-forty feet, well above the jungle canopy. They were steep sided and hard to walk up or down, actually dangerous in places. We walked a lot and got to the top of every pyramid we found.

The first night there we rented hammocks, but decided to camp out on the green grassy lawn in the designated campground. It was a pleasant place with large shade trees and several open shelters roofed with palm leaves. These were used for slinging hammocks and storing packs while visiting the ruins

During the night, I awoke startled with fear by the loud roaring of an animal in the woods. I thought I was about to be attacked and eaten. Other campers woke too, and that's how we found out that the dreadful noise was from howler monkeys. They seemed harmless but sounded scary. They went roaring by on their way through the tree tops to another place in the jungle.

Then we found the grass and all our gear sopping wet from heavy dew. We scrambled into a dry shelter nearby, and spent the rest of the night trying to stay warm in whatever extra dry clothes we had with us.

"Never again," I muttered. "The air here has too much water to stay dry at night."

In the morning, drops like rain dripped off the eaves of the shelter. But that changed fast after the sun rose. The air got hot, and we spent another muggy day in the jungle.

We left Tikal early one morning, snagging a ride with a park ranger who was returning to Flores. He dropped us off at the intersection where the right fork went on to Flores and the left fork went to the border with Belize. The traffic going to Belize was desultory, and we waited for a long time between potential rides. As a result, quite a few travelers were stuck at this place trying to get ongoing rides. At one point, a car from Flores stopped and three women got out and began trying to hitch a ride.

When they saw us, they waved and came over to talk. That's when I recognized them as the three pretty blonde Danish girls we had met in Sayaxché. For safety's sake, they wanted to join us in traveling to Belize. We agreed and shortly after that, a pickup stopped to give us a ride. To this day, I am not sure if the pretty women had anything to do with the driver's decision to stop for us or not. He certainly had many other choices, but he stopped for our group.

I was not too surprised when all the women ended up in the cab of the pickup, and Josh and I made do in the back where we had to share space with the gear of five people plus a large four-by-four foot silvery box already in the bed of the pickup. The box was too big to sit on, so Josh and I sat squeezed between the box and the sides of the pickup where we endured a weary, bone-jarring ride. About ten miles from the border, a police checkpoint stopped us. We all got out and showed the officer-in-charge our papers, and these he stamped indicating that we had left Guatemala legally.

Next to the checkpoint, the army had a base with a few buildings, a parade ground, and a barbed wire fence surrounding these. At each corner, a man stood guard in a little four by four feet thatched shelter. A dozen or more men stood around smiling, talking among themselves, and showing off to the girls. All seemed to be going well until the officer spoke to our driver and pointed to the silvery box.

All of a sudden, I felt tension in the air and wondered what was in that box. Thoughts of guns or illegal contraband ran through my mind as I waited for the disaster to fall, whatever it was. The driver climbed into the back of the pickup, lifted its lid, and reached in with his hand. Everyone went silent, waiting to see what he had in the box. I held my breath.

Out came a colorful wrapper on a stick, and it took me a second to realize that it was an ice cream bar. We had hitched a ride with the ice cream man. It wasn't long before everyone one was eating ice cream bars, including the officer, and we had an impromptu party right there in the road. The girls picked flowers along the edge of the road and placed a blossom into each rifle barrel. Never in my wildest dreams could I imagine a scene of such fun, happiness, and goodwill in that wild setting in the middle of nowhere, ignited by a simple ice cream bar.

A little later, we entered Belize, and by the time Josh and I got our passports properly stamped, the young

Danish women were gone. We never saw them again. We arrived in Belize City, the capital a couple of days later. Somehow we had formed an attachment to a young man, an American, I think. His name was Larry and his only good attribute was the ability to speak American English well. I didn't like him, but Josh who was perhaps more friendly or tolerant than I, encouraged him to travel with us to Caye Caulker. It was a small island off the coast, about an hour's boat ride from Belize City.

In Belize City, on the way to catch the launch out to Caye Caulker, all Larry could talk about was getting some "grass," meaning marijuana, I suppose. Josh and I were always very careful not to antagonize people or talk about doing anything illegal, especially in a foreign country. But this guy blabbed to anyone he met about his project to get some "grass." We were almost to the boat terminal when someone grabbed Larry by the arm and persuaded him to enter a grim-looking bar on the riverbank, and he went with them. Josh and I followed, but I had grave misgivings and alarms sounded throughout my body signaling danger.

The interior of the tavern was dark, dirty, and smelled foul. Several men sat at tables slouched over their drinks, and I half expected one of them to produce a knife and rob us. Somehow we were ushered to a back deck built over the river, and I felt a little better out in the open, in bright light. But how were we to get back out to the road without going through that menacing hellhole of a tavern? Just then, salvation came floating up to the deck. It was the launch that we had hoped to catch to Caye Caulker.

"Do you folks want a ride out of there?" asked the boat operator. "You're not in a very good place," he said in the understatement of the day.

Josh and I yelled out our desire to get out of there and get to Caye Caulker. Without hesitation, the launch pulled in alongside the deck, and we scrambled aboard to safety. Josh and I thanked the boat operator, but that dummy Larry was bemoaning that he had paid good money for some worthless grass. He showed it to me and, sure enough, his grass was clippings from someone's lawn. I was so mad I never spoke to him again, and after we arrived at the island we never saw him again, even though the island was very small.

Caye Caulker was a fun place, small enough to walk everywhere, and almost everyone spoke English of some sort. Josh prowled about day and night, but I mostly sat under the palm trees listening to the light breezes that rustled through the fronds and watched the ocean waves pound the barrier reef. Everything I needed was close at hand. The local people sold pastries and fresh-squeezed orange juice out of the windows of their houses. Rum was available almost everywhere, and restaurants were nearby. It's a wonder that Josh and I ever got around to leaving. But finally, we had to leave to catch our plane back home.

39) Ruins at Tikal

40) Ruins at Tikal

Chapter 25
Climbing White Giants, Peru

Our camp for the night was in a small valley closed-in on three sides by high ridges and peaks. The verdant green pastures on the valley floor were made even greener by contrast to the huge mountains and ridges around us covered in a thick mantel of brilliant white snow. Earlier we had passed a few head of beef peacefully grazing on the lush grass of the valley.

"I thought we would be camping higher," said Janet pointing to the cattle. She was one of the three women in our party of seven, climbing and hiking in the Cordillera Blanca, the White Mountains of Peru.

"Well," I said, "We're above fourteen thousand feet, higher than Mount Rainier back home. How high do you want to be?"

"Really?" she said. "How weird to think of cattle grazing here on green grass at such high elevations. Higher than our highest mountains at home. They must have big lungs."

"Thick, fur coats too," I said, shivering in the late afternoon sun.

I knew that after sunset the air would get cold enough to freeze the water in our water bottles. Our camp near the head of the valley was just a couple hundred feet below the snowline. This was to be our base camp for three or four days of hiking and climbing in the area. The mountains we hoped to climb were considerably higher than anything we had in the United States, except Alaska.

At last the *arrieros*, the two men who loaded and unloaded the burros, and guided us to where we wanted to go, stopped for the night. We had twelve burros with us that carried most of our personal gear as well as tents, sleeping bags, and food. As soon as each burro was relieved of its load, it moved off and started to graze on the thick grass. The seven of us on the trip put up our tents and moved in with our own packs. A little later, we fixed supper on our stoves, and sat around in twilight, relaxing, eating, and going over the day's events.

The next day we went out to scout the head of the U-shaped ridge that formed the end of the little valley where we were camped. Only three of us went; the others decided to rest a day in camp and perhaps take a leisurely hike up one of the side ridges enclosing our small valley. Many climbers tried to get used to high altitudes by climbing or hiking high during the day and sleeping lower at night. "Climb high, sleep low" was a mountaineer adage. According to the small map we had, the low point on the ridge, the col, at the head of our little valley was about sixteen thousand five hundred feet high. Two peaks at well over Eighteen thousand feet lay to the right of the col, and two other higher peaks, lay to the left of the col. None were in sight from camp.

For years, I had wanted to climb a six thousand meter peak and also reach twenty thousand feet high. The closest six thousand meter peak on the ridge to the left of the col had the unpronounceable name of Tocllaraju, but was only 19,906 feet high. Rats! The other six thousand meter peak, Pallkaraju, was farther out on the ridge at 20,163 feet high. Of course, I wanted to climb that peak since it fulfilled both my height criteria of climbing a six thousand meter peak that was also one that was over twenty thousand feet high.

We climbed a short distance beyond the snow line to reach a broad glacier that wound its way up to the top of the ridge at the end of our valley. The snow on the glacier was steep and still very hard from freezing overnight. Later on, the heat of the sun would turn the hard snow to mush. We finally decided to use crampons and stopped to put them on before entering a field of séracs and crevasses. These séracs were towers of ice ten or more feet high formed as the glacier fell over a steep rock cliff way below its surface. Normally, we tried to stay away from séracs and crevasses because of the difficulty of traveling through them, and séracs were notoriously unstable at times. No one liked the thought of a sérac suddenly tipping over on top of an unsuspecting climber. But the broken area was large, and we saw no way to get around it, so we prepared to go through the mess.

As I waited impatiently for the others to finish fastening their crampons to their boots, a shadow passed overhead, momentarily blocking out the sun. Quickly looking up for the source of the shadow, I caught a glimpse of a giant bird just before it disappeared behind a snowy slope. I couldn't believe its size. It was huge with a wingspan of at least ten feet, bigger than any bird I had ever seen flying. It reappeared almost immediately, flying over us again, tightening a circle that seemed to have us as the center of its attention. I never did see the bird flap its wings. It just floated effortlessly around and around us. And it seemed to get lower and closer as I watched.

"That's a condor," said Harry, Janet's brother. We three shared a tent on the trip. "They generally don't bother anything that's alive. They go for dead meat."

Just then a second condor joined his brother, and now we had two of those giant birds interested in us enough to stick around.

"I think we better move around a little to prove we're not just dead meat," I said, getting up on my feet.

The others finished fastening their crampons and hoisted on their packs. As we started walking on, the condors made one last pass and soared out of sight. I don't know if I could have fended off those giant birds if they decided I was close to death.

It took a long time for us to wend our way through the sérac towers and open crevasses. We all agreed to try and find a way around those obstacles on the way back. In early afternoon, we got to the top of the glacier where it joined the ridge just below the col. Looking around we found a small flat bench, eight feet by eight feet, right at the top of the glacier, suitable for a possible bivouac spot.

It backed into the steep slope leading to the top of the ridge, and the front edge dropped off down the equally steep glacier that we had just climbed. The view down the glacier and out over the valley was spectacular. In the distance, huge white peaks lay in jumbled confusion across the skyline. And closer we saw the greenery where our camp lay far below.

This small bench might have to serve as our campground for a couple nights, and we marked the perimeter with wands, which were one-quarter inch round bamboo, three feet long, with a piece of red flagging attached to one end. Then we carefully deposited some extra food we had brought with us at the bottom of a small depression where the glacier met the rock. If we had to camp out here, at least we wouldn't get hungry.

After lunch we climbed to the top of the ridge. Beyond lay another valley similar to the one where our base camp was located, and beyond that lay giant white peaks and a bewildering network of ridges that spread in all directions. A few rock faces lay exposed, but almost everywhere I looked a deep mantle of brilliant white snow covered everything. I was impressed and awed to see that much snow lying about, a truly wild wilderness. Close to the right of the col a prominent peak over eighteen thousand feet lay exposed on the ridgeline. The second peak to the right shown on our map lay out of sight behind the first one that was clearly visible.

The closest peak to the left of the col was one of the six thousand meter peaks and was partly hidden behind an intervening ridge of snow. But the other six thousand meter peak, that was also over twenty thousand feet, lay completely out of sight, and I had my first misgivings about being able to bag it. Everything looked further away than my optimistic, imagination had assumed from our small-scale map. Climbers were usually pretty optimistic, and I was at the top of that list, but looking at the vast distances between peaks and ridges lying at such high elevations, I had to squash a little pang of unease that arose from the pit of my stomach.

"Let's get out of here," said Harry at last.

"I agree," said Janet.

Without a word, I turned back and we headed down the glacier toward our camp. By now, the snow was very soft, and we took off the crampons. But we still remained roped up while on the glacier. On the way back, we scouted a little to one side of the field of sérac towers and crevasses, and found a much easier and safer way to go.

When we returned to our camp in the little green valley, it was already in deep shadow and the late afternoon air was cold. We put on coats, hats, and gloves, and ate our supper quickly before the food cooled off too much to be appetizing. I noticed the *arrieros* didn't put on any extra clothes, and when I asked about that, they shrugged. And one said "no have," and spread out his arms with his hands palm up. They each wore a wool sweater, which they never took off no matter how hot it got during the day. They wrapped up in a blanket at night, and lay out on the ground in the open. I figured they must freeze almost every night and thaw out during the day.

Then one of them pointed to a scorched circle where a fire had burned the grass, and made a pantomime of sleeping. I had seen many of those scorched places on the hillsides throughout the trip and now realized what they were. The *arrieros* and other people like them lit fires in the grass at night then lay in the embers to gain a little warmth. I thought about that a little, when I nestled down in my warm, cozy sleeping bag and zonked off to sleep.

Early the next day, all of us except one headed up toward the bivouac spot we had found the day before, planning to camp overnight there and climb some of those really big mountains. We carried packs that included a tent and sleeping gear, plus food, ropes, helmets, and climbing gear. The extra weight slowed us down, and I had to experiment to find the right combination of breathing and speed to keep going without too many stops to rest and recover my breath.

We arrived at the bivouac spot before noon, set up camp, and ate a quick lunch. Since the peaks we wanted to climb lay hidden behind the ridge above our camp, Harry, Janet, and I who had been there the day before discussed the possible climbs with the other three who had stayed in camp. We arrived at a consensus to climb the first six thousand meter peak on the ridge to the left of the col, and if all went well, take a look at the higher peak further out on the ridge beyond it. That would involve climbing two six thousand meter peaks in one afternoon which might be as much as five thousand feet of elevation gain. That would be a tremendous feat even at lower elevations and almost impossible at these high elevations. But mountaineers tend to be optimistic when planning climbs using small maps only. Wait until we actually saw those remote ridges and peaks from the top of the col.

The party was badly separated already by the time I reached the top of the col. One person was not feeling well, and another person was going very slowly, but two people were already out of sight, ahead of me making their way to our first objective that was visible above an intervening ridge. I wasn't tied to anyone in particular and decided to move ahead to catch up to Nadine and Bruce, the lead couple.

The others agreed to come along as best they could. When I reached the top of the intervening ridge, I saw the entire six thousand meter peak ahead and about halfway across the cirque beyond the ridge, the two tiny figures that were Nadine and Bruce. That's when the true scale of the distances we had to travel became evident and I knew we would be lucky to bag just one six thousand meter peak for that day. I yelled and they waved for me to come ahead, but they didn't stop. The route was easy, simply a matter of rest stepping and breathing, and once a good rhythm was established, I wouldn't have stopped either.

By the time I reached eighteen thousand feet I had to take in more breaths of air to keep going. The pace was maddeningly slow, but when I tried to push on faster, my legs hurt so badly I had to stop. Stopping was not an efficient way to climb anything, and the object was to keep moving at all costs. So it was a balancing act to breathe enough and yet keep moving.

I caught up to them about two hundred feet below the summit and without stopping the three of us soon arrived at the top. A blanket of snow covered the summit just like all the rest of the route we had followed. There was not a rock in sight anywhere, nothing but brilliant white snow, and the word boring came to mind. It was hard for me to feel any elation; six thousand meters felt similar to climbing Mount Rainier back home, except that Mount Rainier was more fun. This climb had been long, tiring, mostly monotonous, except for a few exciting places maneuvering around huge crevasses.

Farther out on the ridge we saw the second six thousand meter peak. It was a long distance away with about a thousand feet of drop from where we stood. No way were we going to make that summit today. So without much discussion we turned back .

On the way back across the cirque, we met Harry and Stan still climbing and agreed to wait for them on the ridge until they had climbed the peak, were off the summit, and started back toward camp. On the ridge, we waited with Janet, the sixth member of our party who was still not feeling well, and would not be climbing any further that day. When we returned to our bivouac spot, it was late and already in shade from the ridge. Our base camp in the valley was already in deep shadows, and the air was cold without the sun. We made a quick supper and got ready for a night out on the glacier.

We had carried in a three-man tent, which was way too small to handle six people. So we decided that four of us would squeeze into the tent for the night, and Harry and I would sleep out in the open on the glacier next to the tent. After leveling a sleeping platform, we spread out a plastic tarp on the snow with our foam pads and sleeping bags on top, and then laid out the coiled ropes at our feet. I thought this would give Harry and me a feeling of security from sliding down the glacier feet first during the night.

We didn't slide anywhere, but I still woke up in the middle of the night, scared to death, thinking I was about to go careening out of control down the steep slope of the glacier trapped in my sleeping bag. During the night, the glacier woke me up with all sorts of noises, creaks, and pops as it moved ponderously downhill. I never thought of a glacier moving at all, but apparently this one did, and the noise it made was loud, scary, and it continued all night. Harry was awake a lot too, but when I mentioned glacial noises to those who had slept inside the tent, they hadn't heard a thing.

We were up early the next day and decided to climb the smaller peaks to the right of the col. We went for the higher eighteen thousand foot peak first first, and climbed it with no problems. By the time we came back to pick up the second peak, the day had gotten very warm and the snow had melted to where we were floundering in knee-deep snow and dropping in up to our hips in places. Instead of making a frontal assault straight up to the summit, we climbed a low ridge to the right of the peak thinking the top or backside of the ridge might have firmer snow. We wallowed our way up, almost swimming in the snow to gain the ridge. But the snow on top of the ridge was just as deep and soft and the back of the ridge was impossibly steep to navigate. The summit of that nondescript peak just wasn't worth the energy and time it would take to get it, so we abandoned the project and headed back down to our bivouac spot.

There we silently packed our gear and left that hostile place, and were back to our camp in the green meadows by late afternoon. That evening it didn't take much discussion or persuasion to decide to move our camp down to a lower elevation where the air might be warmer and the peaks were not as high.

42) Climbing a big peak (Photo by Harry Morgan)

42) Near the top (Photo by Harry Morgan)

43) Base Camp (Photo by Harry Morgan)

44) A peak over 18,000 ft. (Photo by Harry Morgan)

Chapter 26
Picking up Pieces of Silver, Peru

Gasping for breath on the trail at sixteen thousand feet, I had to stop. Way down below, I saw the main trail where I had left my friends to go alone on this side trip. We were hiking and camping in the Cordillera Blanca, a section of the Andes in Peru. I had no idea where this trail led, and it was simply curiosity that led me onward and upward. Now that I had expended so much energy getting this far, I couldn't quit until I saw where the trail ended. Looking up ahead, I saw some buildings about two hundred feet above, and concluded that they were probably mine buildings. "Okay, I'll go and see a mine."

Just as I was about to start out again, a wild boar came trotting down the trail. When he saw me, he stopped abruptly about fifteen feet away, as surprised to see me as I was to see him. He was an ugly-looking creature with great curving tusks and coarse hair now raised up on his back. Although he was much smaller than a domestic pig, he looked mean and nasty. Looking at him made me think of stories of how wild boars would charge without provocation and tear away flesh with those sharp tusks.

We both stood very still staring at each other wondering what to do next. He didn't budge or run away like most animals I've met in the wilds and that was disconcerting. I wasn't about to challenge him by proceeding up the trail, and he apparently didn't want to challenge me either. Finally, almost by mutual agreement, we each sidled off the trail to the right and walked slowly past each other through light brush to regain the trail beyond. Once back on the trail, I hurried on my way, and glancing back, saw the boar trotting away at a good speed. He also peered over his shoulder to make sure I was no longer a threat.

When I got to the buildings, I saw that the largest of them was a large living quarters, with dorm and kitchen for several men. There were other small storage and equipment buildings scattered about. Off to one side, was a three-sided shed with the open side facing a tremendous view out over the whole valley with those giant white mountains across from me thrusting into a deep blue sky, forming an impenetrable barrier.

I thought the place was abandoned, so I was surprised to see two little men sitting side by side in the shed. They showed no surprise to see me, and continued concentrating on getting their Coke fix. They had gourds filled with cocoa leaves, water, and ashes. They stirred and chopped the mix with a small stick, and occasionally licked the sticks clean of the resulting mash. The little men sat on a high bench with their feet off the ground and their legs dangling down. Their lips were green, a green froth gathered at the corners of their mouths, and I thought they might be elves. With the help of the cocaine released from the raw cocoa leaves by the potash and water, they were able to work the silver mine located well over sixteen thousand five hundred feet.

I tried talking to them in Spanish, but I think their language was Quechua, and they spoke very little Spanish. I found out that their job was to process silver ore. They picked out chunks of unprocessed ore from a large pile nearby and hammered off pieces of waste rock to make the ore more concentrated with silver. They spent many hours of the day clinking away at the ore to make it more valuable to ship. Then about once every two weeks, a mule train arrived to take out the processed ore.

The little men graded the ore and placed it in one of three piles, depending on how much silver showed up in the ore. There was a dramatic difference between the piles. The pile with the best or highest concentration of silver actually looked like pure silver, and it glinted brightly in the sunshine. Of course, I wanted a piece of silver from that shiny pile to bring home with me, but they indicated that the price would be $20 per piece. Wow, nothing backward about these men's economics!

I tried to bargain, but to no avail. They waved their arms uphill behind them and grunted out some volleys of Quechuan. I finally understood their suggestion to wander up into the mines and find my own pieces of silver to take home. No charge.

As I climbed up above the shed, I saw that the whole mountainside was peppered with openings leading into mining shafts, a labyrinth of them. I entered several and picked up pieces of silver ore. Even in the gloom of the mine tunnel, the silver glinted, and it was easy to find the ore. There was so much laying about it was hard to choose the very best specimens.

Suddenly, the elevation got to me. I became lightheaded and dizzy, and felt like I was going to pass out. I quickly ran through the possibilities of what was wrong and boiled it down to the onset of mountain sickness. That was scary, for who would know where I was if I couldn't get back, and I had no confidence in being rescued by drugged miners.

I stopped bending over and looking for silver. I already had plenty by now. I slowly retreated out of the mine and down the hill to the shed where I rested for a bit.

The miners were back at work, and they never looked at me as they clinked away at the ore with their hammers. I knew that the best antidote for mountain sickness was to lose altitude fast. And this I proceeded to do. I went down the trail quickly, losing one thousand feet of elevation, and this made me feel better. When I had no more feelings of light headiness, I relaxed a little, but didn't feel safe until I reached the main trail in the valley below.

I came away with about six pieces of ore, none more than three or four inches across. But today, only the memory remains. I regret that I don't have them to see or touch. All those pieces of silver I worked so hard to get that day, are gone, lost in the turmoil and confusion of living life in the present.

Frank King

45) Descendents of the Inka (photo by Harry Morgan)

Chapter 27
Leaving the Inka* Roads, Peru

Late one afternoon, for no reason at all, one of our pack burros stopped in the middle of the trail and refused to go on. No matter how much the two *arrieros* with us, men who handle pack animals, pulled, pushed, and swore at the burro, it wouldn't budge an inch. Finally, they took the load off its back and tried again to get it to move. Not a chance. That animal stood its ground as if glued to the spot.

Suddenly, without a word, one of the *arrieros* pulled out his knife and cut off the top part of one ear of the burro. Shocked, I watched the piece of ear bounce on the ground, and come to rest among some dried leaves. I winced, but the animal didn't even twitch. Abruptly the *arrieros* turned away, distributed the extra load onto the other burros, and left without another look at the burro who wouldn't go. The rest of us followed leaving the malfunctioning burro behind.

****

*Note: Some scholars think the word "Inca" should be spelled "Inka" which I have chosen to use throughout this book.

Our trail at this point was an Inka road about eight feet wide and paved with flat rocks. It twisted and turned, following the easiest contour to get over a ridge about one hundred feet above us. The burro had stopped in the middle of a flight of curving steps enclosed on both sides by three to four foot high rock walls where ancient Inka masons had carved the road into the steep slope of the mountain.

Before passing out of sight, I took a quick look back at the sick burro; he still hadn't moved an inch, but I noted a couple beads of red blood that glistened in the bright sun. They had oozed from the cut and were caught in the fur part way down its ear. I never found out, and no one ever said why the *arriero* maimed the burro. It must have hurt a little, and it certainly was a cruel act. Maybe the *arriero* was simply pissed off and had taken out his annoyance by hurting the animal.

We stopped for the night just on the other side of the ridge. If only the poor little burro had known our camp would be so close, he might have tried to make it to food and water, and rest up with his burro buddies for the night. I thought the *arrieros* would go back to the stricken burro with food and water, but they made no move to leave camp.

Finally Harry, a good climbing friend, and I went back with a little feed and fodder and some water to see if we could help the burro. He was still there on the steps where we had left him, and nothing we tried convinced him to move. Then suddenly he fell over backward and turned a complete backward somersault down the steps to land on his side on the landing ten feet below at the bottom of the steps. The burro, with some effort, scrambled to its feet and stood very still, looking dejected as I thought a burro might possibly appear if it had such emotions.

"Wow, that was a close call," said Harry. "You almost got crushed by a sick burro."

"I really didn't see much," I said. "I was too busy getting out the way of a bouncing burro body."

But I knew that the burro had almost hit and smooshed me into the rocks, not on purpose, of course. By consensus, and without words, that was the end of our mercy mission with the burro, and we left him standing on the landing looking just as listless as before.

"What do you think will happen to him?" I asked.

"If he doesn't move, eat, or drink he'll die."

"It's hard to believe that something that big would just die right there on the trail," I said. "What a mess."

"I bet that if you came back in a week, there would be nothing left to see," said Harry. "We've seen those giant condors floating over us for days, and I bet it wouldn't take them long to spot a dying burro."

"You're right," I said. "Especially when they invite all their uncles, aunts, and cousins along to join the feast."

No one mentioned the burro again until the end of our pack trip when the owner of the pack train tried to bill us for the cost of a dead burro. We objected, of course, and after lengthy negotiations, reached a settlement.

Due to poor scheduling, I had to cut the last three days of the climbing and camping part of my trip in Peru from my itinerary. I had to leave my climbing friends the next day to get back to Lima in time to meet other non-climbing friends that I was traveling with for the next two months in other parts of South America. So early in the morning, my climbing friends waved me off, and I started the long journey out to civilization and the bus that would take me to Lima.

All morning I followed the Inka road down a couple thousand feet off the ridge to where it entered a long shallow valley. There its character changed to a more modern appearing, plain old dirt road. I came upon the first person I had seen in days who was not a part of our climbing group. He was working alone in an empty field, no houses, no horse, no pickup truck, just him alone, surrounded by bare fields. He was turning the soil over with a five-foot long crowbar. He was small and thin, about six inches shorter than me, and was working close enough to the trail, so that I saw clearly what he was doing.

I stopped to watch, because I had never seen earth dug in this manner. Finally, I couldn't stand it any longer. I went over, and asked him by pantomime if I could try digging with his crowbar. Without a word, he handed it to me. I lifted the heavy steel bar and drove it about six inches into the hard earth like I had seen him do. Then I pried the clod loose and upended it to bury the packed surface and expose the relatively loose bare soil below. I did this a few times, but it didn't take long for my arms to get tired, and I was glad to give the farmer back his crowbar. He went back to work, and when I left, he still hadn't spoken a word to me.

As I walked along, I did a little figuring. His plot of ground was about one hundred feet by two hundred feet, say, one-half acre. I noticed that each clod of dirt was about six by four inches, which totaled six clods per square feet. In order to dig up his twenty thousand square feet of land would require one hundred twenty thousand jabs with that heavy bar.

My arms felt tired after my puny efforts of jabbing the bar six to eight times. So that scruffy little man had to have upper arm muscles like bands of steel. And then I figured if it took ten seconds to dig one clod, each square foot of land took one minute to dig. That translated to 333 hours, and if the little man worked ten hours per day, it would take him over thirty-three days to dig his little plot of ground. What toil!

Further down the trail, I passed a few houses, the first I had seen in over a week. They lay scattered among small plots of farmland bright green with growing crops. At the end of the little valley, the land fell away, and I had wide views of lush farmlands and houses below me. The houses ware tied to one another by umbilical-like trails that led everywhere and nowhere. I saw no roads except for the one I followed, and it disappeared to the right around a shoulder of a low ridge.

Here and there, plots of ripe grain stood in golden contrast to the intense green surrounding them. At first, I was confused how the farmers were able to have some crops ready for harvest while others remained green with growth. The only solution was that this part of Peru was close to the equator and had similar temperatures all year round. Thus, they could harvest wheat in a field next to green growing wheat, or potatoes in a field next to potato plants in blossom.

I munched some lunch on the run, not wanting to waste any time stopping to eat, because I still had a long way to go to get to the village of Chacas which was the end of the line for the one and only bus that went to Lima each day. But I did stop for a few minutes to watch farming families thresh and winnow their ripe wheat.

The scene reminded me of an oil painting done on canvass by one of the great masters of art. The farmers had hand cut the wheat stalks and placed them in piles throughout the golden field that was sandwiched among other diversely-textured crops in various shades of green. Men and women in their colorful costumes brought stalks of wheat to a central threshing area, a circle of hard packed earth. Five or six people stood around the circle and beat the wheat stalks with long poles, while their children ran about and played. The end of the pole was hinged to form a two to three feet long club. As the threshers swung their poles, the club at the end of their poles flailed in an arc that hit the ground flat at each stroke, thereby smashing the grain from the stalks and the husks from the seeds. They laughed and talked while they worked, and I would have loved beating that grain. It looked like fun.

After sufficient beating, the farmers raked the stalks to one side and swept the seeds and husks into a large, round sieve. Two people worked in unison to toss the seed mixture in the air where the gentlest breeze blew away the lighter husks and left the heavier seeds to drop back into the sieve. They repeated winnowing until only pure grain was left in the sieve, and then they poured the seeds into storage baskets. I used the word pure loosely since I'm sure some of the husks ended up in the baskets along with a fair amount of pure dirt. But who would know that after the tortillas were cooked?

As I dropped further into the valley, I passed more houses. I asked an older couple sitting on their porch just a foot or two from the road, "Dondé está Chacas?"

They pointed in the direction I was going and replied, "muy cerca," very near.

They said a lot of other things in Spanish too, but I only understood the "very near." But their idea of very near was different than mine and it took me all afternoon to get to Chacas. The sun was setting behind the mountains to the west when I got there, and I realized that, over the last two weeks I had completed a hike clear through the Andes from west to east.

A chill was in the air, and I knew darkness would come fast because there was so little twilight this close to the equator. So I went searching for the bus and found it parked at one corner of the Plaza de Armas. It sat there empty and forlorn with no one around. After asking several people, I found out it didn't leave until three in the morning. All that hustling down the trail, and now I had about nine hours of free time. I found a little store, but no restaurants. There went my dream of a leisurely luxury meal of fresh food rather than the dehydrated meals I had eaten for two weeks on the trail.

The storeowner gave me directions to a place to eat in a private home just a few blocks from the plaza. I found it just as daylight ended. I was their first customer, and they let me roam about a bit before I settled into a straight-backed chair in the dining room, easily recognized by the long table with several chairs on each side. The walls were adobe, painted white; the roof was made of red tiles, and the floor was packed earth. Chickens and little varmints darted about, coming and going from the kitchen. I studiously sat in my chair and ignored that traffic. Nor did I press my luck and enter the kitchen.

On one wall was a large poster depicting a young, white, pretty blonde beaming at me from her perch on a reed boat floating on a lake. She was extremely buxom showing her breasts barely constrained by a skimpy blouse that was missing two crucial buttons. She waved at me and had an enticing smile that invited me to come join her on a romantic boat ride.

Right next to that poster was a large art print of Jesus with a serene, holy look on his face. With his signature beard, he was dressed in a flowing robe and had one hand raised with two fingers held in a blessing attitude. Looking at the two pictures so close together my emotions were completely confused by the message of holiness side by side with raw sex.

Finally, it was time for supper, but I was the only guest. They served me the first course, runny lentil soup. Before I finished it, several men came in and took seats at the table. They seemed at home there and knew the exact time that dinner was served. The next course came out in a bowl and consisted of four or five little round potatoes surmounted by a tiny haunch of meat. I saw its little leg bone protruding from the meat and wondered what kind of animal I was eating. Later I noted that some of the varmints scurrying around the room were guinea pigs, *cuy* in Spanish, and I deduced that I had just eaten the rear leg of one of their cousins. It was mild tasting with the consistency of pork, and I could have easily eaten more.

The third course was a large mug of tea. I looked around for more, but that was it, the complete dinner. The tea was laced with milk and lots of sugar—yuk! Maybe it was supposed to be dessert. I found out I could get seconds on the tea and grew to like it, a little. The other men at the table drank the stuff with gusto and talked politics. They were discussing the latest news about the teacher's strike against the government.

I had been on the trail for two weeks so I didn't know anything about it. Apparently the teachers wanted more money, and the government didn't want to pay it, so the teachers didn't show up for work on Thursdays, only Thursdays. I never found out why they picked Thursday, but that was their strike day. I thought it was a pretty puny effort that probably wouldn't get them anywhere with the government. However, the bulk of the people in Peru supported the teachers, and as a result, everything in Peru came to a screeching halt every Thursday.

The trains and buses didn't run. Airplane service continued, but with no taxis or cars running, long lines of passengers walked to and from the airport dragging their luggage along. Stores were closed, restaurants too. Everything closed down, and to make sure that traffic stopped running, the people tore up cobblestones at road intersections and left large pieces of broken glass in the roadway.

I happened to be in Cuzco once on a Thursday, and the whole city was eerily quiet. No honking, no traffic, no people, and no noise, except for the dogs and chickens. The dogs barked and howled from all over the city for no reason that I could see, and the dumb chickens crowed their fool heads off. These animal noises perversely made the urban areas sound even more quiet. Many families took the day off and walked out into the countryside on extended picnics for the day. They clogged the road leading upland to Sacsayhuamán, the huge Inka fortress above Cuzco. There they sat around, ate, laughed, and talked, while their children flew kites and ran about among the extensive ruins.

On Friday and every other day of the week, everything was back to normal as if the strange events of Thursday had never happened. The strike finally ended weeks later, and I hoped the teachers got more money for their efforts.

The other men were still discussing the strike when I left the dining room and headed back to the plaza. I shivered in the cold as I walked in the dark with only a few streetlights lighting my way. The plaza was better lighted, but I had no place to sit except for some cold, uncomfortable-looking park benches. The store was closed, but a few people still lingered about. I needed to pee, but felt inhibited by the lights and the people hanging around. So I climbed aboard the bus, held it in, and tried to get comfortable in one of the seats.

It was terribly cold, and I broke out a plastic blanket with one side coated with a silvery material. The manufacturer called it a "space blanket" and touted it to be as warm as a wool blanket. It certainly wasn't warm and fuzzy and should have been relegated to outer space from where it came. The silvery lining was supposed to reflect radiant body heat back to my body, but I felt colder under it than without it.

For convenience and light travel, I had left my big pack with all my warm clothes in it with my climbing friends who had agreed to get it back to Lima for me, thereby saving me a lot of work carrying it out on my back to Chacas. Now I wore everything I had with me, but still needed that sleeping bag, wool sweater, and hat.

The hours passed slowly, and I intermittently shivered or dozed fitfully. At one point, the town shut down the generators, and the plaza went dark as pitch. I got out of the bus to pee and gratefully saw no one loitering about.

Back aboard the bus, I tried to arrange that miserable plastic blanket to give myself some comfort, but I ended up shivering a lot and just stoically waiting it out. The bus was supposed to leave at three o'clock, and surely the running motor would generate some heat. My mantra was to remind myself over and over that this temporary discomfort would pass with time.

Just before three o'clock, I saw a small wavering light approach the bus from across the plaza. My mind was fuzzy from the cold, and the light appeared to be ethereal from another world. It swayed from side to side and bounced up and down, sometimes bright, and sometimes dim. and I was confused whether to stay or run. Fight or flight. Too cold for flight, I stayed and watched, fascinated until it came close enough that I saw the light was a candle with a disembodied palm held behind it to reflect the light forward. How novel. The palm belonged to a man in a dark robe with a hood that made me think of monks. He opened the door of the bus, turned on some lights, started the engine, and then turned on some loud music. Oh joy, I was to have obnoxious music all the way to Lima. But this was action at last, and I waited impatiently for the heat to come my way.

Two other passengers boarded the bus, and promptly at three o'clock, we left the town of Chacas for the long trip to Lima, now on the other side of the mountains. At every little settlement along the way, we picked up other passengers. In between stops, the bus careened from side to side and swooped around curves, losing elevation fast. But in the dark, I didn't fully appreciate the road we traveled. When dawn arrived I saw the steep, narrow gravel and dirt road we followed with its sharp hairpin turns and abrupt drop offs on one side that went down forever. No bus would ever survive a roll down one of those slopes.

I quickly appreciated the scariest places on the road, which were whenever the bus came to a curve too sharp to get around without backing and filling. The driver would stop with his front end out over the cliff, while I strained my legs jamming imaginary brakes on the floor by my seat. After stopping, he ground some gears, and then came the movement I dreaded. Inevitably, the bus rolled forward slightly toward the edge of the cliff and oblivion before the clutch engaged the engine, and we lurched back uphill to safety. In that moment I had visions of me trapped inside that oversized box of glass and steel, rattling about inside as it tumbled off the cliff and rolled a thousand feet down the slope while the radio continued to play that God-awful music to the bitter end.

But the engine took hold each time he stopped to reverse, and the driver backed up his bus until the back wheels were inches from the edge of the same cliff, and now the passengers in the rear seats were sitting out over the void. *How does the driver judge where the wheels of his bus are on the road*? Again, I strained my legs on imaginary brakes to help stop us from going too far. But now, I had gravity on my side, and as soon as the driver changed gears, the bus automatically moved downhill away from the edge of the cliff. Then he cranked the steering wheel over, and the bus lunged down around the rest of the curve, quickly gaining speed as it went. I think he had only two speeds: fast or stop.

The more I looked out the window, the more agitated I became until I finally did what the other passengers were doing They carefully kept their eyes viewing the inside of the bus as if the outside didn't exist, or, they went to sleep which was not an option for me.

In late morning, after traveling on a smooth, paved road for several hours that was relatively flat and straight, we arrived at a bus stop near the ruins of Chavin, and everyone got off to eat. I wanted to see the Chavin ruins, but by now, I was so famished, I chose to eat rather than see the ruins. I didn't miss much since most everything to see was in subterranean rooms or unlit tunnels, and visitors needed good strong flashlights. I tried to order the biggest meal on the Spanish menu, an item called biftek, *Hidalgo*, which I thought was a beefsteak, served with onions and potatoes. Great! What I got was liver, not my favorite meat, smothered in fried onions. But it didn't matter, everything tasted good when I was really hungry.

Aboard the bus again, we began the climb back over the Andes to the west side of the mountains and the Pacific coast. Somewhere along the way the road changed from pavement to dirt and gravel, and we ground our way up in lower gears around hairpin turns, through gorges, and past the everlasting drop offs They were scenic, but scary.

We went up a few thousand feet to the Cahuish Tunnel, the high point on the road at over fourteen thousand seven hundred feet. The traffic in the tunnel was one way and we joined a long line of cars and trucks that entered the tunnel together. Part way through the tunnel, the road doubled as the bed of a sizable stream, and we splashed and bounced through a foot or so of water.

Suddenly, we came to a halt still in the middle of the tunnel, surrounded by water. A few cars ahead, a pickup truck carrying two llamas was dead in the water, literally. Several men waded about trying to make the clunker go, but we sat there with our engine running while the minutes ticked away. I finally realized that, with all the engines idling in the enclosed tunnel, we could all die from the buildup of carbon dioxide and carbon monoxide. So I engaged the driver in a conversation of sorts to convince him to shut off the engine.

My Spanish was so poor and the music so loud, I couldn't convey the danger of engine gases and the need to stop running the motor. Maybe he had never heard of suicide by running an engine in an enclosed space like a garage or a tunnel. I was now the center of attention and humorous entertainment and several passengers nodded, smiled, and encouraged me to continue my performance. But my words and pantomime conveyed an urgency so that several people began to see what was troubling me. When they fully understood, they easily convinced the driver to shut off the motor, but not the music which played on unabated, sounding louder now without the engine running.

Many of the vehicles nearby had already shut down their engines, and the tunnel was quiet as a tomb, except for our on going rock concert. The men ahead continued sloshing about in the water, working on the stalled pickup as their shouts and curses echoed off the bare rock walls of the tunnel. Then suddenly, the pickup grunted to life and limped out of the tunnel. The long line of traffic came to life and snaked its way out of the tunnel into bright sunshine, open space, and fresh air. A few hundred feet beyond the tunnel, we passed the pickup with its two llamas stalled again by the side of the road, this time dead out of the water.

The road west of the Andes improved greatly as it went down thousands of feet to sea level. We finally joined the major north-south highway in Peru and roared into Lima well after dark. So after two full days of travel I had traveled from a remote mountain pass at sixteen thousand feet down to Lima, the largest city in Peru. Ready for more adventures.

46) Headed for the last pass (photo by Harry Morgan)

Chapter 28
In Search of Giant Shrimp, India

In a restaurant in Sri Lanka, I watched a lady at the next table devour the largest shrimp I had ever seen. They put to shame the largest shrimp offered by grocery stores back home. Unfortunately, I had already ordered my dinner, but the next evening I came back and ordered the large shrimp. To my great disappointment, the shrimp were just average size.

"But where are the huge shrimp you had last night?" I asked the waitress. "These are just babies."

"Sorry, so sorry, but fisherman find small shrimp today. Sometimes he find big shrimp, but not often."

Right then, I decide an important goal of this trip was to find and eat the giant shrimp. From that point on, it was part of my repertoire of questions to ask. By the time I got to India, I had brought up the question of giant shrimp many times. The answers were vague and no one seemed to know exactly where they were, The consensus of knowledge pointed to the Indian Ocean.

I stayed in Ernakulam, Kerala a few days, which is on a bay off the Indian Ocean. Someone told me to go to Fort Kochi for shrimp and seafood. They also said there were many things there for a tourist to see. Fort Kochi was across the bay from Ernakulam on a peninsula between the ocean and the bay. I took an early morning commuter ferry and landed at the village of Mattencherry a few kilometers South of Fort Kochi. When I asked about giant shrimp, I was told they were not there, but I should go to see the Mattencherry palace and the Jewish synagogue. Since they were not open yet, I walked around "Jewtown," a place of small, very old shops. Many shops weren't open yet, but a little hole-in-the-wall carpet store was.

"Where can I buy the giant shrimp?" I asked the proprietor

"I don't know," he said. "But take a look at this beautiful carpet. I can give you a special price for being my first customer of the day."

I went in and the owner started showing me his carpets. They were made of silk from northern India. He showed me how to tell authentic silk from manufactured fibers. Silk burns, but other fibers melt. Then he asked me the first of three standard questions that venders used to snare a buyer.

"Do you like these carpets?"

I could say no, and walk out. But I would be lying through my teeth, so I said, "yes."

He brought out a chair for me, and handed me the first of many cups of mint tea. Then he spread out a lot of carpets in front of my chair, all different colors and patterns. If I showed any interest in one, it would remain in prominent sight while the others disappeared under new displays. Finally, he asked the second question.

"Which one do you like the best?"

I could leave now without answering, implying that I couldn't make a determination of what I liked. But it's hard for me to lie, so I said, "there are two I like really well and it's hard for me to choose the best."

Magically, all the carpets disappeared except the two I thought were best. We discussed the merits of each, and I received a second cup of tea. Eventually, I boiled it down to one carpet. Then came the third question.

"How much would you pay for this beautiful carpet?"

Any price I mentioned would be subject to intense pressure upward, so it would have to be lower than the reasonable market value to allow me room for bargaining. If my first price was too high, he would have an easy time gaining something more than the market value, and laugh all the way to the bank. In this case, I decided to let him set the first price, knowing that it would be high, and probably twice the market value. I would have to exert pressure to get it down to a reasonable price. We bargained for quite awhile and the price ended somewhere at about half his first price.

During the bargaining, we drank mint tea, talked about our families, where we had been in the world, and about giant shrimp. I paid for my carpet with a credit card, and he promised to ship it to my house. At this point, we were each taking a risk. He had to assume that my credit was good and that he would eventually get paid, while my risk was that the carpet would actually get to my house. It took some time, but we each got what we wanted.

I walked away from the carpet shop toward Fort Kochi on the northwest coast of the peninsula where I now knew a lot of the local fish and seafood were caught, thinking someone there would know where to buy giant shrimp. It was also close to where I could catch a ferry back to my hotel. So I started walking toward that ferry dock about five miles up the road. It was very hot, and I got very thirsty. Part way there, I passed a beautiful four-star hotel that had a covered patio with a view of the water. It also had cold beer, and I was drawn inextricably to its cool shelter. Shrimp and ferries could wait; some things were more important.

I sat and read my book while I sipped a cold beer. The book was Ann Rand's *Atlas Shrugged*. It was something I could easily lay aside, or just not read for minutes at a time. It was one of those looking around times, when I caught the eye of an Indian man two tables away. He motioned me to come over and join him at his table.   I smiled and was about to decline when he motioned again even more emphatically.   So, I thought, what the hell; the book wasn't that interesting and I was going to go shortly anyway.   I got up and went to meet him.

"My name is Amar," he said, and then he introduced me to the two friends sitting with him. They were drinking tea and he got a cup for me.

"I saw you sitting by yourself," he said.   "You are obviously a tourist, but you seem so at ease and comfortable here.   I was intrigued and wanted to meet you. Are you traveling with friends?"

"No, I'm traveling alone, but I do enjoy India.   Some places are quite hectic, but this area is very peaceful."

He explained this to his friends who were not well versed in English. He talked about this part of India. He had lived here all his life. I talked about Seattle and some of the places I had visited in India. I told him I had to leave soon to catch a ferry back to my hotel. The ferry dock was several miles away, and it would take me some time to walk there. Also, I wanted to find some giant shrimp to buy before I left.

He asked, "Can you wait for a bit? I must take my friends back to their office, but I know where to buy those shrimp and would be delighted to give you a ride there in my car."

I graciously accepted. A valet delivered the car. It was a Mercedes four-door with everything on it, but the kitchen sink. He dropped off his friends, and drove through heavy traffic crossing a bridge to the Ernakulam side of the bay. He wanted me to see his house first.

It was on one of the main arterials set back about forty feet from the street, room enough for a car turnaround. A six-foot chain-link fence protected the yard. The front of the house, the only part seen from the street, was clad in marble and appeared very institutional. The entry opened into a large sitting room, which was the only room I got to see. It was quite formal and cheerless. I met his wife briefly when she served tea and Indian snacks. He and I talked for a bit. Then he said he wanted me to go with him to his club for tea. He excused himself and left me alone a few minutes wondering when this day would end, and if Indian men drank only tea. As I waited, I caught glimpses of his wife as she moved about in the next room, but never once did she come in or look my way.

The clubhouse was not as ostentatious as I thought it would be. We sat at long trench tables while Indian men in uniform served us tea and snacks. As we sat there, his friends would come and sit for awhile and talk in Hindi. My host introduced me to each, but the conversation would turn to Hindi in just a few minutes.

At one point, between friendly visits from his club friends, Amar said, "This club was exclusively for the use of the British before our independence. My Indian friends and I were not allowed in here. The only Indians allowed were servants. Now it is still very exclusive. The British left, but they have been replaced by privileged Indians who are every bit as exclusive as the British. But we still have Indian servants. I am afraid our democracy is not entirely universal."

Finally, we got up to leave, and he said good-bye to his friends.

"Are you married?" he asked, pulling out of the parking area into traffic.

"Yes, actually I'm with my second wife."

"You were divorced? But why?"

"At first there was love, or maybe it was infatuation. It didn't last long. But we had two children and we lived together fairly well for seventeen years. It was as if she had a role, I had a role, and we each played our parts very well."

"But you did leave."

"Yes, I did. When I reached forty years old, I asked myself, is this all there is to life? The answer to that, of course, was no. And shortly after that, we divorced."

"You met my wife," said Amar. "She is Hindu and very conservative. We have two children, but we have never loved each other. Divorce is out of the question. If I tried to do that, she would leave to live with her family and take my two children with her. I would never see them again. No, it is not possible for me."

"You mean that you are stuck forever with a woman you have never loved? Why didn't you at least start out with someone you did care for?"

"My father was very insistent that I marry the woman who became my wife. I delayed as long as I could, but in the end, I could not go against his wishes."

"You were forced to marry this woman by your father? That's hard to believe in these modern times. I thought Indian men and women could now make their own choice."

"Most of the young people of India today do so. And I could have defied my father and not married this woman, but he would have been shamed by my refusal, and I might have been cast out. Then there is the woman who would be rejected, thereby bringing shame to her and her family. No, my friend, I had to marry that woman."

I digested this in silence for a few seconds. Then he said, "Your first wife. Is she well? Do you see her often?"

"I think she's well, but I never see her. There's no reason to see her."

"That is so strange you never see her. Has she remarried?"

"No."

"Then do you send her money and help her?"

"No."

"Oh, but you must. She is alone and needs help. After all, she is the mother of your children."

Fortunately, we had reached the place on the beach where fish and seafood were available for sale. I said good-bye, left his car, and was able to drop that uneasy conversation. I found the giant shrimp in an open air market. I looked at them in amazement for they were truly huge. I had found them, but now I needed to figure out a way to cook them.

I went over to watch the operation of some Chinese fishing nets on the beach. The nets were large and square. A rigid frame supported them to form a shallow upside down pyramid. A crew of four lowered the contraption in the water, and after a reasonable wait for the fish to assemble, raised it out of the water. The hope was that fish would be trapped in the rising net on the way up. I saw very few fish caught, and concluded that it was an awful lot of work for such little gain.

I walked back to see my giant shrimp once more before walking away from the beach across a park area to some food stalls along the road Eyeing the large kettles on the burners in one of the stalls, I asked the cook if he had any shrimp to eat.

"No," he said, "but you can buy them at the fish market across the way on the beach."

"If I buy them and brought them to you, would you prepare and cook them for me?

"Of course, we can prepare you a meal with your shrimp."

"And a couple bottles of beer?"

"We don't have beer here. It is somewhat restricted. But don't worry, I will send my son to a place I know. We will serve you beer."

"Are you sure it's no problem, because I can make do with something else?"

"No, no, it is no problem. You get the shrimp and I will have the beer here when you get back."

As I walked back to the fish market, I mentally calculated how much shrimp to buy. They were sold by the kilogram, but still had their heads on. So, if I bought 3/4 kilogram I would have about 1½ pounds of shrimp which might net out to be about one pound cleaned. That sounded like a reasonable amount. And I ended up with just two giant shrimp and a baby shrimp thrown in for good measure.

True to his word, the proprietor of the food stall served me a two-course meal. The first course was a giant shrimp and the baby with some rice, and a beer. It was so good I had a second course of other giant

Frank King

shrimp, rice, and beer. I ate leisurely under a large shade tree on the lawn of the park. I watched the pattern of leaves moving against the blue sky. I watched the fishing nets bob up and down on the beach in their fruitless effort to catch fish. But mostly I reveled in eating my giant shrimp.

47) Fishing net out of water with fish--maybe

48) Fishing net in the water catching fish—maybe

Chapter 29
The Construction Worker, India

Trapped again in a long line of Seattle traffic, I waited for a halt in the construction ahead that would allow me to proceed. I saw the men and machines digging up dirt on one side of the road, loading it into big trucks, and then hauling and dumping the dirt on the other side of the road. It was basically a cut and fill operation. The day was hot, well, pretty hot for Seattle. I was bored with the wait, and my mind wandered. I guess the heat build-up in the car reminded me of those hot days in India, and my present surroundings faded as my mind transported me back to a land halfway around the world.

I sat on a rickety chair in the meager shade of a runty tree, waiting for Doris, who was off somewhere out of sight. At home, at times like this, I accused her of picking up lint or imaginary dirt. But now it didn't matter, because our jeep ride for a game drive in a nearby tiger preserve hadn't shown up yet. When the jeep arrived, I knew she would magically appear just in time to hop on board.

The shade protected me, a little, from the fierce rays of the midmorning Indian sun burning in a cloudless sky. The day was hot already, and it wasn't even noon. The road out in front carried a desultory parade of a few motorized vehicles and an occasional cart pulled by an ox. But most traffic consisted of people coming and going, shuffling along in the dust. Many of them carried large bundles, and a few herded their emaciated animals. Dust and the smell of animals and their dung filled the hot morning air.

As I watched that scene, almost comatose from the heat, I became aware of two women working on the road. They loaded up a shallow pan with dirt, lifted it to their head, and then carried it across the road and dumped it. It was basically a cut and fill operation.

I perked up enough to watch the details of the work they were doing. The pans were about two feet in diameter and about four inches deep. They bent over, digging the dirt and loading their pans with a mattock. Since they had only one digging tool, they spaced themselves so that while one was digging and loading, the other was dumping. When each woman dumped her load, she lifted the pan off her head and gave it a slight twist as she flung the pan to the ground. In that way, as it fell, the dirt spread automatically, and the pan landed with a thump upside down. She then retrieved the empty pan and went back for another load. There seemed to be no one in charge, but the women worked away continuously, without instruction at a slow, measured pace.

They worked barefoot with their ankles encircled in silvery bracelets that softly jingled as they walked. They wore long colorful Saris of the sheerest cotton that draped their bodies with no apparent fastenings. As they worked, their dresses appeared to be of no hindrance or handicap, and never in disarray. They moved with exquisite grace and beauty as they dug and transported their loads of dirt through the heat, the smells, and the dust.

On their arms, they wore multiple bracelets of every conceivable color that contrasted with their tawny golden skin. The bracelets moved up and down their arms as they worked giving off splashes of color in the bright sunlight. They wore their jet-black hair in one thick braid down the middle of the back. Woven into the braid were colorful cloth and ribbons that fluttered as they worked, and their dangling earrings glinted in the sun when they moved.

They were, by far, the most colorful and graceful construction workers I had ever seen. I watched them, fascinated by their movements as they worked, cool and poised in the hot sun.

Suddenly, I heard a loud honk behind me, and I awoke with a start from my reverie. Ahead of me was a gap where the cars in front had already moved past the heavy, panting machines now at rest. They were belching diesel fumes into the air as they waited impatiently for the column of cars to get out of their way. Reluctantly, I put my car into gear, and left the pageantry, beauty, and color of that other construction site, halfway around the world.

49) Which hippo?

Made in the USA
Charleston, SC
13 July 2012